"With His Pistol
in His Hand"

Gregorio Cortez

"With His Pistol in His Hand"

A BORDER BALLAD AND ITS HERO

by Américo Paredes

UNIVERSITY OF TEXAS PRESS : AUSTIN AND LONDON

Paredes, Américo. "With his pistol in his hand," a border
ballad and its hero. Austin, University of Texas Press
[1958] 274 p. illus. 24 cm. Includes bibliography.
1. El corrido de Gregorio Cortez (Ballad) 2. Cortez,
Gregorio, 1875–1916. I. Title.
PQ7297.A1C63   398.22
58–10853‡

International Standard Book Number 0–292–73432–8 (cloth)
International Standard Book Number 0–292–70128–4 (paper)
Library of Congress Catalog Card Number 58–10853

Second Printing, 1975

To the memory of my father,
who rode a raid or two with
Catarino Garza;
and to all those old men
who sat around on summer nights,
in the days when there was
a chaparral, smoking their
cornhusk cigarettes and talking
in low, gentle voices about
violent things;
while I listened.

Acknowledgments

This book was made possible with the help of many persons, more than I could name in one short page. To the ballad singers of the Lower Rio Grande, who have shared their songs with me over the years, I owe a debt that I could never repay. A few of them are mentioned in the references made to particular variants of *Gregorio Cortez*. I am indebted to the many people who helped me collect information on Cortez. Those who told me their own experiences are mentioned in the bibliography, but I would especially like to express my appreciation to Mr. Valeriano Cortez, who gave me important information about his father, Gregorio Cortez.

Professor Stith Thompson of Indiana University was kind enough to read an early version of the manuscript, and he made suggestions concerning what is now Part Two which helped me eliminate some of its many faults. Professors Mody C. Boatright and Ramón Martínez-López of the University of Texas also made valuable suggestions. Through Professor Boatright's efforts I received in 1954 a research assistantship from the University of Texas to tape-record ballads in the field.

Most especially I would like to acknowledge my debt to Dr. Robert C. Stephenson, who supervised my folklore studies for five years. This book took its initial shape as a doctoral dissertation under his direction, and it owes a great deal to his guidance and encouragement.

AMÉRICO PAREDES

Austin, 1958

Contents

Introduction

This book began as the study of a ballad; it developed into the story of a ballad hero. Thus it became two books in one. It is an account of the life of a man, of the way that songs and legends grew up about his name, and of the people who produced the songs, the legends, and the man. It is also the story of a ballad, *El Corrido de Gregorio Cortez,* of its development out of actual events, and of the folk traditions from which it sprang.

Corrido, the Mexicans call their narrative folk songs, especially those of epic themes, taking the name from *correr,* which means "to run" or "to flow," for the *corrido* tells a story simply and swiftly, without embellishments. *El Corrido de Gregorio Cortez* comes from a region, half in Mexico and half in the United States, known in this book as the Lower Rio Grande Border, the Lower Border, or simply the Border (with a capital B). Some people call it the Rio Grande Valley, but this name is also given a New Mexican area. In Texas, only the American side is usually called the Valley, and the name is associated with cotton, grapefruit, and the tourist industry.

El Corrido de Gregorio Cortez, then, is a Border Mexican ballad, "Mexican" being understood in a cultural sense, without reference to citizenship or to "blood." But we must stress "Border" too. It is as a border that the Lower Rio Grande has made its mark: in legend, in song, and in those documented old men's tales called histories.

Borders and ballads seem to go together, and their heroes are all cast in the same mold. During the Middle Ages there lived in some parts of Europe, especially in the border areas, a certain type of men whose fame has come down to us in legend and in song. On the Scottish-English border there were heroes like Wallace, the rebel against English domination, like Jock o the Side, Hobie Noble, Willie Armstrong, and other Liddesdale and Teviotdale raiders, whose favorite occupation was defying the power of England.

Spain had its popular heroes too, as did Russia, during the periods when each of those countries held a border against the warlike tribes of the East. And if one goes back to the fall of the Roman Empire, one hears of Digenis Akritas, who lived and fought on the borders between the Eastern Empire and the Saracens.

People composed ballads about men like these; legends grew up about them, and they became folk heroes, to be studied and argued about by generations of scholars. To this same class belongs Gregorio Cortez, who lived not in Europe of the Middle Ages but in twentieth-century America. This is his story, the fact and the legend of it: Gregorio Cortez, who defended his right with his pistol in his hand.

"With His Pistol
in His Hand"

Transcribed by Hally Wood

El Corrido de Gregorio Cortez

In the county of El Carmen
A great misfortune befell;
The Major Sheriff is dead;
Who killed him no one can tell.

At two in the afternoon,
In half an hour or less,
They knew that the man who
    killed him
Had been Gregorio Cortez.

They let loose the bloodhound
    dogs;
They followed him from afar.
But trying to catch Cortez
Was like following a star.

All the rangers of the county
Were flying, they rode so hard;
What they wanted was to get
The thousand-dollar reward.

And in the county of Kiansis
They cornered him after all;
Though they were more than three
    hundred
He leaped out of their corral.

Then the Major Sheriff said,
As if he was going to cry,
"Cortez, hand over your weapons;
We want to take you alive."

Then said Gregorio Cortez,
And his voice was like a bell,
"You will never get my weapons
Till you put me in a cell."

Then said Gregorio Cortez,
With his pistol in his hand,
"Ah, so many mounted Rangers
Just to take one Mexican!"

PART ONE
Gregorio Cortez, the Legend and the Life

I: THE COUNTRY

Nuevo Santander

T̶he Lower Rio Grande Border is the area lying along the river, from its mouth to the two Laredos. A map, especially one made some thirty or forty years ago, would show a clustering of towns and villages along both river banks, with lonely gaps to the north and to the south. This was the heart of the old Spanish province of Nuevo Santander, colonized in 1749 by José de Escandón.

In the days before upriver irrigation projects, the Lower Rio Grande was a green, fertile belt, bounded on the north and south by arid plains, situated along a river which, like the Nile, irrigated and fertilized the lands close to its banks and periodically filled countless little lakes, known as *resacas* and *esteros*. Isolated by natural barriers, the country was still unexplored long after the initial wave of Spanish conquest had spent itself and Spain was struggling with the problems created by her earlier successes. Spanish colonization had gone as far north as New Mexico on the west, and to the east it had jumped overseas to Texas. The Lower Rio Grande, known as the Seno Mexicano (the Mexican Hollow or Recess), was a refuge for rebellious

7

Indians from the Spanish *presidios,* who preferred outlawry to life under Spanish rule. Thus, at its earliest period in history the Lower Rio Grande was inhabited by outlaws, whose principal offense was an independent spirit.

Toward the middle of the eighteenth century Spanish official-dom decided that better communications were needed between Texas and Mexico City, routes which would cross the Seno Mexicano. José de Escandón was ordered to colonize the Lower Rio Grande. Four months after his appointment, Escandón was already on his way with parties of exploration.

Escandón was a wise and far-sighted administrator, and his methods were different from those of most Spanish colonizers. The *presidio,* symbol of military authority over settlers and Indians alike, was not part of his plans. The soldiers assigned to each settlement of Nuevo Santander were settlers too, and their captain was the colony's most prominent citizen.

The colonists came from the settled Spanish families of surrounding regions and were induced to settle on the Rio Grande by promises of free land and other government concessions. One of these concessions was freedom from interference by official-dom in the faraway centers of population. The colony of Nuevo Santander was settled much like the lands occupied by westward-pushing American pioneers, by men and their families who came overland, with their household goods and their herds.

The Indians seem to have given little trouble. They were neither exterminated in the English manner, nor enslaved according to the usual Spanish way. They lived in the same small towns as the Spanish settlers, under much the same conditions, and were given a measure of self-government.

By 1775, a bare six years after the founding of Nuevo Santander, there were only 146 soldiers still on duty among 8,993 settlers. There were 3,413 Indians in the towns, not counting those that still remained in a wild state.[1] In succeeding generations the Indians, who began as vaqueros and sheepherders for

[1] William Curry Holden, *Fray Vicente Santa María: Historical Account of the Colony of Nuevo Santander,* Master's thesis, University of Texas, 1924, p. xi.

the colonists, were absorbed into the blood and the culture of the Spanish settlers. Also absorbed into the basically Spanish culture were many non-Spanish Europeans, so that on the Border one finds men who prefer Spanish to English, who sometimes talk scornfully about the "Gringos," and who bear English, Scottish, Irish, or other non-Spanish names.

By 1755 towns had been founded near the present site of Laredo—the only north-bank settlement of the time—and at Guerrero, Mier, Camargo, and Reynosa on the south bank. The colonists were pushing into the Nueces–Rio Grande area in search of pasturage for their rapidly increasing herds. Don Blas María Falcón, the founder of Camargo, established a ranch called La Petronila at the mouth of the Nueces at about this time.

By 1835 there were three million head of livestock in the Rio Grande–Nueces area, according to the assessments of the towns along the Rio Grande.[2] Matamoros, founded near the river mouth in 1765 by people from Reynosa, had grown into the metropolis of the colony with 15,000 inhabitants. The other riverbank towns, though not so large, were correspondingly prosperous. The old province of Nuevo Santander was about to emerge from almost a century of isolation and growth, when war in Texas opened the period of border strife.

The Rio Grande people

Most of the Border people did not live in the towns. The typical community was the ranch or the ranching village. Here lived small, tightly knit groups whose basic social structure was the family or the clan. The early settlements had begun as great ranches, but succeeding generations multiplied the number of owners of each of the original land grants. The earliest practice was to divide the grant among the original owner's children. Later many descendants simply held the land in common, grouping their houses in small villages around what

[2] Cecil Bernard Smith, *Diplomatic Relations between the United States and Mexico*, Master's thesis, University of Texas, 1928, p. 5.

had been the ancestral home. In time almost everyone in any given area came to be related to everyone else.

The cohesiveness of the Border communities owed a great deal to geography. Nuevo Santander was settled comparatively late because of its isolated location. In 1846 it took Taylor a month to move his troops the 160 miles from Corpus Christi to Brownsville. In 1900 communications had improved but little, and it was not until 1904 that a railroad connected Brownsville with trans-Nueces areas, while a paved highway did not join Matamoros with the interior of Mexico until the 1940's.

The brush around Brownsville in the 1870's was so heavy that herds of stolen beef or horses could be hidden a few miles from town in perfect secrecy.[3] Even in the late 1920's the thick chaparral isolated many parts of the Border. Ranches and farms that are now within sight of each other across a flat, dusty cotton land were remote in those days of winding trails through the brush. The nearest neighbors were across the river, and most north-bank communities were in fact extensions of those on the south bank.

The simple pastoral life led by most Border people fostered a natural equality among men. Much has been written about the democratizing influence of a horse culture. More important was the fact that on the Border the landowner lived and worked upon his land. There was almost no gap between the owner and his cowhand, who often was related to him anyway. The simplicity of the life led by both employer and employee also helped make them feel that they were not different kinds of men, even if one was richer than the other.

Border economy was largely self-sufficient. Corn, beans, melons, and vegetables were planted on the fertile, easily irrigated lands at the river's edge. Sheep and goats were also raised in quantity. For these more menial, pedestrian tasks the peon was employed in earlier days. The peon was usually a *fuereño*, an "outsider" from central Mexico, but on the Border he was not a serf. *Peón* in Nuevo Santander had preserved much of its old

[3] *Informe de la Comisión Pesquisidora de la Frontera del Norte*, Mexico, 1877, p. 32.

meaning of "man on foot." The gap between the peon and the vaquero was not extreme, though the man on horseback had a job with more prestige, one which was considered to involve more danger and more skill.

The peon, however, could and did rise in the social scale. People along the Border who like to remember genealogies and study family trees can tell of instances in which a man came to the Border as a peon (today he would be called a *bracero*) and ended his life as a vaquero, while his son began life as a vaquero and ended it as a small landowner, and the grandson married into the old family that had employed his grandfather—the whole process taking place before the Madero Revolution. In few parts of Greater Mexico before 1910 could people of all degrees—including landowners—have circulated and obviously enjoyed the story of Juan, the peon who knew his right, and who not only outwitted his landowning employer but gave him a good beating besides, so that the landowner afterward would never hire a peon who "walked like Juan."

This is not to say that there was democracy on the Border as Americans recognize it or that the average Borderer had been influenced by eighteenth-century ideas about the rights of man. Social conduct was regulated and formal, and men lived under a patriarchal system that made them conscious of degree. The original settlements had been made on a patriarchal basis, with the "captain" of each community playing the part of father to his people.

Town life became more complex, but in rural areas the eldest member of the family remained the final authority, exercising more real power than the church or the state. There was a domestic hierarchy in which the representative of God on earth was the father. Obedience depended on custom and training rather than on force, but a father's curse was thought to be the most terrible thing on earth.

A grown son with a family of his own could not smoke in his father's presence, much less talk back to him. Elder brothers and elder cousins received a corresponding respect, with the eldest brother having almost parental authority over the younger. It was disrespectful to address an older brother, especially the eldest, by his name. He was called "Brother" and addressed in the formal *usted* used for the parents. In referring to him, one mentioned him as "My Brother So-and-So," never by his name alone. The same form of address was used toward cousins-german.

Such customs are only now disappearing among some of the old Border families. In the summer of 1954 I was present while a tough inspector of rural police questioned some suspects in a little south-bank Border town. He was sitting carelessly in his chair, smoking a cigarette, when he heard his father's voice in an outer room. The man straightened up in his chair, hurriedly threw his cigarette out the window, and fanned away the smoke with his hat before turning back to the prisoners.

If the mother was a strong character, she could very well receive the same sort of respect as the father. In his study of Juan N. Cortina, Charles W. Goldfinch recounts an incident which was far from being an isolated case. After his border-raider period Cortina was forced to abandon Texas, and he became an officer in the Mexican army. At the same time his desertion of his wife set him at odds with his mother. Later Cortina returned to the Border and was reconciled with his mother. "They met just across from her ranch on the Mexican side of the river. As they met, the son handed his mother his riding crop, and, as he knelt before her, in the presence of his officers, she whipped him across the shoulders. Then the chastised son, Brigadier General Cortina, arose and embraced his mother."[4]

These same parent-child customs formerly were applied to the community, when the community was an extended family. Decisions were made, arguments were settled, and sanctions were decided upon by the old men of the group, with the leader usually being the patriarch, the eldest son of the eldest son, so that primogeniture played its part in social organization though it did not often do so in the inheritance of property.

The patriarchal system not only made the Border community

[4] Charles W. Goldfinch, *Juan N. Cortina 1824–1892, a Re-Appraisal*, Brownsville (Texas), 1950, p. 67.

more cohesive, by emphasizing its clanlike characteristics, but it also minimized outside interference, because it allowed the community to govern itself to a great extent. If officials saw fit to appoint an *encargado* to represent the state, they usually chose the patriarch, merely giving official recognition to a choice already made by custom.

Thus the Rio Grande people lived in tight little groups—usually straddling the river—surrounded by an alien world. From the north came the *gringo*, which term meant "foreigner." From the south came the *fuereño*, or outsider, as the Mexican of the interior was called. Nuevo Santander had been settled as a way station to Texas, but there was no heavy traffic over these routes, except during wartime. Even in the larger towns the inhabitants ignored strangers for the most part, while the people of the remoter communities were oblivious of them altogether. The era of border conflict was to bring greater numbers of outsiders to the Border, but most Borderers treated them either as transients or as social excrescences. During the American Civil War and the Mexican Empire, Matamoros became a cosmopolitan city without affecting appreciably the life of the villages and ranches around it. On the north bank it took several generations for the new English-speaking owners of the country to make an impression on the old mores. The Border Mexican simply ignored strangers, except when disturbed by violence or some other transgression of what he believed was "the right." In the wildest years of the Border, the swirl of events and the coming and going of strange faces was but froth on the surface of life.

In such closely knit groups most tasks and amusements were engaged in communally. Roundups and brandings were community projects, undertaken according to the advice of the old men. When the river was in flood, the patriarchal council decided whether the levees should be opened to irrigate the fields or whether they should be reinforced to keep the water out, and the work of levee-building or irrigation was carried out by the community as a whole. Planting and harvesting were individual for the most part, but the exchange of the best fruits of the harvest (though all raised the same things) was a usual practice. In the 1920's, when I used to spend my summers in one of the south-bank ranch communities, the communal provision of fresh beef was still a standard practice. Each family slaughtered in turn and distributed the meat among the rest, ensuring a supply of fresh beef every week.

Amusements were also communal, though the statement in no way should suggest the "dancing, singing throng" creating as a group. Group singing, in fact, was rare. The community got together, usually at the patriarch's house, to enjoy the performance of individuals, though sometimes all the individuals in a group might participate in turn.

The dance played but little part in Border folkways, though in the twentieth century the Mexicanized polka has become something very close to a native folk form. Native folk dances were not produced, nor were they imported from fringe areas like southern Tamaulipas, where the *huapango* was danced. Polkas, mazurkas, waltzes, lancers, *contra-danzas*, and other forms then in vogue were preferred. Many Border families had prejudices against dancing. It brought the sexes too close together and gave rise to quarrels and bloody fights among the men. There were community dances at public spots and some private dances in the homes, usually to celebrate weddings, but the dance on the Border was a modern importation, reflecting European vogues.

Horse racing was, of course, a favorite sport among the men. In the home, amusements usually took the form of singing, the presentation of religious plays at Christmas, tableaux, and the like. This material came from oral tradition. Literacy among the old Border families was relatively high, but the reading habit of the Protestant Anglo-Saxon, fostered on a veneration of the written words in the Bible, was foreign to the Borderer. His religion was oral and traditional.

On most occasions the common amusement was singing to the accompaniment of the guitar: in the informal community gatherings, where the song alternated with the tale; at weddings, which had their own special songs, the *golondrinas;* at Christmastime, with its *pastorelas* and *aguinaldos;* and even at some kinds of funerals, those of infants, at which special songs were sung to the guitar.

The Nuevo Santander people also sang ballads. Some were songs remembered from their Spanish origins, and perhaps an occasional ballad came to them from the older frontier colony of Nuevo Mexico. But chiefly they made their own. They committed their daily affairs and their history to the ballad form: the fights against the Indians, the horse races, and the domestic triumphs and tragedies—and later the border conflicts and the civil wars. The ballads, and the tradition of ballad-making as well, were handed down from father to son, and thus the people of the Lower Rio Grande developed a truly native balladry.

It was the Treaty of Guadalupe that added the final element to Rio Grande society, a border. The river, which had been a focal point, became a dividing line. Men were expected to consider their relatives and closest neighbors, the people just across the river, as foreigners in a foreign land. A restless and acquisitive people, exercising the rights of conquest, disturbed the old ways.

Out of the conflict that arose on the new border came men like Gregorio Cortez. Legends were told about these men, and ballads were sung in their memory. And this state of affairs persisted for one hundred years after Santa Anna stormed the Alamo.

Mier, the Alamo, and Goliad

In the conflict along the Rio Grande, the English-speaking Texan (whom we shall call the Anglo-Texan for short) disappoints us in a folkloristic sense. He produces no border balladry. His contribution to the literature of border conflict is a set of attitudes and beliefs about the Mexican which form a legend of their own and are the complement to the *corrido,* the Border-Mexican ballad of border conflict. The Anglo-Texan legend may be summarized under half a dozen points.

1. The Mexican is cruel by nature. The Texan must in self-defense treat the Mexican cruelly, since that is the only treatment the Mexican understands.

2. The Mexican is cowardly and treacherous, and no match for the Texan. He can get the better of the Texan only by stabbing him in the back or by ganging up on him with a crowd of accomplices.

3. Thievery is second nature in the Mexican, especially horse and cattle rustling, and on the whole he is about as degenerate a specimen of humanity as may be found anywhere.

4. The degeneracy of the Mexican is due to his mixed blood, though the elements in the mixture were inferior to begin with. He is descended from the Spaniard, a second-rate type of European, and from the equally substandard Indian of Mexico, who must not be confused with the noble savages of North America.

5. The Mexican has always recognized the Texan as his superior and thinks of him as belonging to a race separate from other Americans.

6. The Texan has no equal anywhere, but within Texas itself there developed a special breed of men, the Texas Rangers, in whom the Texan's qualities reached their culmination.

This legend is not found in the cowboy ballads, the play-party songs, or the folk tales of the people of Texas. Orally one finds it in the anecdote and in some sentimental verse of nonfolk origin. It is in print—in newspapers, magazines, and books—that it has been circulated most. In books it has had its greatest influence and its longest life. The earliest were the war propaganda works of the 1830's and 1840's about Mexican "atrocities" in Texas, a principal aim of which was to overcome Northern antipathy toward the approaching war with Mexico.[5] After 1848, the same attitudes were perpetuated in the works, many of them autobiographical, about the adventurers and other men of action who took part in the border conflict on the American side. A good and an early example is the following passage from *Sketches of the Campaign in Northern Mexico,* by an officer of Ohio volunteers.

[5] See J. Frank Dobie, *The Flavor of Texas,* Dallas, 1936, pp. 125ff., for some of the aims and the effects of this type of work.

The Country

The inhabitants of the valley of the Rio Grande are chiefly occupied in raising stock. . . . But a pastoral life, generally so propitious to purity of morals and strength of constitution, does not appear to have produced its usually happy effect upon that people . . . vile rancheros; the majority of whom are so vicious and degraded that one can hardly believe that the light of Christianity has ever dawned upon them.[6]

In more recent years it has often been the writer of history textbooks and the author of scholarly works who have lent their prestige to the legend. This is what the most distinguished historian Texas has produced had to say about the Mexican in 1935.

Without disparagement, it may be said that there is a cruel streak in the Mexican nature, or so the history of Texas would lead one to believe. This cruelty may be a heritage from the Spanish of the Inquisition; it may, and doubtless should, be attributed partly to the Indian blood. . . . The Mexican warrior . . . was, on the whole, inferior to the Comanche and wholly unequal to the Texan. The whine of the leaden slugs stirred in him an irresistible impulse to travel with rather than against the music. He won more victories over the Texans by parley than by force of arms. For making promises—and for breaking them—he had no peer.[7]

Professor Webb does not mean to be disparaging. One wonders what his opinion might have been when he was in a less scholarly mood and not looking at the Mexican from the objective point of view of the historian. In another distinguished work, *The Great Plains*, Dr. Webb develops similar aspects of the legend. The Spanish "failure" on the Great Plains is blamed partly on the Spanish character. More damaging still was miscegenation with the Mexican Indian, "whose blood, when compared with that of the Plains Indian, was as ditch water."[8] On the other hand, American success on the Great Plains was due to the "pure

[6] [Luther Giddings], *Sketches of the Campaign in Northern Mexico*, New York, 1853, p. 54.

[7] Walter Prescott Webb, *The Texas Rangers*, Cambridge, 1935, p. 14.

[8] Walter Prescott Webb, *The Great Plains*, Boston, 1931, pp. 125–126.

American stock," the "foreign element" having settled elsewhere.[9]

How can one classify the Texas legend—as fact, as folklore, or
as still something else? The records of frontier life after 1848 are
full of instances of cruelty and inhumanity. But by far the majority of the acts of cruelty are ascribed by American writers
themselves to men of their own race. The victims, on the other
hand, were very often Mexicans. There is always the implication
that it was "defensive cruelty," or that the Mexicans were being
punished for their inhumanity to Texans at the Alamo, Mier,
and Goliad.

There probably is not an army (not excepting those of the
United States) that has not been accused of "atrocities" during
wartime. It is remarkable, then, that those atrocities said to have
occurred in connection with the Alamo, Goliad, and the Mier expedition are universally attributed not to the Mexican army as a
whole but to their commander, Santa Anna. Even more note-
worthy is the fact that Santa Anna's orders were protested by his
officers, who incurred the dictator's wrath by pleading for the
prisoners in their charge. In at least two other cases (not celebrated in Texas history) Santa Anna's officers were successful in
their pleading, and Texan lives were spared. Both Texan and
Mexican accounts agree that the executions evoked horror
among many Mexicans witnessing them—officers, civilians, and
common soldiers.[10]

Had Santa Anna lived in the twentieth century, he would have
called the atrocities with which he is charged "war crimes trials."
There is a fundamental difference, though, between his executions of Texan prisoners and the hangings of Japanese army officers like General Yamashita at the end of the Pacific War. Santa
Anna usually was in a rage when he ordered his victims shot.
The Japanese were never hanged without the ceremony of a

[9] *Ibid.*, p. 509.
[10] For a Mexican condemnation of the Alamo and Goliad, see Ramón
Martínez Caro, *Verdadera idea de la primera campaña en Tejas*, Mexico,
1837, published one year after the events.

trial—a refinement, one must conclude, belonging to a more civilized age and a more enlightened people.

Meanwhile, Texas-Mexicans died at the Alamo and fought at San Jacinto on the Texan side. The Rio Grande people, because of their Federalist and autonomist views, were sympathetic to the Texas republic until Texans began to invade their properties south of the Nueces. The truth seems to be that the old war propaganda concerning the Alamo, Goliad, and Mier later provided a convenient justification for outrages committed on the Border by Texans of certain types, so convenient an excuse that it was artificially prolonged for almost a century. And had the Alamo, Goliad, and Mier not existed, they would have been invented, as indeed they seem to have been in part.

The Texan had an undeniable superiority over the Mexican in the matter of weapons. The Texan was armed with the rifle and the revolver. The ranchero fought with the implements of his cowherding trade, the rope and the knife, counting himself lucky if he owned a rusty old musket and a charge of powder. Lead was scarce, old pieces of iron being used for bullets. Possession of even a weapon of this kind was illegal after 1835, when Santa Anna disarmed the militia, leaving the frontier at the mercy of Indians and Texans. Against them the ranchero had to depend on surprise and superior horsemanship. Until the Mexican acquired the revolver and learned how to use it, a revolver-armed Texan could indeed be worth a half-dozen Mexicans; but one may wonder whether cowards will fight under such handicaps as did the Borderers. The Rio Grande people not only defended themselves with inadequate armament; they often made incursions into hostile territory armed with lances, knives, and old swords.[11]

The belief in the Mexican's treachery was related to that of his cowardice. As with the Mexican's supposed cruelty, one finds the belief perpetuated as a justification for outrage. Long after

[11] J. Frank Dobie in *The Mustangs*, New York, 1954, pp. 195 and 261, makes some interesting observations about the Mexican armament of the time.

Mexicans acquired the revolver, "peace officers" in the Nueces–Rio Grande territory continued to believe (or pretended to do so) that no Mexican unaided could best a Texan in a fair fight. The killing of innocent Mexicans as "accomplices" became standard procedure—especially with the Texas Rangers—whenever a Border Mexican shot an American. The practice had an important influence on Border balladry and on the lives of men such as Gregorio Cortez.

The picture of the Mexican as an inveterate thief, especially of horses and cattle, is of interest to the psychologist as well as to the folklorist. The cattle industry of the Southwest had its origin in the Nueces–Rio Grande area, with the stock and the ranches of the Rio Grande rancheros. The "cattle barons" built up their fortunes at the expense of the Border Mexican by means which were far from ethical. One notes that the white Southerner took his slave women as concubines and then created an image of the male Negro as a sex fiend. In the same way he appears to have taken the Mexican's property and then made him out a thief.

The story that the Mexican thought of the Texan as a being apart and distinguished him from other Americans belongs with the post cards depicting the United States as an appendage of Texas. To the Border Mexican at least, Texans are indistinguishable from other Americans, and *tejano* is used for the Texas-Mexican, except perhaps among the more sophisticated. The story that the Mexican believes he could lick the United States if it were not for Texas also must be classed as pure fiction. The Border Mexican does distinguish the Ranger from other Americans, but his belief is that if it were not for the United States Army he would have run the Rangers out of the country a long time ago.

Theories of racial purity have fallen somewhat into disrepute since the end of World War II. So has the romantic idea that Li Po and Einstein were inferior to Genghis Khan and Hitler because the latter two were bloodier and therefore manlier. There is interest from a folkloristic point of view, however, in the glorification of the Plains savage at the expense of the semicivilized, sedentary Indian of Mexico. The noble savage very early crept into American folklore in the form of tales and songs about eloquent Indian chiefs and beautiful Indian princesses. Such stories appear to have had their origin in areas where Indians had completely disappeared.[12] On the frontier the legend seems to have been dichotomized. After the 1870's, when the Indian danger was past, it was possible to idealize the Plains savage. But the "Mexican problem" remained. A distinction was drawn between the noble Plains Indian and the degenerate ancestor of the Mexican.

The legend has taken a firm grip on the American imagination. In the Southwest one finds Americans of Mexican descent attempting to hide their Indian blood by calling themselves Spanish, while Americans of other origins often boast of having Comanche, Cherokee, or other wild Indian blood, all royal of course. The belief also had its practical aspects in reaffirming Mexican racial inferiority. The Comanche did not consider Mexican blood inferior. Mexican captives were often adopted into the tribe, as were captives of other races. But the Comanche had never read the Bible or John Locke. He could rob, kill, or enslave without feeling the need of racial prejudices to justify his actions.

Even a cursory analysis shows the justification value of the Texas legend and gives us a clue to one of the reasons for its survival. Goldfinch puts most Americans coming into the Brownsville-Matamoros area after the Mexican War into two categories: those who had no personal feeling against the Mexicans but who were ruthless in their efforts to acquire a fortune quickly, and those who, inclined to be brutal to everyone, found in the Mexican's defenseless state after the war an easy and safe outlet for their brutality.[13] It was to the interest of these two types that the legend about the Mexican be perpetuated. As long as the majority of the population accepted it as fact, men

---

[12] See Austin E. Fife and Francesca Redden, "The Pseudo-Indian Folksongs of the Anglo-American and French-Canadian," *Journal of American Folklore,* Vol. 67, No. 265, pp. 239–251; No. 266, pp. 379–394.

[13] Goldfinch, *Juan N. Cortina,* p. 40.

of this kind could rob, cheat, or kill the Border Mexican without suffering sanctions either from the law or from public opinion. And if the Mexican retaliated, the law stepped in to defend or to avenge his persecutors.

In 1838 Texas "cowboys" were making expeditions down to the Rio Grande to help the Rio Grande people fight Santa Anna. In between alliances they stole their allies' cattle. McArthur states that their stealing was "condemned by some" but that it was "justified by the majority on the ground that the Mexicans belonged to a hostile nation, from whom the Texans had received and were still receiving many injuries; and that they would treat the Texans worse if it were in their power to do so."[14] In the 1850's and 1860's when the filibuster William Walker—a Tennessean—operated in Central America, he did so to the cry of "Remember the Alamo!"[15] Al Capone in the 1920's, sending his men off to take care of some German shopkeeper who had failed to kick in, might just as well have cried, "Remember Caporetto, boys! Remember the Piave!" But perhaps Scarface Al lacked a sense of history.

This does not explain why the legend finds support among the literate and the educated. The explanation may lie in the paucity of Texas literature until very recent times. Other peoples have been stirred up by skillfully written war propaganda, but after the war they have usually turned to other reading, if they have a rich literature from which to draw. J. Frank Dobie has said that if he "were asked what theme of Texas life has been most movingly and dramatically recorded . . . I should name the experiences of Texans as prisoners to the Mexicans."[16] If it is true that the best writing done about Texas until recent times was ancient war propaganda directed against the Mexicans, it is not strange that the prejudices of those early days should have been preserved among the literate. The relative lack of perspective and of maturity of mind that Mr. Dobie himself deplored as

[14] Daniel Evander McArthur, *The Cattle Industry of Texas, 1685–1918*, Master's thesis, University of Texas, 1918, p. 50.
[15] Dobie, *The Flavor of Texas*, p. 5.
[16] *Ibid.*, p. 125.

late as 1952 in writers about the Southwest also played its part.[17]

Is the Texas legend folklore? The elements of folklore are there. One catches glimpses of the "false Scot" and the "cruel Moor," half-hidden among the local color. Behind the superhuman Ranger are Beowulf, Roland, and the Cid, slaying hundreds.[18] The idea that one's own clan or tribe is unique is probably inherent in certain stages of human development. Sometimes the enemy is forced to recognize the excellence of the hero. Achilles' armor and the Cid's corpse win battles; the Spanish hosts admit the valor of Brave Lord Willoughby, the Englishman; and the Rangers recognize the worth of Jacinto Treviño, the Mexican.

The difference, and a fundamental one, between folklore and the Texas legend is that the latter is not usually found in the oral traditions of those groups of Texas people that one might consider folk. It appears in two widely dissimilar places: in the written works of the literary and the educated and orally among a class of rootless adventurers who have used the legend for very practical purposes. One must classify the Texas legend as pseudo folklore. Disguised as fact, it still plays a major role in Texas history. Under the guise of local pride, it appears in its most blatant forms in the "professional" Texan.

The Texas Rangers

The group of men who were most responsible for putting the Texan's pseudo folklore into deeds were the Texas Rangers. They were part of the legend themselves, its apotheosis as it were. If all the books written about the Rangers were put one on top of the other, the resulting pile would be almost as tall as some of the tales that they contain. The Rangers have been pictured as a fearless, almost super-

---

[17] J. Frank Dobie, *Guide to Life and Literature of the Southwest,* Dallas, 1952, pp. 90–91.

[18] In epic story, however, the enemy is rarely cowardly. Very often it is one of the hero's own side who is the least admirable character—Thersites among the Greeks, the Counts of Carrión among the Castilians, the weeping coward among the Border raiders.

human breed of men, capable of incredible feats. It may take a company of militia to quell a riot, but one Ranger was said to be enough for one mob. Evildoers, especially Mexican ones, were said to quail at the mere mention of the name. To the Ranger is given the credit for ending lawlessness and disorder along the Rio Grande.

The Ranger did make a name for himself along the Border. The word *rinche,* from "ranger," is an important one in Border folklore. It has been extended to cover not only the Rangers but any other Americans armed and mounted and looking for Mexicans to kill. Possemen and border patrolmen are also *rinches,* and even Pershing's cavalry is so called in Lower Border variants of ballads about the pursuit of Villa. The official Texas Rangers are known as the *rinches de la Kineña* or Rangers of King Ranch, in accordance with the Borderer's belief that the Rangers were the personal strong-arm men of Richard King and the other "cattle barons."

What the Border Mexican thought about the Ranger is best illustrated by means of sayings and anecdotes. Here are a few that are typical.

1. The Texas Ranger always carries a rusty old gun in his saddlebags. This is for use when he kills an unarmed Mexican. He drops the gun beside the body and then claims he killed the Mexican in self-defense and after a furious battle.

2. When he has to kill an armed Mexican, the Ranger tries to catch him asleep, or he shoots the Mexican in the back.

3. If it weren't for the American soldiers, the Rangers wouldn't dare come to the Border. The Ranger always runs and hides behind the soldiers when real trouble starts.

4. Once an army detachment was chasing a raider, and they were led by a couple of Rangers. The Mexican went into the brush. The Rangers galloped up to the place, pointed it out, and then stepped back to let the soldiers go in first.

5. Two Rangers are out looking for a Mexican horse thief. They strike his trail, follow it for a while, and then turn at right angles and ride until they meet a half-dozen Mexican laborers

walking home from the fields. These they shoot with their deadly Colts. Then they go to the nearest town and send back a report to Austin: "In pursuit of horse thieves we encountered a band of Mexicans, and though outnumbered we succeeded in killing a dozen of them after a hard fight, without loss to ourselves. It is believed that others of the band escaped and are making for the Rio Grande." And as one can see, except for a few omissions and some slight exaggeration, the report is true in its basic details. Austin is satisfied that all is well on the Border. The Rangers add to their reputation as a fearless, hard-fighting breed of men; and the real horse thief stays out of the surrounding territory for some time, for fear he may meet up with the Rangers suddenly on some lonely road one day, and they may mistake him for a laborer.

I do not claim for these little tidbits the documented authenticity that Ranger historians claim for their stories. What we have here is frankly partisan and exaggerated without a doubt, but it does throw some light on Mexican attitudes toward the Ranger which many Texans may scarcely suspect. And it may be that these attitudes are not without some basis in fact.

The Rangers have been known to exaggerate not only the numbers of Mexicans they engaged but those they actually killed and whose bodies could be produced, presumably. In 1859 Cortina was defeated by a combined force of American soldiers and Texas Rangers. Army Major Heintzelman placed Cortina's losses at sixty; Ranger Captain Ford estimated them at two hundred.[19] In 1875 Ranger Captain McNelly climaxed his Red Raid on the Rio Grande by wiping out a band of alleged cattle rustlers at Palo Alto. McNelly reported fifteen dead; eight bodies were brought into Brownsville.[20] One more instance should suffice. In 1915 a band of about forty *sediciosos* (seditionists) under Aniceto Pizaña raided Norias in King Ranch. Three days later they were said to have been surrounded a mile from the Rio Grande and wiped out to the last man by a force

[19] Goldfinch, *Juan N. Cortina*, p. 49.
[20] *Ibid.*, p. 62.

of Rangers and deputies.[21] About ten years later, just when accounts of this Ranger exploit were getting into print, I remember seeing Aniceto Pizaña at a wedding on the south bank of the Rio Grande. He looked very much alive, and in 1954 I was told he was still living. Living too in the little towns on the south bank are a number of the Norias raiders.

It also seems a well-established fact that the Rangers often killed Mexicans who had nothing to do with the criminals they were after. Some actually were shot by mistake, according to the Ranger method of shooting first and asking questions afterwards.[22] But perhaps the majority of the innocent Mexicans who died at Ranger hands were killed much more deliberately than that. A wholesale butchery of "accomplices" was effected twice during Border history by the Rangers, after the Cortina uprising in 1859 and during the Pizaña uprising of 1915. Professor Webb calls the retaliatory killings of 1915 an "orgy of bloodshed [in which] the Texas Rangers played a prominent part."[23] He sets the number of Mexicans killed between 500 and 5,000. This was merely an intensification of an established practice which was carried on during less troubled years on a smaller scale.

Several motives must have been involved in the Ranger practice of killing innocent Mexicans as accomplices of the wrongdoers they could not catch. The most obvious one was "revenge by proxy," as Professor Webb calls it,[24] a precedent set by Bigfoot Wallace, who as a member of Hays's Rangers in the Mexican War killed as many inoffensive Mexicans as he could to avenge his imprisonment after the Mier expedition. A more practical motive was the fact that terror makes an occupied country submissive, something the Germans knew when they executed hostages in the occupied countries of Europe during World War II. A third motive may have been the Ranger weakness for

[21] J. Frank Dobie, "Versos of the Texas Vaqueros," *Publications of the Texas Folklore Society*, IV, Austin, 1925, p. 32.

[22] See Webb, *The Texas Rangers*, pp. 263ff., for an account of one of these "mistake" slaughters of all adult males in a peaceful ranchero community on the Mexican side, by McNelly.

[23] *Ibid.*, p. 478.

[24] *Ibid.*, p. 87.

sending impressive reports to Austin about their activities on the Border. The killing of innocent persons attracted unfavorable official notice only when it was extremely overdone.

In 1954 Mrs. Josefina Flores de Garza of Brownsville gave me some idea how it felt to be on the receiving end of the Ranger "orgy of bloodshed" of 1915. At that time Mrs. Garza was a girl of eighteen, the eldest of a family that included two younger boys in their teens and several small children. The family lived on a ranch near Harlingen, north of Brownsville. When the Ranger "executions" began, other Mexican ranchers sought refuge in town. The elder Flores refused to abandon his ranch, telling his children, "El que nada debe nada teme." (He who is guilty of nothing fears nothing.)

The Rangers arrived one day, surrounded the place and searched the outbuildings. The family waited in the house. Then the Rangers called the elder Flores out. He stepped to the door, and they shot him down. His two boys ran to him when he fell, and they were shot as they bent over their father. Then the Rangers came into the house and looked around. One of them saw a new pair of chaps, liked them, and took them with him. They left immediately afterwards.[25]

From other sources I learned that the shock drove Josefina Flores temporarily insane. For two days her mother lived in the house with a brood of terrified youngsters, her deranged eldest daughter, and the corpses of her husband and her sons. Then a detachment of United States soldiers passed through, looking for raiders. They buried the bodies and got the family into town.

The daughter recovered her sanity after some time, but it still upsets her a great deal to talk about the killings. And, though forty years have passed, she still seems to be afraid that if she says something critical about the Rangers they will come and do her harm. Apparently Ranger terror did its work well, on the peaceful and the inoffensive.[26]

[25] Specific data concerning sources of material obtained in interviews is found in the Bibliography.

[26] In *A Brief History of the Lower Rio Grande Valley*, Menasha (Wisconsin), 1917, p. 90, Frank Cushman Pierce reports: "On August 3, 1915,

Except in the movies, ruthlessness and a penchant for stretching the truth do not in themselves imply a lack of courage. The Borderer's belief that all Rangers are shooters-in-the-back is of the same stuff as the Texan belief that all Mexicans are back-stabbers. There is evidence, however, that not all Rangers lived up to their reputation as a fearless breed of men. Their basic techniques of ambush, surprise, and shooting first—with the resultant "mistake" killings of innocent bystanders—made them operate at times in ways that the average city policeman would be ashamed to imitate. The "shoot first and ask questions later" method of the Rangers has been romanticized into something dashing and daring, in technicolor, on a wide screen, and with Gary Cooper in the title role. Pierce's *Brief History* gives us an example of the way the method worked in actuality.

On May 17, 1885, Sergt. B. D. Lindsay and six men from Company D frontier battalion of rangers, while scouting near the Rio Grande for escaped Mexican convicts, saw two Mexicans riding along. . . . As the horses suited the description of those alleged to be in possession of the convicts, and under the impression that these two were the men he was after, Lindsay called to them to halt, and at once opened fire on them. The elder Mexican fell to the ground with his horse, but the younger, firing from behind the dead animal, shot Private Sieker through the heart, killing him instantly. B. C. Reilly was shot through both thighs and badly wounded. The Mexicans stood their ground until the arrival of men from the ranch of a deputy-sheriff named Prudencio Herrera, who . . . insisted that the two Mexicans were well known and highly respected citizens and refused to turn them over to the rangers. . . . The citizens of Laredo . . . were indignant over the act of the rangers in shooting on Gonzalez, claiming that he was a well-known citizen of good repute, and alleging that the rangers would have killed them at the outset but for the fact that they defended themselves. The rangers, on the other hand, claimed that unless they would have proceeded as they did,

---

rangers and deputy sheriffs attacked a ranch near Paso Real, about 32 miles north of Brownsville, and killed Desiderio Flores and his two sons, Mexicans, alleged to be bandits."

should the Mexicans have been the criminals they were really after they, the rangers, would have been fired on first.[27]

There is unanswerable logic in the Ranger sergeant's argument, if one concedes him his basic premise: that a Mexican's life is of little value anyway. But this picture of seven Texas Rangers, feeling so defenseless in the face of two Mexicans that they must fire at them on sight, because the Mexicans might be mean and shoot at them first, is somewhat disillusioning to those of us who have grown up with the tradition of the lone Ranger getting off the train and telling the station hangers-on, "Of course they sent one Ranger. There's just one riot, isn't there?" Almost every week one reads of ordinary city policemen who capture desperate criminals—sometimes singlehandedly—without having to shoot first.

Sometimes the "shoot first" method led to even more serious consequences, and many a would-be Mexican-killer got his head blown off by a comrade who was eager to get in the first shot and mistook his own men for Mexicans while they all waited in ambush. Perhaps "shoot first and ask questions afterwards" is not the right name for this custom. "Shoot first and then see what you're shooting at" may be a better name. As such it has not been limited to the Texas Rangers. All over the United States during the deer season, Sunday hunters go out and shoot first.

Then there is the story about Alfredo Cerda, killed on Brownsville's main street in 1902. The Cerdas were prosperous ranchers near Brownsville, but it was their misfortune to live next to one of the "cattle barons" who was not through expanding yet. One day three Texas Rangers came down from Austin and "executed" the elder Cerda and one of his sons as cattle rustlers. The youngest son fled across the river, and thus the Cerda ranch was vacated. Five months later the remaining son, Alfredo Cerda, crossed over to Brownsville. He died the same day, shot down by a Ranger's gun.

Marcelo Garza, Sr., of Brownsville is no teller of folktales. He

[27] Pierce, *A Brief History*, pp. 110–111.

is a respected businessman, one of Brownsville's most highly
regarded citizens of Mexican descent. Mr. Garza claims to have
been an eyewitness to the shooting of the youngest Cerda. In
1902, Mr. Garza says, he was a clerk at the Tomás Fernández
store on Elizabeth Street. A Ranger whom Mr. Garza identifies
as "Bekar" shot Alfredo, Mr. Garza relates, as Cerda sat in the
doorway of the Fernández store talking to Don Tomás, the
owner. The Ranger used a rifle to kill Cerda, who was unarmed,
"stalking him like a wild animal." After the shooting the Ranger
ran into a nearby saloon, where other Rangers awaited him, and
the group went out the back way and sought refuge with the
federal troops in Fort Brown, to escape a mob of indignant citizens.[28] The same story had been told to me long before by my
father, now deceased. He was not a witness to the shooting but
claimed to have seen the chasing of the Rangers into Fort
Brown.

Professor Webb mentions the shooting in 1902 of an Alfredo
Cerda in Brownsville by Ranger A. Y. Baker. He gives no details.[29] Mr. Dobie also mentions an A. Y. Baker, "a famous ranger
and sheriff of the border country," as the man responsible for
the "extermination" of the unexterminated raiders of Norias.[30]

The methods of the Rangers are often justified as means to
an end, the stamping out of lawlessness on the Border. This coin
too has another face. Many Borderers will argue that the army
and local law enforcement agencies were the ones that pacified
the Border, that far from pacifying the area Ranger activities
stirred it up, that instead of eliminating lawlessness along the
Rio Grande the Rangers were for many years a primary cause of
it. It is pointed out that it was the army that defeated the major
border raiders and the local authorities that took care of thieves
and smugglers. The notorious Lugo brothers were captured and
executed by Cortina, the border raider. Mariano Reséndez, the

[28] Letter of Marcelo Garza, Sr., to the author, dated July 7, 1955, and
subsequent conversation with Mr. Garza in Brownsville, December 29,
1957.
[29] Webb, *The Texas Rangers*, p. 464.
[30] Dobie, "Versos of the Texas Vaqueros," p. 32.

famous smuggler, was taken by Mexican troops. Octaviano Zapata, the Union guerrilla leader during the Civil War, was defeated and slain by Texas-Mexican Confederates under Captain Antonio Benavides. After the Civil War, when released Confederate soldiers and lawless characters were disturbing the Border, citizens did not call for Rangers but organized a company of Texas-Mexicans under Captain Benavides to do their own pacifying.[31]

That the Rangers stirred up more trouble than they put down is an opinion that has been expressed by less partisan sources. Goldfinch quotes a Captain Ricketts of the United States Army, who was sent by the War Department to investigate Cortina's revolt, as saying that "conditions that brought federal troops to Brownsville had been nourished but not improved by demonstrations on the part of some Rangers and citizens."[32] In 1913 State Representative Cox of Ellis attempted to eliminate the Ranger force by striking out their appropriation from the budget. Cox declared "that there is more danger from the Rangers than from the men they are supposed to hunt down; that there is no authority of law for the Ranger force; that they are the most irresponsible officers in the State."[33] John Garner, future Vice-President of the United States, was among those who early in the twentieth century advocated abolishing the Ranger force.[34]

In *The Texas Rangers* Professor Webb notes that on the Border after 1848 the Mexican was "victimized by the law," that "the old landholding families found their titles in jeopardy and if they did not lose in the courts they lost to their American lawyers," and again that "the Mexicans suffered not only in their persons but in their property."[35] What he fails to note is that this lawless law was enforced principally by the Texas Rangers. It was the Rangers who could and did furnish the fortune-making

[31] Annie Cowling, *The Civil War Trade of the Lower Rio Grande Valley*, Master's thesis, University of Texas, 1926, pp. 136ff.

[32] Goldfinch, p. 48.

[33] San Antonio *Express*, July 29, 1913, p. 3.

[34] Seguin *Enterprise*, April 18, 1902, p. 2.

[35] Webb, *The Texas Rangers*, pp. 175–176.

adventurer with services not rendered by the United States Army or local sheriffs. And that is why from the point of view of the makers of fortunes the Rangers were so important to the "pacification" of the Border.

The Rangers and those who imitated their methods undoubtedly exacerbated the cultural conflict on the Border rather than allayed it. The assimilation of the north-bank Border people into the American commonwealth was necessary to any effective pacification of the Border. Ranger operations did much to impede that end. They created in the Border Mexican a deep and understandable hostility for American authority; they drew Border communities even closer together than they had been, though at that time they were beginning to disintegrate under the impact of new conditions.

Terror cowed the more inoffensive Mexican, but it also added to the roll of bandits and raiders many high-spirited individuals who would have otherwise remained peaceful and useful citizens. These were the heroes of the Border folk. People sang *corridos* about these men who, in the language of the ballads, "each with his pistol defended his right."

II: THE LEGEND

How they sing
El Corrído de Gregorío Cortez

*T*hey *still sing* of him—in the *cantinas* and the country stores, in the ranches when men gather at night to talk in the cool dark, sitting in a circle, smoking and listening to the old songs and the tales of other days. Then the *guitarreros* sing of the border raids and the skirmishes, of the men who lived by the phrase, "I will break before I bend."

They sing with deadly-serious faces, throwing out the words of the song like a challenge, tearing savagely with their stiff, callused fingers at the strings of the guitars.

And that is how, in the dark quiet of the ranches, in the lighted noise of the saloons, they sing of Gregorio Cortez.

After the song is sung there is a lull. Then the old men, who have lived long and seen almost everything, tell their stories. And when they tell about Gregorio Cortez, the telling goes like this:

33

How Gregorio Cortez came to be in the county of El Carmen

That was good singing, and a good song; give the man a drink. Not like these pachucos nowadays, mumbling damn-foolishness into a microphone; it is not done that way. Men should sing with their heads thrown back, with their mouths wide open and their eyes shut. Fill your lungs, so they can hear you at the pasture's farther end. And when you sing, sing songs like *El Corrido de Gregorio Cortez*. There's a song that makes the hackles rise. You can almost see him there—Gregorio Cortez, with his pistol in his hand.

He was a man, a Border man. What did he look like? Well, that is hard to tell. Some say he was short and some say he was tall; some say he was Indian brown and some say he was blond like a newborn cockroach. But I'd say he was not too dark and not too fair, not too thin and not too fat, not too short and not too tall; and he looked just a little bit like me. But does it matter so much what he looked like? He was a man, very much of a man; and he was a Border man. Some say he was born in Matamoros; some say Reynosa; some say Hidalgo county on the other side. And I guess others will say other things. But Matamoros, or Reynosa, or Hidalgo, it's all the same Border; and short or tall, dark or fair, it's the man that counts. And that's what he was, a man.

Not a gunman, no, not a bravo. He never came out of a cantina wanting to drink up the sea at one gulp. Not that kind of man, if you can call that kind a man. No, that wasn't Gregorio Cortez at all. He was a peaceful man, a hard-working man like you and me.

He could shoot. Forty-four and thirty-thirty, they were the same to him. He could put five bullets into a piece of board and not make but one hole, and quicker than you could draw a good deep breath. Yes, he could shoot. But he could also work.

He was a vaquero, and a better one there has not ever been from Laredo to the mouth. He could talk to horses, and they

34

would understand. They would follow him around, like dogs, and no man knew a good horse better than Gregorio Cortez. As for cattle, he could set up school for your best caporal. And if an animal was lost, and nobody could pick up a trail, they would send for Gregorio Cortez. He could always find a trail. There was no better tracker in all the Border country, nor a man who could hide his tracks better if he wanted to. That was Gregorio Cortez, the best vaquero and range man that there ever was.

But that is not all. You farmers, do you think that Gregorio Cortez did not know your business too? You could have told him nothing about cotton or beans or corn. He knew it all. He could look into the sky of a morning and smell it, sniff it the way a dog sniffs, and tell you what kind of weather there was going to be. And he would take a piece of dirt in his hands and rub it back and forth between his fingers—to see if the land had reached its point—and you would say he was looking into it. And perhaps he was, for Gregorio Cortez was the seventh son of a seventh son.

You piddling modern farmers, vain of yourselves when you make a bale! You should have seen the crops raised by Gregorio Cortez. And when harvesting came, he was in there with the rest. Was it shucking corn? All you could see was the shucks fly and the pile grow, until you didn't know there was a man behind the pile. But he was even better at cotton-picking time. He would bend down and never raise his head till he came out the other end, and he would be halfway through another row before the next man was through with his. And don't think the row he went through wasn't clean. No flags, no streamers, nothing left behind, nothing but clean, empty burrs where he had passed. It was the same when clearing land. There were men who went ahead of him, cutting fast along their strip in the early morning, but by noontime the man ahead was always Gregorio Cortez, working at his own pace, talking little and not singing very much, and never acting up.

For Gregorio Cortez was not of your noisy, hell-raising type. That was not his way. He always spoke low, and he was always polite, whoever he was speaking to. And when he spoke to men older than himself he took off his hat and held it over his heart.

A man who never raised his voice to parent or elder brother, and never disobeyed. That was Gregorio Cortez, and that was the way men were in this country along the river. That was the way they were before these modern times came, and God went away.

He should have stayed on the Border; he should not have gone up above, into the North. But it was going to be that way, and that was the way it was. Each man has a certain lot in life, and no other thing but that will be his share. People were always coming down from places in the North, from Dallas and San Antonio and Corpus and Foro West. And they would say, "Gregorio Cortez, why don't you go north? There is much money to be made. Stop eating beans and tortillas and that rubbery jerked beef. One of these days you're going to put out one of your eyes, pull and pull with your teeth on that stuff and it suddenly lets go. It's a wonder all you Border people are not one-eyed. Come up above with us, where you can eat white bread and ham."

But Gregorio Cortez would only smile, because he was a peaceful man and did not take offense. He did not like white bread and ham; it makes people flatulent and dull. And he liked it where he was. So he always said, "I like this country. I will stay here."

But Gregorio Cortez had a brother, a younger brother named Román. Now Román was just like the young men of today, loudmouthed and discontented. He was never happy where he was, and to make it worse he loved a joke more than any other thing. He would think nothing of playing a joke on a person twice his age. He had no respect for anyone, and that is why he ended like he did. But that is yet to tell.

Román talked to Gregorio and begged him that they should move away from the river and go up above, where there was much money to be made. And he talked and begged so, that finally Gregorio Cortez said he would go with his brother Román, and they saddled their horses and rode north.

Well, they did not grow rich, though things went well with them because they were good workers. Sometimes they picked cotton; sometimes they were vaqueros, and sometimes they cleared land for the Germans. Finally they came to a place called El Carmen, and there they settled down and farmed. And that was how Gregorio Cortez came to be in the county of El Carmen, where the tragedy took place.

Román's horse trade and what came of it

Román owned two horses, two beautiful sorrels that were just alike, the same color, the same markings, and the same size. You could not have told them apart, except that one of them was lame. There was an American who owned a little sorrel mare. This man was dying to get Román's sorrel— the good one—and every time they met he would offer to swap the mare for the horse. But Román did not think much of the mare. He did not like it when the American kept trying to make him trade.

"I wonder what this Gringo thinks," Román said to himself. "He takes me for a fool. But I'm going to make him such a trade that he will remember me forever."

And Román laughed a big-mouthed laugh. He thought it would be a fine joke, besides being a good trade. There were mornings when the American went to town in his buggy along a narrow road. So Román saddled the lame sorrel, led him a little way along the road, and stopped under a big mesquite that bordered on the fence. He fixed it so the spavined side was against the mesquite. Román waited a little while, and soon he heard the buggy coming along the road. Then he got in the saddle and began picking mesquites off the tree and eating them. When the American came around the bend, there was Román on his sorrel horse. The American stopped his buggy beside Román and looked at the horse with much admiration. It was a fine animal, exactly like the other one, but the American could not see the spavined leg.

"Changed your mind?" the American said.

Román stopped chewing on a mesquite and said, "Changed my mind about what?"

"About trading that horse for my mare."

"You're dead set on trading your mare for this horse of mine?" Román said.

"You know I am," the American said. "Are you ready to come round?"

"I'm in a trading mood," said Román. "With just a little arguing you might convince me to trade this horse for that worthless mare of yours. But I don't know; you might go back on the deal later on."

"I never go back on my word," the American said. "What do you think I am, a Mexican?"

"We'll see, we'll see," said Román. "How much are you willing to give in hand?"

"Enough to give you the first square meal you've had in your life," the American said.

Román just laughed, and it was all he could do to keep from guffawing. He knew who was getting the best of things.

So they made the deal, with Román still sitting on his spavined horse under the tree, chewing on mesquites.

"Where's the mare?" Román said.

"She's in my yard," said the American, "hung to a tree. You go get her and leave the horse there for me because I'm in a hurry to get to town."

That was how Román had figured it, so he said, "All right, I'll do it, but when I finish with these mesquites."

"Be sure you do, then," the American said.

"Sure, sure," said Román. "No hurry about it, is there?"

"All right," the American said, "take your time." And he drove off leaving Román still sitting on his horse under the mesquite, and as he drove off the American said, "Now isn't that just like a Mexican. He takes his time."

Román waited until the American was gone, and then he stopped eating mesquites. He got off and led the horse down the road to the American's yard and left him there in place of the little sorrel mare. On the way home Román almost fell off his saddle a couple of times, just laughing and laughing to think of the sort of face the American would pull when he came home that night.

The next morning, when Gregorio Cortez got up he said to his brother Román, "Something is going to happen today."

"Why do you say that?" asked Román.

"I don't know," said Gregorio Cortez. "I just know that something is going to happen today. I feel it. Last night my wife began to sigh for no reason at all. She kept sighing and sighing half the night, and she didn't know why. Her heart was telling her something, and I know some unlucky thing will happen to us today."

But Román just laughed, and Gregorio went inside the house to shave. Román followed him into the house and stood at the door while Gregorio shaved. It was a door made in two sections; the upper part was open and Román was leaning on the lower part, like a man leaning out of a window or over a fence. Román began to tell Gregorio about the horse trade he had made the day before, and he laughed pretty loud about it, because he thought it was a good joke. Gregorio Cortez just shaved, and he didn't say anything.

When what should pull in at the gate but a buggy, and the American got down, and the Major Sheriff of the county of El Carmen got down too. They came into the yard and up to where Román was leaning over the door, looking out.

The American had a very serious face. "I came for the mare you stole yesterday morning," he said.

Román laughed a big-mouthed laugh. "What did I tell you, Gregorio?" he said. "This Gringo Sanavabiche has backed down on me."

Now there are three saints that the Americans are especially fond of—Santa Anna, San Jacinto, and Sanavabiche—and of the three it is Sanavabiche that they pray to most. Just listen to an American any time. You may not understand anything else he says, but you are sure to hear him say, "Sanavabiche! Sanavabiche! Sanavabiche!" Every hour of the day. But they'll get very angry if you say it too, perhaps because it is a saint that belongs to them alone.

And so it was with the Major Sheriff of the county of El Carmen. Just as the words "Gringo Sanavabiche" came out of

Román's mouth, the sheriff whipped out his pistol and shot Román. He shot Román as he stood there with his head thrown back, laughing at his joke. The sheriff shot him in the face, right in the open mouth, and Román fell away from the door, at the Major Sheriff's feet.

And then Gregorio Cortez stood at the door, where his brother had stood, with his pistol in his hand. Now he and the Major Sheriff met, each one pistol in hand, as men should meet when they fight for what is right. For it is a pretty thing to see, when two men stand up for their right, with their pistols in their hands, front to front and without fear. And so it was, for the Major Sheriff also was a man.

Yes, the Major Sheriff was a man; he was a gamecock that had won in many pits, but in Gregorio Cortez he met a cockerel that pecked his comb. The Major Sheriff shot first, and he missed; and Gregorio Cortez shot next, and he didn't miss. Three times did they shoot, three times did the Major Sheriff miss, and three times did Gregorio Cortez shoot the sheriff of El Carmen. The Major Sheriff fell dead at the feet of Gregorio Cortez, and it was in this way that Gregorio Cortez killed the first sheriff of many that he was to kill.

When the Major Sheriff fell, Gregorio Cortez looked up, and the other American said, "Don't kill me; I am unarmed."

"I will not kill you," said Gregorio Cortez. "But you'd better go away."

So the American went away. He ran into the brush and kept on running until he came to town and told all the other sheriffs that the Major Sheriff was dead.

Meanwhile, Gregorio Cortez knew that he too must go away. He was not afraid of the law; he knew the law, and he knew that he had the right. But if he stayed, the Rangers would come, and the Rangers have no regard for law. You know what kind of men they are. When the Governor of the State wants a new Ranger, he asks his sheriffs, "Bring all the criminals to me." And from the murderers he chooses the Ranger, because no one can be a Ranger who has not killed a man. So Gregorio Cortez knew that the best thing for him was to go away, and his first thought was of the Border, where he had been born. But first he must take care of his brother, so he put Román in the buggy and drove into town, where his mother lived.

Now there was a lot of excitement in town. All the Americans were saddling up and loading rifles and pistols, because they were going out to kill Cortez. When all of a sudden, what should come rolling into town but the buggy, driven by Gregorio Cortez. They met him on the edge of town, armed to the teeth, on horseback and afoot, and he on the buggy, holding the reins lightly in his hands. Román was in the back, shot in the mouth. He could neither speak nor move, but just lay there like one who is dead.

They asked him, "Who are you?"

And he said to them, "I am Gregorio Cortez."

They all looked at him and were afraid of him, because they were only twenty or twenty-five, and they knew that they were not enough. So they stepped aside and let him pass and stood talking among themselves what would be the best thing to do. But Gregorio Cortez just drove ahead, slowly, without seeming to care about the men he left behind. He came to his mother's house, and there he took down his brother and carried him in the house. He stayed there until dawn, and during the night groups of armed men would go by the house and say, "He's in there. He's in there." But none of them ever went in.

At dawn Gregorio Cortez came out of his mother's house. There were armed men outside, but they made no move against him. They just watched as he went down the street, his hands resting on his belt. He went along as if he was taking a walk, and they stood there watching until he reached the brush and he jumped into it and disappeared. And then they started shooting at him with rifles, now that he was out of pistol range.

"I must get me a rifle," said Gregorio Cortez, "a rifle and a horse."

They gathered in a big bunch and started after him in the brush. But they could not catch Gregorio Cortez. No man was ever as good as him in hiding his own tracks, and he soon had them going around in circles, while he doubled back and headed for home to get himself a rifle and a horse.

How Gregorio Cortez rode the little sorrel mare all of five hundred miles

He went in and got his thirty-thirty, and then he looked around for the best horse he had. It is a long way from El Carmen to the Border, all of five hundred miles. The first thing he saw in the corral was the little sorrel mare. Gregorio Cortez took a good look at her, and he knew she was no ordinary mare.

"You're worth a dozen horses," said Gregorio Cortez, and he saddled the little mare.

But by then the whole wasp's nest was beginning to buzz. The President of the United States offered a thousand dollars for him, and many men went out to get Gregorio Cortez. The Major Sheriffs of the counties and all their sheriffs were out. There were Rangers from the counties, armed to the teeth, and the King Ranch Rangers from the Capital, the meanest of them all, all armed and looking for Cortez. Every road was blocked and every bridge guarded. There were trackers out with those dogs they call hounds, that can follow a track better than the best tracker. They had railroad cars loaded with guns and ammunition and with men, moving up and down trying to head him off. The women and children stayed in the houses, behind locked doors, such was the fear they all had of Gregorio Cortez. Every town from the Capital to the Border was watching out for him. The brush and the fields were full of men, trying to pick up his trail. And Gregorio Cortez rode out for the Border, through brush and fields and barbed wire fences, on his little sorrel mare.

He rode and rode until he came to a great broad plain, and he started to ride across. But just as he did, one of the sheriffs saw him. The sheriff saw him, but he hid behind a bush, because he was afraid to take him on alone. So he called the other sheriffs

42

together and all the Rangers he could find, and they went off after Gregorio Cortez just as he came out upon the plain.

Gregorio Cortez looked back and saw them coming. There were three hundred of them.

"We'll run them a little race," said Gregorio Cortez.

Away went the mare, as if she had been shot from a gun, and behind her came the sheriffs and the Rangers, all shooting and riding hard. And so they rode across the plain, until one by one their horses foundered and fell to the ground and died. But still the little mare ran on, as fresh as a lettuce leaf, and pretty soon she was running all alone.

"They'll never catch me like that," said Gregorio Cortez, "not even with those dogs called hounds."

Another big bunch of sheriffs rode up, and they chased him to the edge of the plain, and into the brush went Cortez, with the trackers after him, but they did not chase him long. One moment there was a trail to follow, and next moment there was none. And the dogs called hounds sat down and howled, and the men scratched their heads and went about in circles looking for the trail. And Gregorio Cortez went on, leaving no trail, so that people thought he was riding through the air.

There were armed men everywhere, and he could not stop to eat or drink, because wherever he tried to stop armed men were there before him. So he had to ride on and on. Now they saw him, now they lost him, and so the chase went on. Many more horses foundered, but the mare still ran, and Gregorio Cortez rode on and on, pursued by hundreds and fighting hundreds every place he went.

"So many mounted Rangers," said Gregorio Cortez, "to catch just one Mexican."

It was from the big bunches that he ran. Now and again he would run into little ones of ten or a dozen men, and they were so scared of him that they would let him pass. Then, when he was out of range they would shoot at him, and he would shoot back at them once or twice, so they could go back and say, "We met up with Gregorio Cortez, and we traded shots with him." But from the big ones he had to run. And it was the little sorrel mare that took him safe away, over the open spaces and into the brush, and once in the brush, they might as well have been following a star.

So it went for a day, and when night fell Cortez arrived at a place named Los Fresnos and called at a Mexican house. When the man of the house came out, Cortez told him, "I am Gregorio Cortez."

That was all he had to say. He was given to eat and drink, and the man of the house offered Gregorio Cortez his own horse and his rifle and his saddle. But Cortez would not take them. He thanked the man, but he would not give up his little sorrel mare. Cortez was sitting there, drinking a cup of coffee, when the Major Sheriff of Los Fresnos came up with his three hundred men. All the other people ran out of the house and hid, and no one was left in the house, only Gregorio Cortez, with his pistol in his hand.

Then the Major Sheriff called out, in a weepy voice, as the corrido says. He sounded as if he wanted to cry, but it was all done to deceive Gregorio Cortez.

"Cortez," the Major Sheriff said, "hand over your weapons. I did not come to kill you. I am your friend."

"If you come as my friend," said Gregorio Cortez, "why did you bring three hundred men? Why have you made me a corral?"

The Major Sheriff knew that he had been caught in a lie, and the fighting began. He killed the Major Sheriff and the second sheriff under him, and he killed many sheriffs more. Some of the sheriffs got weak in the knees, and many ran away.

"Don't go away," said Gregorio Cortez. "I am the man you are looking for. I am Gregorio Cortez."

They were more than three hundred, but he jumped their corral, and he rode away again, and those three hundred did not chase him any more.

He rode on and on, until he came to a river called the San Antonio. It is not much of a river, but the banks are steep and high, and he could not find a ford. So he rode to a ranch house nearby, where they were holding a baile because the youngest child of the house had been baptized that day, and he asked the man of the house about a ford.

"There are only two fords," the man said. "One is seven miles upstream and the other is seven miles down."

"I will take another look at the river," said Gregorio Cortez. He left the baile and rode slowly to the river. It was steep, and far below he could see the water flowing; he could barely see it because it was so dark. He stood there thinking, trying to figure out a way, when he heard the music at the baile stop.

He knew the Rangers were at the baile now. So he leaned over in his saddle and whispered in the mare's ear. He talked to her, and she understood. She came to the edge of the bank, with soft little steps, because she was afraid. But Gregorio Cortez kept talking to her and talking to her, and finally she jumped. She jumped far out and into the dark water below, she and Gregorio Cortez.

The other bank was not so high, but it was just as steep. Gregorio Cortez took out his reata, and he lassoed a stump high on the bank. He climbed up the rope and got a stick, and with the stick he worked on the bank as fast as he could, for he could hear the racket of the dogs. The ground was soft, and he knocked off part of the top, until he made something like a slope. Then he pulled and talked until the mare struggled up the bank to where he was. After that they rested up a bit and waited for the Rangers. Up they came with their dogs, to the spot where the mare had jumped. When they came up to the river's edge, Cortez fired a shot in the air and yelled at them, "I am Gregorio Cortez!"

Then he rode away, leaving them standing there on the other side, because none of them was brave enough to do what Cortez had done.

He rode on and on, and sometimes they chased him and sometimes he stood and fought. And every time he fought he would kill them a Ranger or two. They chased him across the Arroyo del Cíbolo and into an oak grove, and there they made him a corral. Then they sent the dogs away and sat down to wait, for they wanted to catch him asleep. Gregorio Cortez thought for a little while what he should do. Then he made his mare lie down

45

on the ground, so she would not be hurt. After that Gregorio Cortez began talking to himself and answering himself in different voices, as if he had many men. This made the Rangers say to one another, "There is a whole army of men with Gregorio Cortez." So they broke up their corral and went away, because they did not think there were enough of them to fight Gregorio Cortez and all the men he had. And Gregorio Cortez rode away, laughing to himself.

He kept riding on and on, by day and by night, and if he slept the mare stood guard and she would wake him up when she heard a noise. He had no food or cigarettes, and his ammunition was running low. He was going along a narrow trail with a high barbed wire fence on one side and a nopal thicket on the other, and right before he hit a turn he heard horses ahead. The first man that came around the turn ran into Gregorio Cortez, with his pistol in his hand. There was a whole line of others behind the first, all armed with rifles, but they had to put the rifles away. Then Gregorio Cortez knocked over a tall nopal plant with his stirrup and made just enough room for his mare to back into while the Rangers filed by. He stopped the last one and took away his tobacco, matches, and ammunition. And then he rode away.

He rode on to La Grulla, and he was very thirsty, because he had not had water in a long time, and the mare was thirsty too. Near La Grulla there was a dam where the vaqueros watered their stock. But when Gregorio Cortez got there, he saw twenty armed men resting under the trees that grew close to the water. Gregorio Cortez stopped and thought what he could do. Then he went back into the brush and began rounding up cattle, for this was cattle country and steers were everywhere. Pretty soon he had two hundred head, and he drove them to water and while the cattle drank he and the mare drank too. After he had finished, some of the Rangers that were resting under the trees came over and helped him get the herd together again, and Gregorio Cortez rode off with the herd, laughing to himself.

He rode on and on, and by now he knew that the Rio Grande was near. He rode till he came to Cotulla, and there he was chased again. The little mare was tired, and now she began to limp. She had cut her leg and it was swelling up. Gregorio Cortez rode her into a thicket, and the Rangers made him a corral. But once in the brush, Gregorio Cortez led the mare to a coma tree and tied her there. He unsaddled her and hung the saddle to the tree, and he patted her and talked to her for a long while. Then he slipped out of the thicket, and the Rangers didn't see him because they were waiting for him to ride out. They waited for three days and finally they crept in and found only the mare and the saddle.

How El Teco sold Gregorio Cortez for a morral full of silver dollars

Gregorio Cortez was gone. While all the armed men were guarding the thicket where the mare was tied, he walked into Cotulla itself. He walked into town and mixed with the Mexicans there. He sat on the station platform and listened to other men while they talked of all the things that Gregorio Cortez had done. Then he went to a store and bought himself new clothes and walked out of the town. He went to the river and took a bath and then swam across, because the bridge was guarded. That sort of man was Gregorio Cortez. They don't make them like him any more.

He had only three cartridges left, one for one pistol and two for the other, and he had left his rifle with the mare. But he was very near the Rio Grande, and he expected to cross it soon. Still he needed ammunition, so he walked into El Sauz and tried to buy some, but they did not sell cartridges in that town. Then he thought of trying some of the houses, and chose one in which there was a pretty girl at the door because he knew it would be easier if he talked to a girl. There was not a woman that did not like Gregorio Cortez.

The girl was alone, and she invited him into the house. When he asked for ammunition, she told him she had none.

"My father has taken it all," she said. "He is out looking for a man named Gregorio Cortez."

Gregorio Cortez was embarrassed because he could see that
the girl knew who he was. But she did not let on and neither did
he. He stayed at the house for a while, and when he left she told
him how to get to the Rio Grande by the quickest way.

Now all the people along the river knew that Gregorio Cortez
was on the Border, and that he would soon cross, but no one told
the sheriffs what they knew. And Gregorio Cortez walked on,
in his new clothes, with his pistols in a morral, looking like an
ordinary man, but the people he met knew that he was Gregorio
Cortez. And he began to talk to people along the way.

Soon he met a man who told him, "You'll be on the other side
of the river tonight, Gregorio Cortez."

"I think I will," he said.

"You'll be all right then," said the man.

"I guess so," said Gregorio Cortez.

"But your brother won't," the man said. "He died in the jail
last night."

"He was badly wounded," said Gregorio Cortez. "It was his
lot to die, but I have avenged his death."

"They beat him before he died," the man said. "The Rangers
came to the jail and beat him to make him talk."

This was the first news that Gregorio Cortez had heard, and
it made him thoughtful.

He walked on, and he met another man who said, "Your
mother is in the jail, Gregorio Cortez."

"Why?" said Gregorio Cortez. "Why should the sheriffs do
that to her?"

"Because she is your mother," the man said. "That's why. Your
wife is there too, and so are your little sons."

Gregorio Cortez thought this over, and he walked on. Pretty
soon he met another man who said, "Gregorio Cortez, your own
people are suffering, and all because of you."

"Why should my own people suffer?" said Cortez. "What have
I done to them?"

"You have killed many sheriffs, Gregorio Cortez," said the
man. "The Rangers cannot catch you, so they take it out on other
people like you. Every man that's given you a glass of water has

been beaten and thrown in jail. Every man who has fed you has been hanged from a tree branch, up and down, up and down, to make him tell where you went, and some have died rather than tell. Lots of people have been shot and beaten because they were your people. But you will be safe, Gregorio Cortez; you will cross the river tonight."

"I did not know these things," said Gregorio Cortez.

And he decided to turn back, and to give himself up to the Governor of the State so that his own people would not suffer because of him.

He turned and walked back until he came to a place called Goliad, where he met eleven Mexicans, and among them there was one that called himself his friend. This man was a vaquero named El Teco, but Judas should have been his name. Gregorio Cortez was thirsty, and he came up to the eleven Mexicans to ask for water, and when El Teco saw Gregorio Cortez he thought how good it would be if he could get the thousand-dollar reward. So he walked up to Cortez and shook his hand and told the others, "Get some water for my friend Gregorio Cortez."

Then El Teco asked Gregorio Cortez to let him see the pistols he had, and that he would get him some ammunition. Gregorio Cortez smiled, because he knew. But he handed over the guns to El Teco, and El Teco looked at them and put them in his own morral. Then El Teco called the sheriffs to come and get Gregorio Cortez.

When Gregorio Cortez saw what El Teco had done, he smiled again and said to him, "Teco, a man can only be what God made him. May you enjoy your reward."

But El Teco did not enjoy the reward, though the sheriffs gave him the money, one thousand dollars in silver, more than a morral could hold. He did not enjoy it because he could not spend it anywhere. If he went to buy a taco at the market place, the taco vender would tell him that tacos were worth two thousand dollars gold that day. People cursed him in the streets and wished that he would be killed or die. So El Teco became very much afraid. He buried the money and never spent it, and he never knew peace until he died.

How Gregorio Cortez went to prison,
but not for killing the sheriffs

When the sheriffs came to arrest Gregorio Cortez, he spoke to them and said, "I am not your prisoner yet. I will be the prisoner only of the Governor of the State. I was going to the Capital to give myself up, and that is where I'll go."

The sheriffs saw that he was in the right, so they went with him all the way to the Capital, and Cortez surrendered himself to the Governor of the State.

Then they put Cortez in jail, and all the Americans were glad, because they no longer were afraid. They got together, and they tried to lynch him. Three times they tried, but they could not lynch Gregorio Cortez.

And pretty soon all the people began to see that Gregorio Cortez was in the right, and they did not want to lynch him any more. They brought him gifts to the jail, and one day one of the judges came and shook the hand of Gregorio Cortez and said to him, "I would have done the same."

But Gregorio Cortez had many enemies, for he had killed many men, and they wanted to see him hanged. So they brought him to trial for killing the Major Sheriff of the county of El Carmen. The lawyer that was against him got up and told the judges that Cortez should die, because he had killed a man. Then Gregorio Cortez got up, and he spoke to them.

"Self-defense is allowed to any man," said Gregorio Cortez. "It is in your own law, and by your own law do I defend myself. I killed the sheriff, and I am not sorry, for he killed my brother. He spilled my brother's blood, which was also my blood. And he tried to kill me too. I killed the Major Sheriff defending my right."

And Gregorio Cortez talked for a long time to the judges, telling them about their own law. When he finished even the lawyer who was against him at the start was now for him. And all the judges came down from their benches and shook hands with Gregorio Cortez.

The judges said, "We cannot kill this man."

They took Gregorio Cortez all over the State, from town to town, and in each town he was tried before the court for the killing of a man. But in every court it was the same. Gregorio Cortez spoke to the judges, and he told them about the law, and he proved that he had the right. And each time the judges said, "This man was defending his right. Tell the sheriffs to set him free."

And so it was that Gregorio Cortez was not found guilty of any wrong because of the sheriffs he had killed. And he killed many of them, there is no room for doubt. No man has killed more sheriffs than did Gregorio Cortez, and he always fought alone. For that is the way the real men fight, always on their own. There are young men around here today, who think that they are brave. Dangerous men they call themselves, and it takes five or six of them to jump a fellow and slash him in the arm. Or they hide in the brush and fill him full of buckshot as he goes by. They are not men. But that was not the way with Gregorio Cortez, for he was a real man.

Now the enemies of Gregorio Cortez got together and said to each other, "What are we going to do? This man is going free after killing so many of our friends. Shall we kill him ourselves? But we would have to catch him asleep, or shoot him in the back, because if we meet him face to face there will be few of us left."

Then one of them thought of the little sorrel mare, and there they had a plan to get Gregorio Cortez. They brought him back to court, and the lawyer who was against him asked, "Gregorio Cortez, do you recognize this mare?"

"I do," said Gregorio Cortez. "And a better little mare there never was."

Then the lawyer asked him, "Have you ridden this mare?"

And Gregorio Cortez answered, "She carried me all the way from El Carmen to the Border, a distance of five hundred miles."

Then the lawyer asked him, "Is this mare yours?"

And Gregorio Cortez saw that they had him, but there was nothing he could do, because he was an honest man and he felt that he must tell the truth. He said no, the mare did not belong to him.

Then the judges asked Gregorio Cortez, "Is this true, Gregorio Cortez? Did you take this mare that did not belong to you?"

And Gregorio Cortez had to say that the thing was true.

So they sentenced Gregorio Cortez, but not for killing the sheriffs, as some fools will tell you even now, when they ought to know better. No, not for killing the sheriffs but for stealing the little sorrel mare. The judge sentenced him to ninety-nine years and a day. And the enemies of Gregorio Cortez were happy then, because they thought Cortez would be in prison for the rest of his life.

How President Lincoln's daughter freed Gregorio Cortez, and how he was poisoned and died

But Gregorio Cortez did not stay in prison long. Inside of a year he was free, and this is the way it came about. Every year at Christmastime, a pretty girl can come to the Governor of the State and ask him to give her a prisoner as a Christmas present. And the Governor then has to set the prisoner free and give him to the girl. So it happened to Cortez. One day President Lincoln's daughter visited the prison, and she saw Gregorio Cortez. As soon as she saw him she went up and spoke to him.

"I am in love with you, Gregorio Cortez," President Lincoln's daughter said, "and if you promise to marry me I will go to the Governor next Christmas and tell him to give you to me."

Gregorio Cortez looked at President Lincoln's daughter, and he saw how beautiful she was. It made him thoughtful, and he did not know what to say.

"I have many rich farms," President Lincoln's daughter said. "They are all my own. Marry me and we will farm together."

Gregorio Cortez thought about that. He could see himself already like a German, sitting on the gallery, full of ham and beer, and belching and breaking wind while a half-dozen little blond cockroaches played in the yard. And he was tempted. But then he said to himself, "I can't marry a Gringo girl. We would not make a matching pair."

So he decided that President Lincoln's daughter was not the woman for him, and he told her, "I thank you very much, but I cannot marry you at all."

But President Lincoln's daughter would not take his no. She went to the Governor and said, "I would like to have a prisoner for Christmas."

And the Governor looked at her and saw she was a pretty girl, so he said, "Your wish is granted. What prisoner do you want?"

And President Lincoln's daughter said, "I want Gregorio Cortez."

The Governor thought for a little while and then he said, "That's a man you cannot have. He's the best prisoner I got."

But President Lincoln's daughter shook her head and said, "Don't forget that you gave your word."

"So I did," the Governor said, "and I cannot go back on it."

And that was how Gregorio Cortez got out of prison, where he had been sentenced to ninety-nine years and a day, not for killing the sheriffs, as some fools will tell you, but for stealing the little sorrel mare. Gregorio Cortez kept his word, and he did not marry President Lincoln's daughter, and when at last she lost her hopes she went away to the north.

Still, the enemies of Gregorio Cortez did not give up. When they heard that he was getting out of prison they were scared and angry, and they started thinking of ways to get revenge. They got a lot of money together and gave it to a man who worked in the prison, and this man gave Cortez a slow poison just before Gregorio Cortez got out of jail.

And that was how he came to die, within a year from the day he got out of jail. As soon as he came out and his friends saw him, they said to each other, "This man is sick. This man will not last the year."

And so it was. He did not last the year. He died of the slow poison they gave him just before he was let out, because his enemies did not want to see him free.

And that was how Gregorio Cortez came to die. He's buried in Laredo some place, or maybe it's Brownsville, or Matamoros, or somewhere up above. To tell the truth, I don't know. I don't know the place where he is buried any more than the place where he was born. But he was born and lived and died, that I do know. And a lot of Rangers could also tell you that.

So does the corrido; it tells about Gregorio Cortez and who he was. They started singing the corrido soon after he went to jail, and there was a time when it was forbidden in all the United States, by order of the President himself. Men sometimes got killed or lost their jobs because they sang *El Corrido de Gregorio Cortez*. But everybody sang it just the same, because it spoke about things that were true.

Now it is all right to sing *El Corrido de Gregorio Cortez*, but not everybody knows it any more. And they don't sing it as it used to be sung. These new singers change all the old songs a lot. But even so, people still remember Gregorio Cortez. And when a good singer sings the song—good and loud and clear—you can feel your neck-feathers rise, and you can see him standing there, with his pistol in his hand.

III: THE MAN

A likable young man

𝒞*ortez has become* a legend, as have many other popular heroes before him. But in his case at least it has been possible to go behind the legend to the facts from which it arose. There are still men today who knew Cortez well. More important still, there is a sizable pile of documentary material on the man—in newspaper reports, in letters and official papers—which tells a great deal about his life. And this true story is no less remarkable than the legend which it inspired.

Gregorio Cortez Lira, the son of Román Cortez Garza and Rosalía Lira Cortinas, was born according to the best available information on a ranch between Matamoros and Reynosa, on the Mexican side of the Border, on June 22, 1875. He was the seventh child of a family of eight which included five women and three men. In 1887, when Gregorio was twelve years old, his family left the Border and moved to Manor, Texas, in the Austin area. Two years later Gregorio followed his older brother, Romaldo, to Karnes, Gonzales, and adjacent counties, where they lived a roving life for eleven years, working for the farmers and ranchers of the area, sometimes as vaqueros, sometimes as farm hands.

Gregorio married Leonor Díaz at an early age; his first child, a girl named Mariana, was born in 1891, when Gregorio was only sixteen. By 1901 there were four children: Mariana, ten; Valeriano, one of my informants, eight; Severo, five or six; and Crispín, the baby, about three. Valeriano was born in Manor; so it appears that Gregorio and Romaldo traveled to and from Manor in their round of jobs.

Valeriano remembers that his uncle Romaldo and his father were inseparable. They would get jobs together, one moving when the other moved. Sometimes the families settled at some particular place for a season or two, Gregorio and Romaldo making the rounds of nearby ranches. Valeriano, now an old man, remembers those days with pleasure, the wagon in which they traveled and the noon camps in the shade by small streams as they went from job to job.

In 1900 Romaldo and Gregorio finally decided to settle down and farm on their own. Gregorio, who was now twenty-five and the father of four children, may have been the one who suggested it. Romaldo was older, but he and his wife had no children. W. A. Thulemeyer, who owned a large ranch some ten miles west of Kenedy in Karnes County, rented the two Cortezes some of his land. The brothers settled down to farm, making their homes within a mile of each other. The year 1901 was their first as renters, and by June they had a good corn crop in the making.

According to all reports, Gregorio Cortez was a likable young man, and up to that time he had not been in any trouble with the law. He and his brother were well-known in Karnes County, had been so for eleven years. T. D. Pritchett of Kenedy, a sheriff's deputy, later told the newspapers that Cortez had never been accused of any crime before the death of Morris.[1] But though Cortez had never been in trouble with the law, he had had trouble with American farmers in the vicinity on at least one occasion.

His son Valeriano remembers having been with him one day, not long before Morris' death, when his father and an American

[1] San Antonio *Express*, June 23, 1901, p. 5.

farmer were pitching hay onto an oxcart. The American and his father began to argue. Then they started hitting each other with their fists, and his father knocked the American down. The American got up and grabbed a pitchfork and was going to stick his father when the American women came out of the house and stopped the fight. Valeriano, who was seven, remembers no more about the incident. This, perhaps, may offer a clue as to the reason for some subsequent events.

Though there were probably some people in Karnes County who did not like Gregorio Cortez, he was of a type that many men and most women like. A detailed description of him was printed after his capture in the San Antonio *Express*.

He is tall, slender, and lithe, with the lean muscular appearance of one who has passed through a trying physical ordeal. His shoulders are slightly stooped. His hands and feet are small and well shaped. His head is large and of good shape. It is covered with hair, of which any society "exquisite" might be envious—black as night and tumbling in heavy curls all over his head. His face is long and aquiline, all the features being regular. The forehead is slightly receding, the nose is large and distinctly aquiline, and the cheek bones high. The eyes are brown and bright, but not fierce or unduly prominent in repose . . . his teeth are regular and white. . . . He was easy in his manner and showed no embarrassment . . . it was apparent that Cortez understood English, and later demonstrated that he could speak it . . . he coolly proceeded to give the officers a detailed statement. . . . He talked unaffectedly and was at pains to make himself clear, often repeating statements over and over to make himself understood. Where his statements seemed at variance with the facts as known by the officers, he argued the point and usually succeeded in removing the doubt.[2]

The lack of partiality in this description is best appreciated if one knows that on the same page the *Express* had lamented the fact that Cortez had not been lynched when he was brought to San Antonio.

The *Express* report described Cortez as tall, and during the

[2] *Ibid.*, June 25, 1901, p. 1.

chase he was often said to be six feet two. At Huntsville his height was recorded as five feet nine inches, his weight as 144 pounds. Like Cortina, Cortez was relatively small, wiry rather than broad. In the words of the San Antonio *Express,* he was "possessed of remarkable powers of endurance and skill in eluding pursuit."[3] His enemies themselves remarked more than once after his capture on his nerve and his inventiveness during the chase, as well as on the dignity of his bearing and his self-confidence, that refused to be shaken even before the majesty of the law. At the same time, he had the power to charm many of his former enemies, including some Texas sheriffs, into becoming his friends.

But at one in the afternoon on the twelfth of June, 1901, the farthest thing from Gregorio Cortez's mind must have been judges and sheriffs. He had just finished the noon meal and was lying full length on the floor of the front gallery of his house on the Thulemeyer land, his head on his wife's lap. Sitting outside with them were his mother, his brother Romaldo, and Romaldo's wife. The children were inside, still eating. It was hot and clear; the corn was tall and promised a good harvest. There was cause to be contented. It was at that moment that Sheriff Morris appeared, looking for horse thieves.

The sheriff is interpreted to death

Sheriff W. T. (Brack) Morris was an experienced hunter of men. He was forty-one years old and had spent half of his life as an officer of the law in Texas. "When he had just reached manhood's estate"[4] he had joined the Texas Rangers and had risen to sergeant in the Ranger force. He had become sheriff of Karnes County in 1896, and in 1901 was serving his third term in office. He was a small man but was reputed to be very fast and very accurate with the revolver, and one imagines that in his years as Ranger and sheriff he had had occasion to use it with deadly effect.

[3] *Ibid.*
[4] *Ibid.,* July 7, 1901, p. 13.

58

A day or so before June 12, Morris had received word from Sheriff Avant of Atascosa County, asking him to look for a horse thief from Atascosa who had been trailed to Karnes. Sheriff Avant did not know the man's name. "That he was a medium-sized Mexican with a big red broad-brimmed Mexican hat" was all the information that was passed on to Morris.[5] At this point the search for the thief takes on a very familiar aspect. The officers of the law go out looking for a Mexican, any Mexican. But in fairness to Morris it must be said that he did not go about the country shooting at every Mexican on horseback that he saw. He followed a trail to Kenedy, and on the morning of the twelfth began to check up on local Mexicans who had acquired horses in recent weeks.

As interpreter, Morris had one of his deputies, Boone Choate, who was supposed to be an expert on the Mexican language. Choate appears to have been one of those men who build up a reputation for knowing the Mexicans better than they know themselves on a few bits of broken Spanish and a lot of "experience." If one goes over court records, investigations of claims, and other documents concerning relations between Mexicans and Anglo-Texans, one finds that jail sentences, decisions on claims, and even the "facts" of history have often been based on statements by men who have qualified as experts on Mexican affairs without even knowing the Spanish language. Boone Choate, perhaps through no fault of his own, was one of these men. A number of people might not have died had Choate either known more Spanish or known enough to know what he did not know.

Through Boone Choate, Morris questioned several Kenedy Mexicans and finally got to a man named Andrés Villarreal, who had recently acquired a mare, not by purchase but by trade. Villarreal told the officers that he had traded a horse for the mare to a man named Gregorio Cortez; so Morris decided to check this new lead. Later investigations proved that Cortez had legally acquired the mare, and that Villarreal knew the mare's

[5] Judge Henderson's opinion, Court of Criminal Appeals, Case No. 2270, p. 179.

history when he talked to Morris. Perhaps Morris did not trust Villarreal's word and wanted to check on Cortez for himself. Or perhaps Morris had heard recent reports about the man's being a troublesome Mexican, as one would imagine from Valeriano Cortez's story of his father's fight with the American farmer.

One cannot tell what Morris' intentions were. He did not swear out a warrant for Cortez's arrest, though he had time enough to do so, but that in itself means little. A "peace officer" of that day and of that part of Texas who brought in a Mexican without shooting him or beating him up was considered extremely just and fair, and "a friend of the Mexicans." To require that he also bother about such things as warrants was asking too much. However, it is extremely probable that when Morris and his deputies decided to pay a visit to Gregorio Cortez they were more interested in questioning him than in bringing him to jail. Morris simply wanted to know more about the mare that Gregorio had traded to Villarreal.

The Morris expedition was not typical of the rustler-hunting parties one reads about. Morris was accompanied by two of his deputies, John Trimmell and Boone Choate. According to later testimony, only Morris and Trimmell were armed; Choate declared that he had not carried a pistol when he accompanied Morris to the Cortez farm. The three went not on horseback but in the sheriff's surrey.

Half a mile from Gregorio's house were some pens and a gate with several roads leading away from it. At this point Trimmell got out of the surrey. This was an odd move on the part of Morris and his men if they were out, as was later claimed, to arrest a pair of cunning and dangerous horse thieves. Choate later testified that Trimmell had been left at the pens to cut off the retreat of the Cortezes. Since the half-mile between the house and the gate was covered with brush, this seems like a particularly useless maneuver that only served to divide the sheriff's forces. It is most probable that Trimmell was left at the pens to do some investigating of his own, while Morris and Choate went up to the house to talk to the Cortezes about the mare.

The Man

The house was set in a small clearing in the middle of a mesquite thicket. There was a fenced yard in front, about the width of a city street, and beyond the fence was the road. Beyond the road there was mesquite brush again. The surrey pulled up even with the house and stopped. This was still the time when all men went about armed, even in populous and metropolitan San Antonio. Gregorio, lying on the gallery floor with his head on his wife's lap, had a revolver stuck in his belt, in front. Romaldo was not armed. When the surrey stopped, Gregorio sat up and slid the gun around his belt until it was about even with his hip pocket. He said to Romaldo, who was sitting on the steps, "See what they want."

Romaldo went and talked to the men, and then came back and called Gregorio. According to Boone Choate, he (Choate) asked for Gregorio Cortez, and Romaldo walked back a few steps and called to Gregorio in Spanish, "They want you." *Te quieren*, literally "you are wanted," is a common way of saying, "Somebody wants to speak to you." To Choate, however, this was evidence that both Cortezes knew that Gregorio was a wanted man.[6] Whether Choate communicated his suspicions to Sheriff Morris is not made clear.

Gregorio came up at Romaldo's call, and both stood near the fence, Romaldo leaning on a fence post and Gregorio, apparently suspicious, standing a few feet away. Choate then asked Gregorio if he had traded a horse to Villarreal, and Gregorio said, "No." He was telling the truth; he had traded a mare. Why Choate, a ranchman presumably, confused a horse with a mare is not clear. A plausible guess, in view of other evidence about Choate's shaky command of Spanish, is that he did not know or could not think of the word for mare *(yegua)* and used *caballo* (horse) instead.

When Gregorio said "No," Sheriff Morris got off his surrey, climbed through the fence, and approached the Cortezes, telling Choate to inform Romaldo and Gregorio that he was going to arrest them. He was to the right of the two men and about twelve feet from them when Choate translated his statement.

[6] Court of Criminal Appeals, Case No. 2270, pp. 169–183.

At this point Gregorio said something in Spanish which included the words *arrestar* (to arrest) and *nada* (nothing). Choate, who at Gregorio's trial at Karnes rendered the statement as "A mi no me arreste nada," translated it as "No white man can arrest me."[7] After learning from defense witnesses that *nadie* and not *nada* means "no one," Choate changed his wording in later trials to "A mi no me arreste nadie," still mangling the verb. Probably made aware that Mexicans do not think of Anglo-Americans as "white," he also changed his translation to "No one can arrest me." What Cortez probably said, and so his defense argued, was "You can't arrest me for nothing." But whatever he may have said, Morris apparently understood the words to be "No white man can arrest me."

In the next few seconds Morris shot Romaldo Cortez, shot at Gregorio and missed, and was in turn shot by Gregorio. All eyewitness accounts agreed as to this sequence of events. The details, however, varied. Choate testified that Gregorio, after boasting that he could not be arrested, reached for his gun. Morris, who was caught unawares with his arms hanging loosely at his sides, then drew his own weapon, shot Romaldo, who "kind of ran at Morris like he intended to catch him,"[8] and after that shot at Gregorio and missed. Gregorio then shot the sheriff.

To accept this story one must believe that Morris was careless enough to be caught napping seconds after he told two suspected criminals that they were under arrest. One must also believe that Morris was so fast on the draw that he could start drawing after Gregorio—himself a handy man with a gun—and not only beat him to it but shoot twice, in two different directions and at two different targets before Gregorio could get off a shot. These things are possible though not probable. But one must also believe that Morris, faced by two opponents, one in the act of drawing a pistol and the other "kind of running" at him, would shoot first not at the man with the gun but at the unarmed man.

Valeriano Cortez remembers that his father slipped his pistol behind him when the surrey drew up. Both Cortezes were in

[7] San Antonio *Express*, October 10, 1901, p. 6.
[8] Court of Criminal Appeals, Case No. 2270.

their shirtsleeves, and as far as one can tell Morris did not know that either of them was armed. It seems that even Romaldo was not aware that Gregorio had a pistol.

It is highly probable that Morris also thought both Cortezes were unarmed and that he drew his pistol to shoot Gregorio because Gregorio did not want to be arrested. Sheriff Morris was a kind and popular man, newspaper reports said after his death, but the customs of his time did not require that he extend his kindness to Mexicans. When the sheriff drew, Romaldo ran at him, trying to protect his brother whom he thought unarmed like himself, and Morris had to shoot Romaldo first. The bullet entered Romaldo's mouth at an angle, came out through his cheek and lodged in his shoulder, indicating that Romaldo, a much bigger man than Morris, had run at Morris in a crouch with the idea of grappling with the sheriff.

After Morris shot Romaldo he turned back to Gregorio and found him with a pistol in his hand. Surprised, Morris shot hastily, so hastily that he missed at a distance of ten or twelve feet. Cortez shot immediately afterward. The heavy impact of his forty-four almost knocked Morris down. Morris fired two or three more times, but his shots went wild, and Gregorio shot him again. Now Morris began "to reel and stagger, going down the wire fence towards the gate."[9] He fell before he reached the gate, and Cortez caught up with him and shot him again as he lay on the ground.

Meanwhile Boone Choate was getting out of the surrey as fast as he could. Here he was, faced with the old familiar situation between Anglo-Texan and Mexican, except that the roles had been reversed. In this case the Mexican had the six-shooter, while Choate was unarmed except for possibly his whittling knife. Under these circumstances, Boone Choate preferred to "travel with rather than against the music" made by "the whine of leaden slugs." In words less colorful, he ran. He ran into the chaparral "where it was thickest," according to his own testimony, and headed toward the pens, a half-mile away, to the other deputy, Trimmell.

[9] *Ibid.*

Deputy Trimmell was armed. According to tradition, between the two they should have vastly outnumbered Cortez. But they both threw tradition to the winds and retreated in the direction of Kenedy to get more satisfying odds. Or perhaps they acted according to another branch of tradition; it seems that they were already convinced that it was not Cortez alone but a whole gang of Mexicans that had killed Sheriff Morris.

Cortez picked up Morris' pistol and left him lying by the gate. Morris was still alive, though wounded three times—in the right arm, in the left shoulder, and in the region of the lower intestines. The wound in the arm was the most serious because an artery was severed. Romaldo was taken inside the house. They washed his face, loaded him into the sheriff's surrey, and drove off to Romaldo's house. Valeriano was sent to round up the *remuda*.

Thus, within a few minutes after Morris fell and Choate ran away the whole Cortez family left the house. If Choate and Trimmell had returned at that point, they would have found no one there but Morris, slowly bleeding to death from the wound in his arm. Some time later Morris struggled to his feet, apparently seeking aid. He staggered aimlessly out of the gate and wandered into the chaparral, where he fell and was no longer able to get up. Morris died there, some two hundred yards from the place where he had been shot.

At Romaldo's house, Valeriano came up with the *remuda,* and his father saddled a sorrel mare for himself and a horse for Romaldo. The surrey was turned loose on the road, and a wagon was hitched up. The women and children got on the wagon, heading for the house of a friend on the outskirts of Kenedy. Gregorio helped Romaldo on horseback, and they went into the brush, intending to reach the same destination by a longer route.

The wagon had not gone very far when the first posse appeared from Kenedy. Gregorio had instructed ten-year-old Mariana to tell the possemen that the family was from a ranch closer to town than the Thulemeyer ranch. The posse, and others that followed, believed her and let the family pass without any more questions.

The long walk

It was about ten miles in a straight line from the Cortez place to Kenedy. Gregorio planned to hide in the brush about halfway to town and wait until nightfall to slip Romaldo into Kenedy for medical aid. Riding through the brush was difficult and slow, doubly difficult because Romaldo kept falling from his horse. Finally Gregorio stopped deep in the brush and laid Romaldo down under a tree.

The wounded man was getting feverish. He kept mumbling through his swollen mouth that he wanted a gun, and that they should go back and fight the *rinches* together. While they were under the tree they heard the breaking of brush. Romaldo began mumbling louder, and Gregorio moved away from the tree, closer to the noise, but the mounted men passed by.

From early afternoon until dark the two lay in the brush less than five miles from the Cortez place, while a posse of at least fifty men combed the area for them all afternoon and night. Not only did the posse fail to find the Cortezes five miles away; they failed to find Morris two hundred yards from where he was shot until the next morning. It seems that the posse was not looking for a couple of men but for a whole "Cortez gang," made up of unknown numbers of Mexican desperadoes. Until someone stumbled on Morris' body next morning, it was believed that Morris had been spirited away by the gang for unknown reasons.

The possemen did discover the whereabouts of the Cortez family. They came storming into the house on the outskirts of Kenedy, and Valeriano, who was then eight, remembers that they were very angry. He has a vivid recollection of two or three possemen with very fierce faces, who raised up their rifle butts over him as if to crush in his head. Valeriano crawled under a table, and one of the women came and threw a bedcover over it, in the manner of a tent. All four children cowered under the table while the men were in the house.

After dark Gregorio and Romaldo resumed their journey to Kenedy. By then Romaldo could no longer sit his horse. Gregorio with much difficulty got Romaldo into the saddle and climbed up behind him, abandoning his mare in the chaparral. But Romaldo kept slipping off the saddle, and Gregorio was so much lighter that he could not hold Romaldo up once he started to fall. Finally Gregorio had to abandon the horse too, and carry Romaldo. It took him from dark until one o'clock to cover the five miles to Kenedy. He slipped into the house unobserved, left Romaldo with the family, and then began his flight.

When Gregorio Cortez left Romaldo in Kenedy, he had two horses hiding in the brush, but he left afoot and headed not south but north. His pursuers expected him to ride toward the Border; so he walked in the opposite direction. His plan was to hole up for a few days in Gonzales County, where he had many friends, and then go to Austin and Manor among relatives, finally losing himself in north Texas. The least he could hope for if he made it to San Antonio or north of the Colorado was a fair trial. Where he was he could expect nothing but a rope at the nearest tree. He was successful in his ruse. The posses struck south, and the newspapers reported, "The trail of the Mexican leads toward the Rio Grande."[10]

Cortez became celebrated for his prodigious ride to the Border, but very little was made of his equally prodigious walk in the other direction. From Kenedy in Karnes County to Ottine in Gonzales it is about sixty-five miles in a straight line. Cortez must have covered half again that distance. A conservative estimate would be eighty miles. He made it in about forty hours, an average of two miles an hour for forty straight hours, through brush and other rough country; and for this hiking feat Cortez was wearing a pair of low-cut shoes with narrow, pointed toes.

The first few miles he made very slowly, perhaps because of the posses in the vicinity. He made the eight miles from Kenedy to Runge by eight next morning and entered town for breakfast at a Mexican restaurant on the outskirts of town. Apparently Cortez was unaware that Runge was Sheriff Morris' home, and that the town was holding Morris' funeral and an indignation meeting later that same day. It was probably the most dangerous breakfast that Cortez ever ate.

[10] San Antonio *Express,* June 13, 1901, p. 1.

After leaving Runge he made better time. By noon of the fourteenth, about thirty-four hours after he had left Kenedy, he was at Belmont, about fifty-five miles from Kenedy by direct route. There he ate at a friend's house and rested for a while, and in the afternoon he began to walk again, this time toward Ottine and the Schnabel ranch, where he expected to hide with another friend of his, Martín Robledo.

Cortez arrived at the Robledos about sundown, and one of the first things he did was to slip off his shoes.

After supper he told Martín Robledo about the killing of Morris, and it was agreed that he should hide with the Robledos for a few days. The Robledo place was in an isolated and wooded spot, and Cortez was pretty sure he had fooled his pursuers.

The Battle of Belmont

There were seven other persons at the Robledo house: Martín Robledo and his wife, their three sons— Bonifacio, eighteen; Tomás, sixteen; and Encarnación, thirteen; Ramón Rodríguez, a half-grown boy living with the Robledos; and a visitor, Martín Sandoval. After dark the four men—the two older Robledos, Sandoval, and Cortez—sat outside on the gallery. Young Bonifacio Robledo had a pistol stuck in his belt and joked about what they would do if the *rinches* showed up.

"Shall we run or shall we fight?" Gregorio is supposed to have asked young Robledo.

"We'll fight," Bonifacio answered.

All this was just talk. Cortez considered himself pretty safe. As he sat on the Robledo gallery in his bare feet the last thing he seems to have expected was the early arrival of a posse.

And he would probably have been correct but for Robert M. Glover, the sheriff of Gonzales County. Glover and Morris had been good friends, and when Glover heard of Morris' death, he started out for Karnes City. Instead of attempting to trail Cortez, he went for information about his whereabouts to the most likely source. "He went to the home of a Mexican woman who he suspected had information as to the whereabouts of the murderer ... and his gang."[11]

There were three Mexican women whose "home" was then Karnes City and who knew about Cortez's whereabouts. These were Cortez's mother, his wife, and his sister-in-law, all three of whom had been put in jail at Karnes City that morning, along with the children and the wounded Romaldo. Which of the three he questioned Glover did not say.

The woman, whoever she was, at first refused to talk, but "under pressure" told Glover where Cortez was going, so that Glover knew his destination before Cortez reached it. What sort of pressure Glover used, whether it was physical or psychological, there is no way of telling.

Glover left for Gonzales immediately, picking up a posse along the way. A member of the posse was Henry Schnabel, the owner of the ranch on which the Robledos lived and a Gonzales County constable. At the moment that Cortez was arriving at the Robledo house, the posse was leaving Gonzales for Ottine on the train. By the time Cortez came out on the gallery of the Robledo house to rest his feet, the posse was in the brush behind the house, preparing their plan of attack and, the defense later was to claim, fortifying themselves for the task ahead with a "black bottle" they had bought at Ottine.[12]

How much whiskey the posse drank and whether the sheriff and his men were appreciably affected by what they did drink is something that only a member of the posse could have answered. It appears that the rumor went around Gonzales some time later that "the black bottle they bought at Ottine was what did the work," and the defense in the Gonzales trial sought to prove that the sheriff and his posse had been drunk, but the evidence was excluded as mere hearsay.[13]

The Robledo house faced south, with the gallery in front. As Glover's posse approached from the north and rear, the four men at the house were sitting on the gallery at the southeast corner.

[11] *Ibid.*, June 16, 1901, p. 1.
[12] Court of Criminal Appeals, Case No. 2397.
[13] *Ibid.*

Glover divided his posse of eight to surround the house. Deputy Swift was to approach from the rear. Glover and Crispín Alcantar, the one Mexican in the posse, took the east side, and the other five went around the west. All dismounted except Glover. Their plan decided upon, the posse according to the testimony of Deputy Howard "rushed up to the house in a run."[14]

As Glover reached the southeast corner and while the other five were approaching the southwest corner, the shooting began. Cortez claimed that the posse rushed up firing its guns and that he answered. The possemen said that someone at the house fired first. But all agreed that the firing began at the southeast corner and took place between Glover and Cortez.

At the first shots the two Robledos and Sandoval ran into the brush. Glover and Cortez kept firing at each other until Glover fell dead from his horse. Then Cortez ran into the brush and right into a patch of grass burrs. He quickly took off his vest, tore it in two, bound the pieces over his bare feet, and ran into a nearby field. From his hiding place he could hear heavy firing at Martín Robledo's house.

The action which followed was described by the San Antonio *Express* the following day as "a tale of bravery unsurpassed on the part of the officers and of desperation on the part of the Mexicans." The *Express* added, "That more of the officers were not killed is little short of a miracle. . . . The Mexicans had the advantage."[15]

The real story appears to have been far from glorious. After Glover fell, Cortez, Sandoval, and young Robledo all took to the brush. Old Robledo ran to the edge of it and stood watching helplessly. The "bandit gang" that now faced the brave posse was composed of a woman and three boys, all unarmed and inside the house. At the first sound of firing from the southeast corner of the house, where Glover and Cortez were having their duel, the five possemen at the southwest corner also opened fire, toward the southeast corner, and Swift opened the back door.

Mrs. Robledo and the three boys were running back and forth

[14] *Ibid.*
[15] San Antonio *Express*, June 16, 1901, p. 1.

inside the house, thrown into a panic by the firing. Swift saw in the next room "two men running back and forward, and he did not like their maneuvers." One of the "men," the Rodríguez boy, came running into the back room, and Swift shot him. Behind Rodríguez came one of the Robledo boys, but Mrs. Robledo was right behind and "came in between said party and witness, and he could not shoot again."[16]

Outside, the five possemen on the west side were having a good-sized war of their own. If the first reports that they gave the papers of their desperate, hand-to-hand battles with Mexican cutthroats had any basis in fact at all, the posse must have been chasing each other around tree trunks and behind barns, burning ammunition at a tremendous rate. The *Express*'s comment that it was a miracle more of the officers were not killed sounds all too true. Here is one of the fights as reported by the *Express*.

> The desperate nature of the encounter . . . is shown by the individual fight which Tip Davis, deputy sheriff had with a Mexican at the same time. Davis and the Mexican came to close quarters, each of them being armed with a sixshooter. They met at a small tree, and shot at each other around this tree several times. The Mexican escaped, but Davis is sure he hit him.[17]

When Swift fired inside the house at the Rodríguez boy, the five desperately fighting men on the west side thought that Mexicans were attacking them from that quarter too, and they fired into the house, missing Swift but hitting Refugia Robledo, who was standing in front of Swift to prevent him from shooting down her sons. At about the same time Constable Schnabel, one of the five on the west side, fell dead near the barn, his face half-blown away by a discharge so close to him that it left powder-burns upon his skin.

The shooting stopped, leaving on the field two officers dead— Glover by the hand of Gregorio Cortez, Schnabel by that of one of his own comrades-in-arms. On the Mexican side a woman and

[16] Court of Criminal Appeals, Case No. 2397.
[17] San Antonio *Express*, June 16, 1901, p. 1.

a boy were wounded, both noncombatants. Captured were Martín Robledo, his wounded wife, his two youngest sons, and the wounded Rodríguez boy. "The capture of the five," the *Express* reported with unconscious irony, "is regarded as hardly less wonderful" than the bravery shown by the officers in the fight.[18] Thus ended the Battle of Belmont, "a tale of bravery unsurpassed."

But the posse were not yet through. They wanted information, and they may also have wanted a little revenge. They took it out on Encarnación Robledo, thirteen. The *Express* describes how it was done.

Friday night, before the posse left the ranch, they endeavored to wring from the younger of the robber's boys information concerning the plans of the three who escaped. The boy refused to talk. He was hung up to a tree until his tongue protruded and life was nearly extinct, but he steadfastly declined to reveal any of the secrets of the gang.[19]

That the boy knew no "secrets" to reveal is of course obvious. But to the men pursuing Cortez this was only additional evidence of the desperate sort of characters that belonged to the "Cortez gang."

"That they are game and desperate," the *Express* told its readers, "is proven by the refusal of the Roblero [sic] boy, in the face of death by hanging, to disclose any of the information desired by the officers."[20]

The five prisoners, glorious prize of the Battle of Belmont, were rushed to San Antonio to keep other good citizens of Gonzales from finishing the work begun by the posse on the youngest Robledo boy. Mrs. Robledo was promptly charged with the murder of Schnabel. Deputy Tom Harper, who later changed his testimony and against whom unproved charges were made that he had killed Schnabel himself, testified that he had seen the Robledo woman fire at Schnabel from the window, and that

[18] *Ibid.*
[19] *Ibid.*
[20] *Ibid.*

he had fired twice at her when he had seen Schnabel fall. Mrs. Robledo was never tried on the charge. In fact, none of the five "desperate characters" captured that night was ever brought to trial.

On the Robledo premises, the brave officers told the newspapers, they found an "arsenal" of ten Winchester rifles and "a lard bucket full of cartridges." A couple of days later the ten rifles had become eight. By the time of the Gonzales trial a month later, the ten rifles had become one Winchester rifle and one single-barreled shotgun, more in keeping with the normal country household of the time. The weapons had not been used the night of the shooting, Deputy Swift testified.[21] It was evident by that time that except for Cortez's shooting on Glover all the firing had been done by the brave and fearless officers, who had merely followed a long-established custom, that of shooting first and looking afterward.

The long ride

Meanwhile Gregorio Cortez lay in a field, his feet wrapped in pieces of his vest, while the shooting died away at the Robledo house. After a while he crept back to the scene, entered the house, and got his shoes. This time he headed for the Rio Grande. He walked directly south to the banks of the Guadalupe River, about ten miles, to the house of another friend, Ceferino Flores. It was early on the morning of Saturday, June 15. In the two and one-half days since he had killed Sheriff Morris, Cortez had walked nearly one hundred miles. He was to walk no more for several days. Flores took Morris' pistol and hid it, giving Cortez his own. He also gave Gregorio his own mount and his saddle. It was another sorrel mare, the second of three mares that Cortez was to ride in his flight.

He left Flores' house on the mare, pursued by a posse. Bloodhounds chased him across the Guadalupe River before they left off, but the posse stopped to give Ceferino Flores the rope treat-

[21] Court of Criminal Appeals, Case No. 2397.

ment and Cortez escaped. Flores got two years in the penitentiary for his part in the affair.

Cortez was now on his way to the Border. Between early Saturday morning and Sunday evening the sorrel mare carried him from the Guadalupe to the San Antonio River. In a straight line it is less than fifty miles. Cortez traveled many times the distance in those two days and one night. Long afterward all he remembered was riding and riding, doubling back, stopping to shoot, then riding again, circling about, leaving false leads when he could, and riding again.

The little mare was fleet and strong, but by Sunday morning she showed signs of giving out. Sunday noon, as he crossed the Cíbolo creek near Stockdale, his trail was picked up by a fresh posse. For the next six hours he galloped, running in circles and zigzags in the area between Stockdale and Floresville, with the posse sometimes less than five hundred yards behind him. About six in the afternoon the sorrel mare stopped and refused to go any further. He had barely dismounted when she fell dead.

Cortez slipped saddle and bridle off the mare, got behind a thick tree trunk and waited. The posse stopped some distance away, dismounted, and broke into small groups, but he managed to elude them in the brush until dark. Then he slipped away, carrying the saddle until he came to a pasture where he saw another mare, a brown mare which looked tall to him, though it has been later described as a "Spanish mare, not much over thirteen hands high."[22]

Cortez saddled the little brown mare, cut the pasture fence with a file, and started on the last lap of his ride. He was just outside of Floresville, about one hundred miles from Cotulla, where he was to leave the mare. His pursuers later estimated that he rode at least three hundred miles in getting from Floresville to Cotulla, through brush and rough country, over barbed wire fences and rivers, in three days.

The little brown mare made a name for herself. Time and again posses sighted Cortez, and every time the mare ran away from them. In the end the posses had to stop for fresh horses.

[22] Dobie, *The Mustangs*, p. 236.

At least six horses were killed by one posse in pursuing Cortez and the little mare.

Meanwhile Cortez moved toward the Rio Grande and safety. The latter part of the chase became a blur, and later he could remember but few details. He would be chased by one posse in one county and run until he lost them, only to have another one pick up his trail and chase him again, often in the direction from which he had come. Hundreds of men were out looking for him.

Aside from the dogs, probably the greatest handicap that Cortez and the brown mare faced was the Corpus Christi-to-Laredo railroad, which had been built in 1882. No matter how much Cortez hid his trail, no matter how he twisted and turned, it was evident that he was moving toward Laredo. Special trains moved up and down the tracks, bearing men, horses, and dogs, which kept in touch with other searching parties by telephone and telegraph. Whenever Cortez was sighted a posse with fresh horses would be transported to the scene by rail. And when his trail was lost, all the pursuers had to do was board a train, travel a few miles in the direction of Laredo, and take up the search again.

To ride through such a network of organized pursuit required a remarkable rider and a remarkable horse. Cortez and the little brown mare were well matched for the job, as the men who pursued them testified.

"The only hope," the San Antonio *Express* said in a page-one story on June 19, "seems to be to fill up the whole country with men and search every nook and corner and guard every avenue of escape. . . . The country is stirred as it perhaps never was before. In many places business has been practically suspended and all the men are out scouring the country." Next day the *Express* reported that "new men are joining in the hunt every day and this keeps the woods full of searching parties."

Ex-sheriff E. G. Reagan of Live Oak County said in the *Express* for June 23 that the pursuit of Cortez equalled the excitement and activity of the Indian depredations of former years. He called the little brown mare "the best bottomed animal in the world."

The Man

Sheriff John Vann of Kerr County, leader of another posse that chased Cortez, thought him "certainly the smartest at eluding pursuit that I know anything about."

Since Glover was killed, Southwest Texas has swarmed with men in pursuit of him. Some of the best trailers in the country have been following him, and he has thrown them all off. His methods are peculiar. He traveled a great deal at night and never followed the trails. He staid [sic] in the brush as much as possible. His trail would run along straight and smooth for several miles, and the trailers would be certain that he was following a certain general direction, when the trail would start at right angles. Then it would double back. Another trick of Cortez was to stop, walk around in a circle, then reverse, then cross his circle and step on a grassy place. This trick gave the trailers the most trouble, and they lost hours picking up the trail again.[23]

From Floresville Cortez rode twenty-five miles along the San Antonio looking for a fording place. When he heard dogs behind, he cut off his shirt tails, blindfolded the mare, and forced her into the river and to the other side. The mare kept ahead of all the horses that chased her, but whenever he could Cortez ran into the brush. He cut across pastures, filing in two the upper strand of wire and making the mare jump over the lower. Several times he rounded up cattle and used them to cover up his trail; and once, desperate with thirst, he did drive a bunch of cattle up to a waterhole near which were several armed men, who took him for a vaquero from a nearby ranch.

But the time came when the little brown mare could no longer go on. She dragged her hind legs when she jumped over fences, and once she cut herself on the wire and began to limp. Cortez rode her into a thicket near Cotulla, took the saddle off, and hung it to a *coma* tree. A posse was right behind him when he entered the thicket.

The news went out that Gregorio Cortez had at last been trapped. By ten o'clock on Thursday, June 20, the little brown mare had been found, and the thicket in which Cortez had dis-

[23] San Antonio *Express*, June 23, 1901, p. 5.

appeared was surrounded. Careful arrangements were made to flush him out of his hiding place. But the next day news came that the chase was still on. While the posses sat around the thicket, waiting for him to come out, he had slipped away in the direction least expected of him, to the town of Cotulla, out of which many of the possemen had come.

When the little brown mare's strength gave out, Cortez's will to survive seems to have given out too. At this point, he later told officers, he was so tired and sleepy and so weak from lack of food and water that he decided he could no longer go on. He sat down in the thicket and waited for the posses to catch up with him. But after he waited for two hours and the posses did not come, he regained some of his strength and self-confidence and decided to go on. The Rio Grande was almost within reach.

He slipped out of the thicket in full daylight and walked into Cotulla. Later the men who pursued him talked about his "remarkable nerve" in entering this and other towns along the way toward the Rio Grande. But as in his flight north after the killing of Morris, Cortez took what he considered was a calculated risk. If all the armed men in the vicinity were out scouring brush and hills for him, guarding bridges and pasture gates, the safest place for him was in the towns, where they were not.

Cortez had with him his *morral*, the feed bag of woven ixtle that the Border ranchero used as a catchall. In the *morral* Cortez put his pistols. Hanging it from his shoulder, he walked into the town of Cotulla at noon on June 20, trying to look as much as possible like any ranchero walking into town. But his tattered clothes and exhausted condition gave him away to the Mexicans he met.

He stopped at the house of a Mexican woman, who gave him food and water, and then continued his walk through the town. Below Cotulla the Nueces River cuts across the Cotulla-Laredo road. Here there was a bridge, like all others in south Texas guarded by men on the lookout for the fugitive. Cortez went below the bridge, took a bath in the river, crossed to the other side and rested a while. Then he followed the railroad tracks to the town of Twohig. At Twohig a posse had just left town, going east.

"A Mexican woman told me the officers were after a man that looked like me," Cortez later told his captors. "I told her they weren't looking for me, but she said I had better get away quick, because I looked like the man they were after."[24]

But he was too tired to travel any more that day. He went to the outskirts of Twohig, lay down by a water tank, and slept all the night of the twentieth, all day the twenty-first, and all the next night, while the posses were waiting for him to come out of the thicket at Cotulla. By 2:30 P.M. of the twenty-first, the posses were convinced that he was not in the thicket. The tracking began again, facilitated by the fact that Cortez was on foot and that his worn, broken shoes left easily recognizable prints.

In spite of this he hid his trail effectively. The posses on June 22 were quoted in the *Express* as reporting that "owing to the many circuitous routes made by Cortez and his success in almost completely wiping out his tracks, very slow progress was made today." The same report indicated that the posses were beginning to lose heart. They were sure that Cortez had got another horse, from another member of his numerous and widespread "gang," and had disappeared across the Rio Grande. That was the only way they could explain his total disappearance. Men were beginning to return to their homes, saying that if he was captured now it would be only through an accident.

The capture

Cortez got up from his long sleep early on the morning of June 22. It was his twenty-sixth birthday. He walked into the little ranch village of El Sauz and bought a new pair of trousers and a shirt and converted what American money he had left ($1.50) into Mexican currency. He changed his clothes, threw away his tattered shirt, wrapped his pistols in his old pair of trousers, and put the bundle in his *morral*.

[24] *Ibid.*, June 25, 1901, p. 4.

He was now some thirty miles from the Rio Grande, in a region of sheep and cattle ranches and coal mines. The ranches and the mines attracted many laborers from Mexico, who crossed more or less at will in those days before stringent immigration regulations. The country was full of strange Mexicans walking around from job to job. Cortez's plan was to masquerade as a newly arrived laborer and to work his way down to the Rio Grande, where he would cross without exciting attention either from Americans patrolling the river or from Mexican authorities, who had an extradition agreement with the United States.

He left the railroad tracks and the towns and turned southwest, to hit the Rio Grande above Laredo, near the location of the old Spanish settlement of Dolores. He walked all morning without molestation, for the posses were then picking up his trail at Cotulla. At noon he arrived at the sheep camp of a man named Abrán de la Garza. That was as far as he was to go.

In gaining the north bank of the Rio Grande, Cortez had gained a great deal—the assurance of a trial for the killings of which he was accused. In the Laredo area he was out of the "lynching belt" and in Border Mexican territory. Local posses were beginning to take over the chase, and these were largely made up of Texas-Mexicans, led by men like Sheriff Ortiz of Webb County and Assistant City Marshal Gómez of Laredo.

But while this new state of affairs assured Cortez of personal safety in case of capture, it also made his capture more probable. In Karnes and Gonzales counties his movements often had been an open secret among the Mexicans, but a secret they did not share with officers. Mexicans in that area looked upon local law enforcement agencies as an alien force, in the same way that Borderers looked upon the Texas Rangers. On the Border, however, the law was at least partly Mexican, and though sympathy was predominantly with the fugitive the formerly closed circle now had its breaks. When Cortez arrived at the sheep camp, his almost exact whereabouts were known to authorities in Laredo, and they were riding to intercept him.

There was also the matter of a reward. One thousand dollars in reward money had been contributed by the Governor, by citizens of Karnes, and by others. The reward seems to have been in the mind of Jesús González, known as *El Teco,* when he saw Cortez arrive at Abrán de la Garza's sheep camp at noon on June 22. González knew him well, and scarcely had Cortez sat down when González was on his way to inform the nearest searchers where they could find the fugitive.

Two hundred yards from the sheep camp a party of Texas Rangers headed by Capt. J. H. Rogers had encamped for the noon meal, unaware that the object of their search was so close to them. González offered to lead them to Cortez. Rogers and K. H. Merrem, a posseman and former Texas Ranger, went with González to the sheep camp, and a few minutes later Gregorio Cortez was under arrest.

The chase had taken ten days, during which Cortez walked at least one hundred twenty miles and rode more than four hundred on the brown and the sorrel mares. He had been chased by hundreds of men, in parties of up to three hundred. He had killed two sheriffs and fought off many posses. But for his capture all that was needed was one Texas Ranger, with the incidental assistance of another man, a former Ranger. Or so the papers said.

According to the first newspaper reports, González went with Rogers and Merrem and pointed out the hut in which Cortez was hiding. Rogers sent Merrem to the rear of the hut to cut off the wanted man's avenue of retreat. He then crept up to the door, threw it open suddenly and "threw down" on Cortez, who was caught completely by surprise and offered no resistance.

To Rogers' credit it must be said that he later corrected the story in an article published in the San Antonio *Express,* June 25, 1901. But the factual account, which corresponds to Cortez's own version and comes pretty close to what tradition tells, has been ignored, while the first version showing the Texas Ranger in his generally accepted heroic role lived on as fact.

On April 6, 1952, the Austin *American-Statesman* published an article on Cortez by J. Frank Dobie. It was illustrated with a drawing showing the capture. Cortez is shown sitting on the floor of a hut. At the door is a grim-faced Texas Ranger, his left hand pushing the door open, his right holding a six-shooter, his cartridge belt hanging so dangerously low about his thighs that if he takes a step forward the belt is sure to slip down to his ankles and hobble him. In the text, "Railroad" Smith, via Mr. Dobie, has Cortez say, "I cannot walk more. I find ole house and nobody there. I fall on floor and I am sleep when I hear, 'Hands up.' Now I am here for feefty year for keel man that I do not keel."

This version of the capture shows the Ranger in his legendary role, but more than legend seems to have been involved in the heroization of the Rangers at that particular time. At the beginning of the twentieth century, the strong men of the Border must have been disturbed at the turn of events. Mexicans on the north bank were taking over their own affairs, making it extremely hard for the fortune-maker to use local authorities for purposes of intimidation. At the same time, the railroad would soon come into Brownsville, bringing a new era of "development." More than ever in their history the Rangers were needed on the Border.

And at just this time a movement was afoot to do away with the Ranger force entirely. People not directly interested in the "development" of the Border, especially East Texans, were saying harsh things about the Rangers, and they were being joined by Texans from other parts of the state. John Nance Garner, later Vice President of the United States and then a young politician, was among those who opposed the continuation of the Rangers. On April 18, 1902, the Seguin *Enterprise* ran an angry editorial denouncing Garner for having "stood with the East Texas element that have been fighting the ranger force for the last twenty years."

English-language papers on the Border were especially active in puffing up Ranger participation in the Cortez chase. The Brownsville *Herald* not only ran the legendary version of the capture, without correction, but it also gave a grossly inaccurate account of an encounter between Rangers and "the Cortez gang" at Benavides on June 18. According to the San Antonio *Express* of June 19 a posse under Ranger Sanders met three Mexicans near Benavides and killed one, captured one, and wounded the third. The *Herald* reported it on the same day as a desperate battle between Sanders, "a mere boy" and all by himself, and the three Mexicans, over whom the Ranger triumphed single-handed.

On June 28 the *Herald* made its point on the editorial page.

> Those who object to the maintenance of the state ranger force should take notice that it was a ranger captain that caught the fleeing desperado who killed Sheriffs Morris and Glover.

Rogers' own version of the capture of Cortez, as told to the San Antonio *Express*, was as follows.

> We came in sight of the ranch house. In the open yard around it were several men and when we got within about fifty yards of them, we threw down our Winchesters on them and told them to surrender. Of course, I didn't know but that Cortez was in the crowd. The vaquero seeing this, told me Cortez was in the house. He rode on ahead and entered the house. In a moment he appeared at the door, Cortez with him.
>
> "Here's your man," said Gonzales, and that was all there was to it. Cortez made no attempt at resistance. . . . No especial credit is due to me for the capture. Somebody else would have got him if I hadn't.[25]

Two points are left unexplained in Captain Rogers' account. Unless one takes the Wild West concept of the Ranger seriously, it seems odd that Rogers, with a whole posse at his command, should go for Cortez accompanied only by Merrem; that is, unless one assumes that Rogers already knew that Cortez would not or could not resist. The behavior of González is also unexplained. While the Ranger nervously "throws down" on a group of equally nervous Mexicans outside, the vaquero calmly walks into the house and brings the wanted man out. Either González was an extremely brave man, or he knew that Cortez was helpless.

Some variants of the Border *corrido* say that Cortez surren-

[25] *Ibid.*, p. 1.

dered. A Mexico City broadside ballad, the Spanish-language newspapers, and the Border prose legend say he was betrayed. After his capture Cortez did not act like a man who has just surrendered. He denied his identity until he was positively identified. In a statement to Sheriff Ortiz of Webb County soon after his arrest, he said he had been "unfortunately and accidentally captured."[26]

At that time it appears that Cortez still thought that González was his friend and that the Rangers had just happened by at the wrong moment. After his release from prison Cortez told the *Imparcial* reporter who wrote the Chapa pamphlet that he had been betrayed.[27] González took his pistols to get some ammunition, he stated, took them to Rogers, and Rogers came and arrested him.

The Mexicans in the Laredo area were bitter toward González. Under the heading, "Ostracized by his people," the Laredo *Times* ran an article that was widely reprinted in other Texas papers.

The Times knows from an authentic source that Jesús González, the cowboy who assisted in the capture of Gregorio Cortez, has been entirely ostracized from his circle of Mexican friends at the coal mines on account of having rendered such assistance, effecting the capture of one of his countrymen. He has been declared as a traitor and is repeatedly and continuously insulted by certain individuals every time he meets them. Threats have been made that they were going to kill him.[28]

González did not get the thousand dollars, all in shiny silver coins inside a *morral*. Ranger Captain Rogers suggested that all the money go to González, and at first his suggestion was enthusiastically approved, according to the Karnes County *News* of July 26.

[26] Corpus Christi *Caller*, June 28, 1910, p. 1.
[27] An untitled pamphlet by the Chapa Publishing Company, San Antonio, undated and unpaginated, c. 1914.
[28] Quoted in the Brownsville *Herald*, August 13, 1901.

The Man

The entire amount of the reward will go to the Mexican cowboy. . . . None of the men who were in the chase were in it for the money there was in making the capture, and the entire $1000 will be given to the Mexican cowboy, not only because he deserves liberal treatment but to encourage others of his class to follow his example and assist the officers in the arrest of lawbreakers. This disposition of the reward by those who had a right to claim it meets with general approval.

But there was a change of mind and heart once the citizens of Karnes had thought it over. In the end González got about $200. The rest was divided up among others, including a Karnes County deputy who took no part in the capture. Captain Rogers refused to accept his share.

Aftermath

Now the "arch fiend," as one newspaper called Cortez,[29] was at last caught, and the people between the Colorado and the Nueces received the news with expressions of joy and relief. Beeville reported a "general feeling of relief and much rejoicing." Gonzales reported "great relief and rejoicing." Karnes was "jubilant over the news."

The citizens of Karnes, however, were more than a little miffed when Cortez was taken to San Antonio instead of to Karnes City. They went to the station to wait for the prisoner, and only three possemen got off the train. This hurt the citizens of Karnes deeply. No one, they assured the world at large, had been at the station with any intention of harming a hair of Cortez's head. But as a matter of pride they felt that he should have been lodged at the Karnes City jail.

A justice of the peace from Karnes County made a demand on Bexar County Sheriff Tobin for Cortez. On advice from Karnes County's own Sheriff Hunter, who had succeeded Morris, Tobin ignored the demand. The justice, also named Tobin, was insistent, and finally Judge Wilson of the 24th District Court stepped

[29] Seguin *Enterprise,* June 14, 1901, p. 3.

in and ordered the prisoner kept in San Antonio until further orders came from him. The Karnes County Tobin then wrote an indignant letter to the San Antonio *Express,* claiming that Sheriff Tobin and Judge Wilson had exceeded their authority.

For a few days the eagerness of the people of Karnes to get their hands on Cortez was almost indecent. Finally they seemed to become reconciled to the idea that he would hang legally. They were consoled by the certainty that the prisoner would hang one way or the other, "as from the evidence all know that justice will finally be meted out to its fullest extent."

The egos of the people between the Colorado and the Nueces had been sorely manhandled that June by Gregorio Cortez, and it was in the nature of things that they should seek revenge. The confusion and the tendency to shoot first did not end with the Battle of Belmont. A summary of just those reports appearing in the San Antonio *Express* between June 14, when Glover's posse tried to eat each other up, and June 20, when the little brown mare was recovered at Cotulla, gives one an idea as to what was going on back home while posses led by Manuel Tom, the trailer, were pursuing Cortez toward the Rio Grande.

June 14—Glover and Schnabel are killed. Mrs. Robledo and the Rodríguez boy are wounded; the youngest Robledo boy is hanged.

June 15—Attempts to lynch the five "desperate characters" captured at the Robledo house are foiled by bringing the captives to San Antonio.

Deaths of Glover and Schnabel are explained by the fact that "the Mexicans had the advantage."

From Gonzales County comes the news that the Mexicans are "uneasy" and are going about armed. All Mexicans are ordered disarmed.

June 16—In the Guadalupe bottoms one Mexican is killed, one wounded, and four are arrested as members of the "Cortez gang."

At Ottine, near Belmont, one Mexican is killed, one is wounded who later dies, and one is arrested as a member of the "Cortez gang."

Sheriff Jackman of Hays County sends out the "cheering news" that he is hot on the trail of Gregorio Cortez. Cortez is riding a roan horse and is armed with three six-shooters. He is heading toward

Austin and cutting all telephone and telegraph wires along his way. Posses from Austin, San Antonio, and other points converge upon the rider of the roan.

At Yoakum a posse is organized to go to Kilworth because there are many Mexicans at Kilworth, according to people who know the country.

June 17—A posse from Runge, Sheriff Morris' hometown, returns from the chase of Cortez, having given up because "the fugitive had all the advantage, as he was being supplied with fresh horses all the time." (Cortez walked part of the time this posse was out looking for him. He rode the sorrel mare the rest of the time.)

Eight hundred "thoroughly armed" possemen gather in Gonzales County to combat the "Cortez gang," which is reported to be numerous and armed with "the latest improved 30x30 Marlin Winchester rifles."

At Belmont one Mexican is hanged to death, another is shot dead, one is wounded by rifle fire, and a fourth has his skull fractured by a rifle barrel. All were, of course, members of the "Cortez gang." The hanged man refused to disclose information about the gang and was "hung to unconsciousness" repeatedly until he failed to revive. Three hundred men "were in the crowd who participated in this."

At Beeville the opinion is that some good will come out of the shooting of Morris, Glover, and Schnabel. It will lead to the clearing out of the undesirable element.

June 18—At San Diego one Mexican is killed, one is badly wounded, and a third is captured. They were members of the "gang."

At Willow Springs a Mexican is reported killed. The charge is that he was a member of the "Cortez gang."

One Mexican is reported killed at Benavides, and it is said he belonged to "the gang that killed Sheriff Glover of Gonzales."

June 19—The Cortez gang grows more formidable. It is reported that "this gang of thieves and desperadoes has allies and accomplices almost from the Rio Grande to the Colorado river."

Gonzales reports that another of the slayers of Glover has been reported killed and still another captured.

June 20—"Little doubt" is expressed that Cortez "is at the head of a well organized band of thieves and cutthroats." Sheriff Moss of Refugio County tells reporters that he shot a horse from under Cortez in a desperate encounter with him several years before. (Documentary evidence is that Cortez had never been in any sort of trouble before the death of Morris.)

From San Diego comes the news that the Mexicans killed there by Texas Rangers had nothing to do with Cortez. Gonzales comments on that piece of news: "But they were all probably horse thieves, anyway."

Cortez is reported at Cotulla, and the accounts of the "Cortez gang" in the Colorado-Nueces area end abruptly, never to be mentioned again. The last word is a cry of injured innocence from Gonzales: "The report has gotten out that several Mexicans in this county have been killed and one hung to avenge the death of Sheriff Glover. This report is not true."

Not all the dead and wounded were Mexicans, as overzealous posses tried to get Cortez by shooting at everything they saw. Besides the death of Schnabel, the serious wounding of posseman Robert Benton was reported in Kenedy. Benton made the mistake of moving around in the dark, and he was blasted with buckshot by his friends. Cortez was then at Floresville, thirty miles away.

With the "arch fiend" in jail, the State of Texas held prisoner almost every known member of the Cortez family, from Cortez's mother to his three-year-old son, Crispín. Cortez's father seems to have been no longer living. The mother, Romaldo, the wives of Gregorio and Romaldo, and Gregorio's children had been thrown into the Karnes City jail the morning after authorities discovered Romaldo at the house in Kenedy. Other members of the family were rounded up and jailed during the chase.

Valeriano, Gregorio's son, still remembers his days in the Karnes City jail. The adults were kept in separate cells while he, his ten-year-old sister Mariana, and his six-year-old brother Severo were put together in one cell. Three-year-old Crispín was allowed to be with his mother. For the first few days the children were kept locked up in their cell. Later the three eldest were allowed to play in the jail corridor for part of the day, before being locked in again.

Only little Crispín, the three-year-old, was allowed beyond the doors of the jail. The jailer had a little boy just Crispín's age, and the two were allowed to play together in the jail yard. Valeriano remembers how enviously he and the other two older children would look out their cell window at the two little ones at play.

Some time after the capture of Gregorio, his three eldest children were released, but their mother, Crispín, and the other adults were kept in custody until October, four months after their arrest, when Gregorio was sentenced to death at Karnes City. On September 11 a San Antonio woman named Francisca García came to the sheriff's office in San Antonio, asking that something be done for the older children of Cortez. She had been taking care of them, but she was poor and had run out of means to support them. Both their father and their mother were still in jail.

The deputies at the sheriff's office suggested that she see the Humane Society. If the woman did, it must not have been Humaneness Week, because nothing more is ever heard about the matter.[30]

No charges were ever filed against any other member of Cortez's family except one older brother, Tomás, arrested in Manor during the chase after Gregorio, who was sentenced to five years in the penitentiary. The charge was horse theft.

The battle of the courts

Soon after the capture of Cortez a form letter began to circulate among the Mexicans of Texas and to appear in newspapers as far away as Mexico City. It was signed by the president and the secretary of the Miguel Hidalgo workers' society of San Antonio and was the first appeal for financial aid in the long legal fight over Cortez.

The letter of the San Antonio workers was a model of simplicity and restraint. It announced the beginning of a fund for the defense of the accused man. Cortez, the letter stated, faced a shameful death which he might not deserve. "If he is a criminal," it said, "let him be punished. But only after he has been

[30] San Antonio *Express*, September 12, 1901, p. 7.

given a fair trial. And for him to get a fair trial, money is necessary. This is a sad truth, but it is a truth."[31]

The fund-raising campaigns in behalf of Cortez united Mexicans from the south banks of the Rio Grande to San Antonio
and beyond—rich and poor, workers and professional men,
townspeople and rancheros. Money was collected through direct
donation, through the workers' societies, and through special
benefit performances. Cortez became a symbol to the Mexican
people of Texas. His legal fight was a continuation of the fight
and flight that had carried him from Karnes County to the Border "in defense of his right." And those who had participated vi-
cariously in the flight now participated in the court battles in a
more concrete way.

On the Border, where defending one's right had been a watch-
word of border conflict for half a century, and where Cortez was
recognized as a native son, the feeling of oneness was the strongest. And it was in this atmosphere that *El Corrido de Gregorio
Cortez* was made, by some unknown *guitarrero* perhaps, who
strummed it bar by bar, hummed it line by line, repeating each
quatrain over and over until it took the first of its many shapes.

Pablo Cruz was one of the first men to take up the fight in defense of Cortez. Cruz, editor and publisher of *El Regidor* of San
Antonio, co-ordinated the fund campaigns, hired lawyers, and
was the guiding spirit of the movement until he died in 1903,
still in the middle of the fight, not living to see Cortez acquitted
of the murder of Morris. Col. F. A. Chapa, editor and publisher
of *El Imparcial,* also of San Antonio, took the place of Cruz and
led the battle until 1913, when Cortez was pardoned and released.

In Mexico City a broadside was used to solicit funds. Cortez
is made to talk through the ballad singer directly to the audience
in an appeal for funds, and the name of Pablo Cruz is mentioned.

Pablo Cruz se distinguió	Pablo Cruz distinguished himself
como íntegro mexicano,	As an upright Mexican;

[31] *El Popular de Mexico,* Mexico City, July 25, 1901, p. 1.

88

este prominente hermano	This prominent brother
que su ayuda me impartió.	Who gave me his aid.
Participo esta noticia	I make this news known
a gente culta y honrada . . .	To honest and cultured people;
los de lista enumerada,	Those who put themselves on this
la suerte le sea propicia.	numbered list—
	May fortune be kind to them.

One can see the blind singers on every corner of the markets of Mexico, grinding away at the ballad, while a little boy or a girl holds the "numbered lists" and collects the coins. It is doubtful that the *ciegos* ever sent much money to Pablo Cruz. On the Border and deeper in Texas there is no record of ballads being used to collect funds.

The *ciegos*, by the way, were not the only ones cashing in on Gregorio Cortez. Three days after his capture the following advertisement appeared in the San Antonio *Express*, June 25, 1901.

> FOR SALE—Gregoria [sic] Cortez, sheriff killer,
> photographed as captured, send 25 cents.
> Photographer T. E. Mitchell, Laredo, Tex.

Not all people who came to Cortez's aid were of Mexican descent. A curious ambivalence developed in the Anglo-American attitude toward him, even while the chase was on. Many people found it hard not to admire the courage, skill, and endurance of the hunted man. And after the excitement died down, some Texans changed their opinions about the case. The Chapa pamphlet says that there were many Anglo-Americans among the people who contributed to Cortez's defense. As the pardons committee would later note, the sheriffs who had Cortez in custody began by hating him as a sheriff killer and ended by becoming his friends. Some very prominent Anglo-Texans were to come to his aid, among them the Hon. F. C. Weinert, who was Texas secretary of state at the time Cortez was pardoned and who interceded in his behalf. Weinert was from Seguin, in the middle of the Cortez-inflamed area.

The lawyer who worked the hardest to get Cortez justice in

the courts was R. B. Abernathy of Gonzales, the county where the Belmont gunbattle took place and one of the two counties in which prejudice against Cortez was the strongest. Cortez later was to remember Abernathy among his lawyers. Abernathy worked for four years in a cause that could make him neither rich nor popular. He could not even be accused of courting the Mexican vote because at that time Mexicans were denied the right to vote in the primaries in Gonzales and neighboring counties.

Still, when Cortez first came to trial there were hundreds of people who apparently had given up the idea of lynching the man only because they expected to see him hanged legally without delay. It is a curious commentary on the workings of the human mind that the people of Karnes and Gonzales chose to hang Cortez not for the killings of Morris and Glover—for which he was responsible—but for the murder of Schnabel, whose death it was already common knowledge had been caused by one his fellow possemen.

The trial, which began at Gonzales on July 24, 1901, was remarkable in many ways. Mexicans were allowed on the venire, though none was chosen for the jury. One Negro was chosen juror. The trial itself, though, was another story.

Sheriffs and sheriffs' deputies poured into Gonzales for the trial, with the frankly avowed anticipation of seeing Cortez sentenced to death. They occupied the major part of the spectators' seats. To indict Cortez for the murder of Schnabel the ridiculous charge against Mrs. Robledo was dropped, in return for a "confession" that she had seen Cortez kill Glover on the east side of the house and then run around the house and kill Schnabel on the west side. To clinch the case Manuel Tom, the trailer, testified that Cortez had confessed to him about being by the barn, on the west side where Schnabel was killed. On being asked the Spanish word for barn, the best Tom could do was say *casa*, the word for house.

The testimony was a formality anyway, the jurors apparently having come with their minds made up. All but the twelfth juror. He was impressed by the arguments for the defense, and he hung up the jury for a long time. When a quick verdict did not materialize, the sheriffs, according to the *Express* of July 31, left "very much disappointed."

Juror A. L. Sanders, the man who believed Cortez innocent, stuck to his guns. Finally word was conveyed to him that there was a serious illness in his family and that he was greatly needed at home. The other eleven jurors, who wanted to hang Cortez, suggested a compromise. Sanders gave in, and the prisoner got fifty years on a charge of second-degree murder.

It was a verdict that satisfied no one, least of all the defendant. "When the verdict was read to Cortez," the *Express* reported on August 1, "he was very indignant." It was also reported that "Cortez used very strong language against the court and jury on the way from the courthouse to the jail."

Juror Sanders was not satisfied either. He went to the defense lawyers and told them his story. Cortez's lawyers promptly filed a motion for a new trial, basing their petition on what Sanders had told them. The judge just as promptly denied the motion and fined Sanders one hundred dollars for contempt of court.

There were other people who were even less satisfied with the verdict. One week later, on August 9, Romaldo Cortez, whom Sheriff Morris had wounded, died in the Karnes City jail. The official report was that Romaldo had died of his wound "after two months of intense suffering." Morris' shot had gone into Romaldo's open mouth at an angle. It came out through his left cheek, knocking out some teeth, and lodged in his shoulder. Scarcely a wound to kill a two-hundred-pound man in the prime of life. Valeriano Cortez remembers that in their first few days in jail his uncle was well enough to walk about in his cell and to joke with the jailer. Two months later, however, he died.

Two days after Romaldo's death in the Karnes City jail, an attempt was made to take Gregorio Cortez out of the Gonzales jail to lynch him. Sheriff F. M. Fly, successor to Glover, who frustrated the attempt, declared that most of the mob of 300 to 350 men were from Karnes County.

One week after the lynching attempt, at Runge, Morris' home town, deputy sheriff A. A. Lyons killed one Mexican and wounded another, who disappeared into the brush with Lyons after him and was not heard from again. Lyons testified that the two Mexicans had cursed him; one of them had struck at him with his coat, and the two had surrounded him, placing him "at a great disadvantage." He had then shot them down. He did not claim that the Mexicans were armed, and they did not attack him except for striking at him with the coat. Lyons did not anticipate any "trouble whatsoever in clearing himself of any charges that may be made against him."[32] None were made.

With Lyons' valiant success against a superior Mexican force which placed him "at a great disadvantage" (apparently a favorite expression of the time), physical expression of chagrin against the way the Cortez affair was going seems to have come to an end. Later protests seem to have been all verbal.

On January 15, 1902, the Texas Court of Criminal Appeals reversed the Gonzales verdict. The court expressed doubt that Cortez could have been at two places at one time and disapproved of Manuel Tom's unique translation of *casa* as "barn."[33] Cortez was not tried again for the death of Schnabel.

Cortez meanwhile had been taken to Karnes City and very speedily sentenced to death for the murder of Sheriff Morris. There was no violence during the trial (October 7–11, 1901), the prevailing sentiment appearing to be that the prisoner should be hanged only after a fair and impartial trial. The sheriffs again poured in, and the families of Morris and Glover were sat in the front row, where the prosecution could point them out to the jury. The jury took only two ballots, one for the degree of murder and one for the penalty. Eight months later (during which time Cortez was dangerously ill of pneumonia at the Columbus jail in Colorado County) the Court of Criminal Appeals reversed the Karnes verdict on the grounds of prejudice.[34]

The case was moved to Goliad, but before Cortez was tried

[32] San Antonio *Express*, August 19, 1901, p. 3.
[33] Court of Criminal Appeals, Case No. 2397.
[34] Court of Criminal Appeals, Case No. 2270.

there he was taken to Pleasanton and given two years for horse theft in a quick and a sloppy trial, according to the Court of Criminal Appeals.[35] The conviction was reversed, but not before it served its purpose. At the Goliad trial Cortez was referred to as a convicted horse thief who had killed Morris when the latter had attempted to arrest him.

The Goliad jury failed to agree, with seven for first-degree murder, four for second-degree murder, and one for acquittal. The case went to Wharton County, where it was dismissed by the district judge of Wharton for want of jurisdiction. It then went to Corpus Christi, where it was tried April 25–30, 1904.

There a jury of Anglo-American farmers found Cortez not guilty of murder in the death of Sheriff Morris, agreeing with the claim of the defense that Morris had attempted an unauthorized arrest, and that Gregorio had shot the sheriff in self-defense and in defense of his brother.

"After the reading of the verdict," the *Express* reported on May 1, "Cortez turned in his seat, bowed to the jury and said, 'gracias' which in his native tongue is thanks. He seemed deeply touched."

The weekly Corpus Christi *Caller* on May 6 said that "the verdict seemed to meet with general approval from our citizens, in fact, the sentiment of those who heard the trial in most instances favored an acquittal." This was a far cry indeed from the first trial at Gonzales.

The verdict was a victory not only for Cortez but for all Mexicans in Texas. Especially interested were the Borderers, who for half a century had seen respectable citizens transformed into outlaws by the application of "Ranger law," according to which a man was killed if he did not defend himself, or was tried for murder and hanged if he did.

Meanwhile Cortez had been found guilty of the murder of Glover in a trial at Columbus, but had been given a life sentence instead of the expected sentence of death. The case had been appealed, and lawyers were of the opinion that the decision would be reversed in view of the Corpus Christi acquittal, since

[35] *Southwestern Reporter*, Vol. 74, p. 907.

Cortez had been found guilty of the murder of Glover on the assumption that he had murdered Morris and was a fugitive from justice instead of being a fugitive from lynch law.

The defense, however, had built its case around the contention that Cortez had not fired the shots that had killed Glover. The Court of Criminal Appeals upheld the conviction,[36] and Cortez entered the Huntsville penitentiary on January 1, 1905, to serve a life sentence for the murder of Glover.

The legal battle in his behalf had stretched out over three and one-half years, during which time Cortez had been in eleven jails in eleven counties of Texas, never having been out on bond. Though the final outcome was his going to prison for Glover's death, in the Morris case he and the people who had fought with him had won a significant victory. The fight for a commutation or a pardon immediately began.

"Through thick and thin"

In the Karnes City trial, Leonor Cortez had been the chief witness in her husband's defense. At the Goliad trial eighteen months later, her name had disappeared from the list of defense witnesses. At the Corpus Christi trial the defense felt it necessary to explain why Leonor no longer appeared as a witness for the defense. Encarnación Díaz, Cortez's father-in-law, was put on the stand to testify that his daughter was no longer the wife of the defendant and "was prejudiced against her former husband."

In view of the way that most of the other defense witnesses in the Cortez case sooner or later either left the country or changed their minds, the first thought that occurs is that Leonor Cortez had been somehow convinced to change her allegiance by the "influential citizens of Gonzales and Karnes counties," as the *Express* frequently called them, who were doing all in their power to see Cortez hanged. When Cortez married again, by implication at least he accused his former wife of having aban-

[36] Court of Criminal Appeals, Case No. 2696.

doned him. His new bride, he said, was the only person who had stuck to him through all his adversities.

But there is another side to the question. At least once again Cortez was to refer to still another woman as the only person who had stuck to his cause through thick and thin. Both women (and there may have been at least a third) made public statements that they had loved Gregorio for many years, and that they had been engaged to be married to him before the killing of Morris and Cortez's subsequent troubles had broken up their romance. This seems to throw a different light on Leonor Cortez's "abandonment" of her husband. It also reveals an interesting side of the personality of Cortez.

Gregorio was a good-looking young man (he was twenty-six on the day he was captured), and he had a frank, engaging personality that affected not only women but men, even men who were hostile to him at first. When he settled down near Kenedy to work a farm, Cortez had behind him ten or eleven years of roaming in company of his brother Romaldo. In many of his trips Gregorio's family was not along.

It seems that like the wandering sailor the wandering vaquero made love to many girls along his way and made promises to them that the girls believed, not knowing about the family back home. It is amusing to imagine what happened when the whole state was filled with news of the exploits and the capture of Gregorio Cortez. It would only be natural for each of Gregorio's sweethearts to rush to him, each feeling that her place was beside him in his hour of greatest need, though Cortez may have wished by then that he had never heard of any of them. Such a situation would complicate the life of any man, and it would have taxed the powers even of Gregorio's agile and inventive mind.

The wife probably remained ignorant of Gregorio's several "engagements" until after the trial at Karnes, having been in jail herself all that time, as was most of the family. But after her release she must have felt herself extremely wronged. After months of incarceration she was compelled to provide for her children in a hostile country, all because of a husband who was at that moment surrounded by sweethearts, girls who had not suffered for him but who were trying to push her aside and appear in the public eye as Gregorio's faithful and true companions. At the Corpus Christi trial the defense claimed that Leonor was prejudiced against Gregorio. From the few facts that have survived about his way with women, one can well imagine why.

On June 15, 1904, the Court of Criminal Appeals affirmed the life sentence given Cortez for the murder of Sheriff Glover, and on December 17 a rehearing on the case was denied. Cortez prepared himself for the trip to Huntsville. On December 23 he married in the Columbus jail. His bride was Estéfana Garza of Manor, who had come to Columbus for the ceremony with his mother. The marriage was performed by the county judge, and was witnessed by the sheriff and other county officials. The bride was described as having stood by Cortez "through all his troubles . . . and used her utmost endeavors to secure his freedom. She gained the respect of all the attaches of the jail here because of her undying devotion to the man she loves."[37]

Cortez apparently had also gained the respect of attachés of the jail. Not only did Sheriff Bridge arrange for his marriage in jail, but he and his bride were given the whole upper story of the jail for themselves, as a honeymoon suite, during the week that went by from the date of the marriage to the day—January 1, 1905—when Cortez left Columbus for Houston and Huntsville.

The Houston correspondent to the San Antonio *Express* reported on January 2 the arrival of Gregorio Cortez, "the famous Mexican," and expressed the hope that "the clemency of the State's chief executive is invoked in his behalf. Cortez is well liked by the jail officers here," the Houston correspondent went on to say. "He never gave them any trouble, and they always treated him kindly. When he arrived last night, he gave the hand of Night Keeper Trammell a hearty shake and evidenced a gladness to see him."

His ability to make friends went with Cortez to Huntsville.

[37] San Antonio *Express*, December 24, 1904, p. 2.

So did his ability to adapt himself. When he was received at Huntsville he gave his occupation not as vaquero or farmer but as barber, and he seems to have been allowed to exercise that trade during his years in prison. His certificate of prison conduct reads, "Occupation, barber; habits, temperate; education, limited." In things other than books his education was wide.

The pardon

In July 1913 the efforts to secure a pardon for Cortez were at last successful. Governor O. B. Colquitt signed the necessary papers on July 7, and on July 14 Gregorio Cortez was free, having been a prisoner for twelve years, nine of them at Huntsville. The story went that Colquitt, a softhearted man, had been induced to pardon Cortez by appeals to his sentiments. Many Texas-Mexicans who are too sophisticated to accept any other part of the Cortez legend believe that Cortez was pardoned through the personal intercession of Col. F. A. Chapa, the publisher of *El Imparcial*.

It is pretty certain that Colquitt was a "pardoning governor"; he celebrated his fifty-first birthday by granting fifty-one pardons on December 16, 1912.[38] That he was "softhearted" may be deduced from a study of his correspondence. Many a tearful letter from a mother or a wife seems to have had its desired effect on the governor. And Colquitt was on quite friendly terms with Chapa; there is a regular and cordial correspondence between them during these years.[39]

But the records show that a great many people, some as influential as Chapa or more so, were also supporting pardon efforts for Cortez. And it also seems that in Cortez's case Governor Colquitt was not especially softhearted. The pardon papers dealing with the case (in which Chapa's name does not appear)

[38] George Portal Huckaby, *Oscar Branch Colquitt: A Political Biography,* Doctoral dissertation, University of Texas, 1946, p. 329.
[39] Colquitt Letters, Texas State Library, Austin.

show that the Board of Pardons Advisers recommended a full pardon. Colquitt, however, granted Cortez only a conditional pardon.[40]

Colquitt may have had his political ear to the ground; Karnes and Gonzales counties at least were sure to be indignant. Another reason may have been the letter that Cortez addressed to Colquitt on June 23, two weeks before the pardon was signed. The letter, though respectful, was not of the repentant, tearful type that Colquitt may have got used to expecting from applicants for pardons.

In a last appeal to the governor Cortez promised to be a good citizen and never to enter again that part of the state where his troubles had arisen, "to prevent any hard words or feeling being aroused by any act of mine." But he went on to say, "Deep regret I have always felt for the sad occurrence, but repentance I have never felt, for I could never bring myself to the hypocritical state as to so plead to gain an end that was my just due."[41]

Cortez's belief in his right had not been shaken by twelve years in prison. His attitude, however, may have offended Colquitt.

As a leader of Texas-Mexicans, Chapa was probably very influential in Cortez's defense, but the pardon seems to have depended finally on Cortez's qualities as a man and on the general feeling that his sentence was unjust. The prison chaplain, the warden, and the chief clerk at Huntsville were among those writing the governor. The report of the Indeterminate Sentence Committee stated that Cortez "has won the esteem and the personal friendship of every man with whom he has come in contact in the penitentiary and all of the men there are anxious that executive clemency be extended him."[42] The warden wrote the governor that he "would very much like to see this man pardoned."[43]

The Board of Pardons Advisers recommended a full pardon

[40] State of Texas v. Gregorio Cortez, Application for Pardon No. 28220.
[41] *Ibid.* The letter is recorded in English translation.
[42] *Ibid.*
[43] *Ibid.*

with restoration of citizenship, and in its recommendation stated that "Secty. of State, Hon. F. C. Weinert, who is familiar with its history has ever contended that applicant is innocent."[44] The Indeterminate Sentence Committee added, "It is very doubtful indeed if this man would ever have been convicted of the murder of Sheriff Glover but for the prosecution on the part of the Sheriffs Association which at that time amounted to practical persecution."[45]

Three letters among the pardon papers are of interest aside from their function as part of the appeals apparatus. All three are addressed to the governor. One is by Ben E. Cabell, chairman of the Board of Prison Commissioners; the other two are by Cortez and by a young woman named Esther Martínez. From the typing and from peculiarities in spelling and punctuation, it appears that all three letters were typed by the same person. The letters signed by Esther Martínez and Cortez obviously were dictated in Spanish and translated by someone else, apparently someone who did not know English very well. Esther Martínez is mentioned in another place in the pardon papers. At the bottom of the recommendation of the Board of Pardons Advisers appear the words, "Represented by: Esther Martinez, his sweetheart (see her letter)."

Cabell's letter is typed on the back of the letter signed by Cortez. It introduces the bearer, Esther Martínez, to the governor. Cortez's letter, dated June 23, tells the governor that "this letter will be presented to you by Senorita E. Martinez." It is in this letter that Cortez expresses deep regret but no repentance.

As revealing of his character as his unrepentant attitude is Cortez's introduction of Esther Martínez. It was Esther, he tells the governor, "to whom I was engaged to marry at the time this trouble arose. She alone has remained true, devoted and faithful to me during all of my long and terrible 14 years of sad misfortune." Cortez promises "to see this noble young lady rewarded" by marrying her if he is released. No mention is made of course of Leonor Díaz, to whom Cortez was married

[44] *Ibid.*
[45] *Ibid.*

when the trouble arose, nor of the devoted and faithful Estéfana Garza, whom he had married in 1905, just before entering Huntsville.

Esther Martínez's letter to the governor is a "plea of a woman for the man she going to marry." It begins, "Honorable and dear Sir: As I do not speak English, I use this method of introducing myself to you, and addressing you of what I wish to talk with you about." She must plead Gregorio's case because she has no money to employ lawyers. "When he got into his trouble we were sweethearts and engaged to be married, I have lived single, and have been true to him . . . and I very much want him. If you will give him to me, I will stand responsible for his acts in the future."

In content the letter is much like many others received by Colquitt. The hispanicized English and the apparently strong belief of Esther's that Texas governors "gave away" convicts to girls who asked for them make the letter different. Toward the end she again repeats her plea: "Please Sir, give him to me."

On July 14, 1913, Gregorio Cortez signed his acceptance of the pardon in a very shaky hand. At thirty-eight he had spent almost a third of his life in prison, and all because he had traded a mare for a horse, just as the legend says.

The last days

The Chapa pamphlet gives a fairly complete account of the movements of Cortez the first few weeks after he came out of the penitentiary. It does not record that Gregorio rewarded Esther Martínez with marriage. The pamphlet mentions her only once, in the section listing the people who worked the hardest to obtain the liberty of Cortez.

Cortez first went to Houston, to thank Professor D. J. J. Mercado and others who had worked in his favor. In Houston, as in other Texas cities, his presence attracted crowds of Mexicans. From Houston Cortez went to Austin, to thank Colquitt personally for having pardoned him.

Representatives of the Austin workers' societies accompanied him to the governor's office, and Cortez presented his thanks. The governor is said to have answered that he did only what he thought was just.[46] English-language newspapers mentioned the visit of Cortez "and a number of relatives" to the governor.[47] Mrs. Nora Aréchiga, 1009 East 9th Street, Austin, prepared a dinner for Cortez that day. She remembers him as tall, thin, quiet and polite.

From Austin Cortez went to San Antonio to thank Colonel Chapa and other San Antonians. He was interviewed by Rodolfo Treviño, probably the author of the Chapa pamphlet. The Mexicans of San Antonio gave a great festival in benefit of Cortez, who was ill and needed medical attention. The program is not recorded, but it is said to have been composed of speeches, readings, and music. There were songs by the Solsona brothers, who accompanied themselves on the guitar.

It is doubtful that the people who came to the Cortez benefit at San Antonio heard *El Corrido de Gregorio Cortez*. Such functions leaned toward the genteel. But the audience may have heard it at the San Antonio haymarket after the benefit was over. Along the Border the ballad was already old, and with the release of Cortez the last part of the legend was about to be told, to be handed down with due modifications during the next forty years.

By September Cortez's health was much better, and he left San Antonio for Nuevo Laredo, on the Mexican side of the Border, "to establish residence there," according to the Chapa pamphlet.

Anglo-American reaction to the release of Cortez varied from the sympathetic to the vitriolic. Reaction at Houston and at Austin seems to have been favorable. In the area of the killings the reaction was not uniform, as may be seen from Beeville's two weekly papers, both of which carried accounts of the pardon.

[46] The Chapa pamphlet.
[47] Houston *Chronicle*, July 19, 1913, p. 5, and San Antonio *Light*, July 19, 1913, p. 1.

The Beeville *Picayune* contented itself with reprinting an undated article from the Laredo *Times* to the effect that Cortez, "a criminal whose daring deeds of murder in Southwest Texas about twelve years ago, threw the populace of several communities into a veritable reign of excitement and a desire to avenge the wrongs," had been pardoned. A short, objective account of the Cortez affair followed.[48]

The Beeville *Bee* was considerably disturbed about the matter. In an editorial entitled "Dangerous Murderer Pardoned," the *Bee* castigated both Cortez and Colquitt. The editorial reviewed Cortez's "heinous deeds," erroneously crediting a Karnes County jury with having sent Cortez to prison for life for the murder of Morris, a misstatement perpetuated in subsequent newspaper accounts.

Governor Colquitt has signed a document, known as a pardon, which gives to this Mexican, who took the lives of American citizens, liberty. The governor's signature to this said document endangers the lives of Texas citizens. Who knows but this blood thirsty murderer may deprive more children of a protecting hand in the death of a father? . . . The Mexican, who broke the laws of the state, and with murder in his heart killed those who had the right, and were empowered by the governor of this state, to bring him to justice, is free. He walks on Texas land a free man! Think of the horror of the children of those dead men, grown to young manhood and young womanhood, when they learned the news of that murderer's release!

Governor Oscar Branch Colquitt has pardoned many; he has had a reputation as a "chicken-hearted" governor. He has allowed tears, trickling down the wrinkled cheeks of old and infirm mothers to move him to pardoning a wayward son. Who can understand the emotion that prompted him to release from the penitentiary, where he was sent for life by twelve good Texas men, brave and true (God knows they were lenient enough with him), the state's most heinous coward and murderer?[49]

Two months later Cortez was not "walking on Texas land." He was in Nuevo Laredo, "establishing his residence." Mexico

[48] Beeville *Picayune,* August 7, 1913, p. 1.
[49] Beeville *Bee,* August 15, 1913, p. 4.

was scarcely the place for one to establish residence in the fall of 1913. In February President Madero had been assassinated and the whole north was up in arms against his successor, Huerta. Matamoros, on one end of the Lower Border, had fallen to Carranza on June 3; Nuevo Laredo, on the other end, was still held by Huerta troops. There was fighting in between.

Valeriano Cortez, Gregorio's son, states that his father went to Nuevo Laredo in response to a request by Colonel Chapa that he join the Huerta forces. When he arrived at Nuevo Laredo the Huertistas took Cortez for a spy. He was almost shot before he could identify himself with papers provided for him in San Antonio. The Huertistas then shaved his head, put him in a uniform, and made him an infantry soldier, thus living up to the tradition of all armies of putting the round pegs in the square holes.

Later, however, Cortez was put on horseback, given a squad of *rurales,* and sent out into the brush to skirmish with revolutionary bands. Cortez had chosen an unpopular and a losing side; apparently he took it up merely out of gratitude for some of his benefactors. Eventually he was wounded. He may also have been captured, as rumor has it, and escaped before his execution. He did return to Texas to convalesce, and was at Manor for some time with his son Valeriano.

Cortez did not tell his son many details about his revolutionary experiences. Most of his stories of the Revolution were about the speed, intelligence, and the training of the horses he rode. After he recovered from his wound, Cortez left for Anson, in Jones County, some twenty miles north of Abilene. At Anson, in the home of a *compadre* of his named Cipriano Rodríguez, he died in 1916. He had just married again. During the evening, as wedding festivities were going on, he suddenly complained of pain, turned black, and died.

It is not clear whom Cortez had married. It may have been a third faithful sweetheart, or it may have been Esther Martínez. Her home was Big Spring, about 100 miles west of Anson.

Valeriano Cortez believes his father was poisoned. If poison it was, it must have been administered later than 1913. It is most probable that Cortez died from natural causes—a heart attack perhaps. The hard life he had lived for fifteen years, with hardships, privations, wounds, and imprisonment, the festivities at the time of his death (which certainly must not have been dry), and the sudden pain would make one think so.

Thus died Gregorio Cortez, at the age of forty-one, after three years of freedom but very few days of peace. The last fifteen years of his life were not of the sort that lead to longevity. He was buried in a little cemetery eight miles outside of Anson. Tomasita Macías, 2509 East 3rd Street, Austin, a niece of Cortez who lived in Anson in the 1920's, lost a child in 1925 and buried it in the Anson cemetery by the side of her uncle. At that time, Mrs. Macías says, there was still a headstone with the name of Cortez on the grave.

And there Cortez lies, more than five hundred miles from the Border on which he was born, and which he once desperately tried to reach on the little brown and the little sorrel mares.

Epilogue

The descendants of Cortez still live in Texas, in Houston and Galveston. After Leonor Cortez was released from the Karnes City jail, her other children were restored to her. The family had to stay in Kenedy because they could not afford to move somewhere else, and to support her children the mother had to take in washing from the people who hated her husband and were doing everything in their power to see him hanged.

Threats were made against their lives, and for some reason the family lived in terror of being poisoned. With childish logic Valeriano used to believe that the poison would come in one of the bundles of clothing from the houses of his father's enemies. The fear of poison seems to have haunted the family. Valeriano believes that both his uncle Romaldo and his father were poisoned.

Later Mariana and Valeriano were taken to the home of Gregorio's parents in Manor. An Anglo-American rancher, whom Valeriano remembers only as Joe, adopted Severo and raised him among his sons. Years later, when both were men, Severo told Valeriano of an experience he had while working cattle on his adopted father's ranch.

According to Severo he met another young cowboy, and they became good friends. They worked together, ate together, and slept side by side at the camp. One day they started talking about their families, and Severo learned that the other cowboy was Sheriff Morris' son. They talked the matter over and decided to say nothing to the other cowboys, and when the job was over each went his separate way.[50]

Of Cortez's four children by his first wife, all except Severo are living. Crispín, who seems to have stayed closest to his mother, lives in Galveston, where his mother died during World War II. Mariana and Valeriano live in Houston.

Valeriano's sons, Gregorio and Louis, are veterans of World War II. Gregorio fought the Germans with his rifle in his hand. He saw service in the United States infantry in Europe and was seriously wounded. Louis belonged to the air unit that dropped the atom bomb on Japan. Theirs is a different world.

On the Border the world also has seen its changes since the days of Gregorio Cortez. One year before Gregorio's death—in 1915—came Aniceto Pizaña's uprising and the beginning of the bloody period known locally as the "border troubles." The "troubles" lasted into the 1920's, by which time the boom was in full swing and efforts were being made to turn the Rio Grande Valley into a combination Florida and California, complete with Hollywood. The Mexican did not always fit into the new scheme of things, except perhaps as a colorful addition to the landscape.

After 1915 he again found himself in many places pushed into the depressed class, both economically and politically. He worked his way up again during the 1920's and the early 1930's. There was no longer any thought of revolt; there were no new

[50] Sheriff Morris left a daughter and two sons. The eldest, Harper Morris, is now sheriff of Karnes County, as his father was before him.

ballad heroes. The new leaders were all political leaders. But the old state of mind continued, even though in some of the upriver towns the Mexican controlled local politics.

Until the rise of Hitler in Germany and the beginning of World War II, a majority of Border Mexicans continued to think of themselves as a people apart. Unlike other American minorities, they directed their energies not toward being accepted into the majority but toward maintaining their own individual rights as members of an aloof enclave struggling to keep its own identity.

On the Mexican part of the Border, fundamental changes were taking place in the 1930's. The south-bank people had turned more and more to farming after the freezes and the drouths of the 1890's, but the chaparral had remained much the same, with the same tight little folk groups. The land reforms of the Cárdenas administration broke up the old patriarchal holdings and brought in many new people, most of them agrarian *fuereños* from the south.

The brush disappeared, and the character of land and people changed. The country became a flat, dusty expanse of cotton land, and the people a diverse conglomeration from many parts of Mexico. The settled folk groups of near relatives, on which the half-destroyed folk aggregations of the north bank had homed in a cultural sense, began to disappear.

On the Texas bank physical changes also were taking place. New people had settled in most of the country; grapefruit orchards and truck farms replaced the chaparral. Still, on the Texas side cultural isolation remained.

But with the advent of World War II greater numbers of north-bank Borderers began to think of themselves seriously as Americans. Like the unreconstructed Southerner—whom he resembled in some respects—the Border Mexican was surprised to find that the peoples of Europe and the Pacific thought of him as just another American.

In World War II, the Anglo-Texan and the Texas-Mexican fought in the same units against a common foe, an enemy whose acts in Europe made the worst Ranger painted by Border folklore look like an amateur. In the Pacific, Texas-Mexican and Anglo-Texan fought side by side against an enemy that made for himself an Alamo out of every bunker and every cave; and after living together through the great atrocity that was the Pacific War, perhaps neither Anglo nor Mexican got excited over what had happened one hundred years before, or even what had happened in the times of Pizaña in 1915.

Brownsville's World War II hero was a Border Mexican. Armed with the modern equivalent of the Ranger's Colt, a machine gun, he displayed such Spanish-Indian cruelty toward the German army that he was awarded the Congressional Medal of Honor. And all good Texans in Brownsville received him on his homecoming with festivities and parades. His deeds were not celebrated in *corridos;* legends were not made about him. For he was not the hero of the Border folk but of the American people.

Thus the old folk communities straddling the international line at the Rio Grande were absorbed into their respective countries. The era of border conflict passed, but its heroes survived in the *corridos* and the legends, to linger in the memories of a new generation until the last old man dies.

And perhaps they will live longer than that—as long as men esteem dignity and courage, even in defeat. In such a way have the English celebrated the Scottish folk heroes, between whom and the English, as the ballad of Wallace says, there was once "an ill seed sown."

IV: THE HERO'S PROGRESS

Theme and variations

For more than half a century the Rio Grande people have remembered Gregorio Cortez, and in that time the figure of a folk hero has been shaped out of historical fact. It has been the vivid, dramatic narrative of the *corrido*—a well-established form—that has kept the image of Cortez fresh in the minds of Border people, but something needs to be said about the amorphous body of narrative that makes up the prose legend.

The stories that make up the Cortez legend are anecdotal for the most part, arising from the singing of the *corrido*, it would seem. Yet, though by-products of it, they have in their turn influenced the *corrido*. And because of their many variations they have been responsible for the growth of Gregorio Cortez as a folk hero. It is the legend that has developed the heroic figure, which the ballad keeps alive.

Chapter II has attempted an idealized, formal version of the legend. Chapter III has presented the facts of the life of Cortez as far as they are known to me. In this chapter I mention other variants of the legend, compare fact with fancy, and attempt to show how the latter grew out of the former. Because they are so closely intertwined, one cannot discuss the legend without making some references to the *corrido*. Such general remarks will be treated more fully in Part Two of this book, which attempts a critical study of *El Corrido de Gregorio Cortez* and considers its position in the balladry of the Lower Border.

Both ballad and legend apparently began in 1901, almost immediately after the capture of Cortez at Abrán de la Garza's sheep camp. In the half-century since then, nothing seems to have been added to the ballad, which on the contrary has lost much of its original detail. The legend, on the other hand, has grown considerably. This is due, no doubt, to its lack of precise form and to the way that it is usually passed from one person to another.

There is no standard version of the legend and it is never, as far as I know, told complete at one sitting. Each individual hears and learns the parts one at a time. A singing of the ballad may lead to the telling of part of the legend, or a part may be told in relation to some other ballad with a similar theme. Even a chance conversation, such as one on horses, may lead to the narration of some part of the legend—Román's horse trade or the speed, endurance, and faithfulness of the little sorrel mare.

It is up to the individual hearer to put the separate parts together, and to choose from among the versions those he prefers or those that seem the true ones to him. The legend as it appears in Chapter II is my own creation. I have put together those parts that seemed to me the farthest removed from fact and the most revealing of folk attitudes. But there are other variants, which may be considered now.

The most significant have to do with the reasons for the killing of Morris. I have heard at least six variants to this part of the legend, the one about the two sorrel horses and the sorrel mare being the best and the most detailed. Another leaves out the horse trade altogether. Román Cortez and Leonor, Gregorio's wife, are riding in a buggy when they meet the Major Sheriff and two of his deputies, who are looking for smugglers. The sheriff searches the buggy and to do so pulls Leonor down. Román objects and the sheriff shoots him. Then Gregorio appears and kills the sheriff and one of the deputies, while the other deputy runs away. Gregorio puts his wife and Román in the buggy, takes them to a safe place, and then rides the buggy for some distance. He comes to a friendly ranch and is given a horse, and from then on he keeps changing horses until he reaches the Border. When he gets to a ranch house, all he has to say is "I am Gregorio Cortez" and he is given a fresh horse.

This variant comes a little closer to fact in some respects. The sheriff actually was out looking for wrongdoers, and he had two deputies with him. The killing of the deputy was probably transferred from the Belmont incident, in which Glover and his deputy, Schnabel, were both killed. Leonor Cortez may very well have been mistreated after the shooting of Morris; here the result is made the cause. The surrey which Morris rode is given to the Cortezes. In the matter of the smuggling, so far from the border line, the Border narrator is applying local conditions to those of unknown parts of the country.

Another variant has Román and Gregorio working as field hands for an American. They do their work well, but the American demands even more than a man can do. He gets abusive and Román objects. The American shoots Román, and Gregorio shoots the American and then kills the sheriff who comes to arrest him. The story is sometimes told in a slightly different way. Cortez is working alone, and the American slaps his face, whereupon Cortez kills him. These versions diverge the most from actual events.

A fifth variant comes pretty close to fact. The sheriff comes to the Cortez house looking for some stolen cattle. Román and Gregorio have just finished butchering one of their own steers, and the hide is hanging on the fence. The hide happens to be of the same color as the stolen cattle; so the sheriff shoots Román as a rustler, after which Gregorio shoots the sheriff and his deputy. In still another variant, the sheriff is out looking for mule thieves. He stops Román on the road, questions him and shoots him. Gregorio runs out of the house and shoots the sheriff.

There are probably many more variants, since I have made no attempt to collect them all. These, however, are some of the most common ones. In all of them the point emphasized is that Cortez was peacefully pursuing his own business when the sheriff or another American showed up and committed some outrage. That actual facts coincide with this central point is not the question here; in all events the peaceful man minding his own business is essential to the concept of the Border hero.

There is much variation in oral accounts concerning Cortez's personal appearance, even among people who knew him well. Those who knew him describe him as opposite to themselves. Short men describe him as tall; tall men say he was short. Fair men call him dark; dark men call him fair. In height and complexion Cortez was somewhat in-between. Prison records put his height at five feet nine inches, neither short nor tall. His complexion appears to have been neutral, dark from a North European's point of view, light from a Mexican one. When captured and when released from Huntsville, Cortez was well sunburned. During his four-year sojourn in county jails he lost a great deal of his tan. All these things explain the variation in details given by people who actually knew Cortez. They are a commentary on the extreme elasticity of reminiscence and of oral report, even when based on direct observation.

More interesting still are the descriptions given of Cortez by people who have known him only in legend. If people who knew him tend to describe him as their opposite, those who did not know him describe him as being like themselves. A short, very dark man told me that Cortez had been just a little dark man, *chiquitito y prietito*. Ah, but what a man! All heart and testicles; that is to say, all kindness and courage.[1] A fair, blue-eyed Anglo-American who as a little boy once met Cortez, and who admired the man, remembers him as fair. In some parts of the Border where the ideal *norteño* type is the tall dark man with green or tawny eyes, Cortez is said to have been a tall dark man with *ojos borrados*. The variant according to which Gregorio is a field hand was given to me by laboring people.

[1] According to folk physiology the heart is the seat of man's kinder virtues. Courage and fighting spirit reside in the testicles. A typical ranchero belief, since steers and geldings do not fight for mates.

Thus it appears that as the story moves farther away from fact into legend, the narrator identifies himself personally with Cortez.

The way Cortez got out of prison also has its variants. Some do not mention President Lincoln's daughter, making his rescuer merely an American girl. The story is basically the same, having as its core the belief that the governor of Texas will give a prisoner to any pretty girl who asks for him at Christmas. One variant has Cortez released through the efforts of Sarita Kenedy, daughter of Mifflin Kenedy (founder of the Kenedy Ranch and partner of Richard King) and of his Border Mexican wife, Doña Petra Vela.

Sarita Kenedy, later Mrs. Sarah Spohn of Corpus Christi, must have been in her thirties when Cortez rode for the Border, and was middle-aged when Cortez regained his freedom. There is no evidence that she had anything to do in the Cortez case. However the Kenedys, perhaps because of their Mexican connections, did have a reputation as benefactors of Texas-Mexicans. It may very well be that Mrs. Spohn, known to this day to Border people as Sarita Kenedy, was one of the many who contributed to the defense or to the release of Cortez, and that for this reason the legend was attached to her name.

The least romantic variant has Cortez released through the personal intercession of Col. F. A. Chapa of San Antonio. Colonel Chapa is said to have been a member of Teddy Roosevelt's Rough Riders, as well as a leader of his people in San Antonio. When everything else failed and Cortez went to prison, Colonel Chapa talked to his friend the governor, and the governor pardoned Cortez for the sake of his friendship with Chapa. (All variants agree, by the way, that Cortez was imprisoned for one year only, and that he died a year after his release.) As has been said, Chapa worked hard in favor of Cortez. But from the pardons documents it is evident that Colquitt's personal feelings had little or nothing to do with the actual granting of the pardon.

One concludes that the variants of the Cortez legend reflect the Border Mexican's identification of himself with his hero. Attitudes and interests of different kinds are mirrored in different variants. The story about the horse trade is fittingly elaborate. Trading horses was a subject of supreme interest to all horseback people. In American frontier literature, for example, the horse trade has been a fertile subject for humor.

Smuggling was commonplace on the Border, as were efforts to stop it, especially by American authorities. One is not surprised to find in one variant of the Cortez story that the sheriff stops the Cortezes to search for smuggled goods. Another variant makes Cortez a day laborer insulted by his boss, reflecting the point of view of the laborer, whose numbers increased as the land ceased to be cattle country and was turned to citrus and truck farming, and still later to cotton.

Thus the laborer made of Cortez a laborer, the farmer a farmer, the vaquero a vaquero, the suspected smuggler a smuggling suspect—each applying his own situation, his own disagreeable contacts with the Anglo-American, as the reasons for Cortez's defending of his right. The short man saw Cortez as short, the dark man as dark; and the tall man saw him tall. The man that the *corrido* shows at bay saying, "So many mounted rangers, all against one Mexican" became in the legend a synthesis of the Border Mexican, who saw himself collectively in Cortez.

Before leaving the matter of variants, one might mention an Anglo-American one. In *The Mustangs* J. Frank Dobie records the end of Gregorio Cortez as told to him by R. R. Smith of Jourdanton. "Gregorio Cortez did not remain in the penitentiary at Huntsville for 'feefty year.' A governor pardoned him. He became a horse thief and was killed out near El Paso."[2]

That the Anglo-American variant should attribute to Cortez a criminal's end is not surprising. Surprising is the fact that another, much more convenient and much more opprobrious possibility should have been passed by. In April 1917, four years after Gregorio Cortez Lira was released from prison and less than one year after he is said to have died at Anson, a man by the name of Gregorio Cortez was convicted of the rape of his own daughter at Del Rio.

[2] Dobie, *The Mustangs*, p. 238.

It took a great deal of investigation, and the lucky finding of a bill of particulars on the case, for me to establish the fact that these two were entirely different and unrelated men. Newspaper readers in 1917 could very justifiably have confused the two. But no such thing seems to have happened. In Anglo-American legend it is the Negro who is the rapist. The Mexican is the horse thief, and it is as a horse thief that the Smith-Dobie variant has Gregorio die.

Fact and fancy

The legend of Gregorio Cortez is made up of three kinds of ingredients: of straight fact, of fact exaggerated into fiction, and of pure folklore, found in easily recognizable motifs. Many of the more realistic parts of the story, though often invented in the case of other Border heroes, appear to have been true about Cortez. He was a good shot and a superb rider, a man of nerve, ingenuity, and endurance. Some of the things with which legend credits him appear to have been fact, such as his use of cattle to cover up his trail and his walking into town to escape pursuit in the brush. The broad outlines of the ideal border-conflict hero were actually present in Cortez, and they were incorporated into the legend as they were.

Other parts of the legend are mere exaggerations of the kind that one often finds in and out of folklore. Cortez killed two sheriffs; legend has him kill dozens. He was actually chased by hundreds of men, and in one or two cases posses (or mobs, rather) of three hundred men were reported scouring the country for "accomplices." In legend Cortez fights off posses made up of three hundred men each. Cortez did leap into the San Antonio River with the little brown mare, though the leap was not so high and he had to blindfold her with a piece of his shirt-tail.

The story of his driving a herd of steers to water to get near a tank guarded by possemen seems to be true, though somewhat exaggerated. Occasionally Cortez did meet lone officers or small groups of them, who were sufficiently impressed by what the newspapers said about him to go for additional help rather than tackle him alone. In the legend groups of twenty or thirty men are afraid to approach him. Blown-up facts of this kind make a good part of the legend, as is probably the case with the stories of every popular hero.

The purely folkloric elements in the legend of Cortez, motifs which can be compared to those found in other folklores, very often owe their presence to some little fact, perhaps unimportant in itself, that serves as a nucleus around which legend grows.

One of the purely legendary parts of the story has to do with the sharp horse trade that Román pulls on the owner of the little sorrel mare. It is one of the most detailed passages in the legend, and one of the most important to the structure of that particular version of it. The horse trade causes the deaths of the Major Sheriff and Román. It provides the mare with which Cortez reaches the Border, and the mare is the cause of Cortez's going to prison.

At first glance the episode seems to have been pure invention. Court records show, however, that the killings of Romaldo and Sheriff Morris did in fact arise out of a horse trade. Gregorio and not his brother had traded a mare for a horse, not a horse for a mare, to a man named Villarreal. It was about this trade that Morris came to see Gregorio Cortez the day Morris and Romaldo were shot. This incident provides the framework upon which the detailed story about Román and his sorrel horses and the little sorrel mare are woven.

The sorrel mare herself is a synthesis of four different mares which figured in the events. There was the mare, of unknown color, which Cortez traded to Villarreal. Cortez left home after the shooting of Morris on a sorrel mare that he owned. He rode her only about five miles, halfway to Kenedy, completing the journey on foot with his wounded brother. Of the two mares which Cortez did ride to the Border, one was a sorrel and the other—the fleetest and most enduring—was brown.

The little brown mare received a great deal of publicity in the English-language newspapers, but in the Border legend she is amalgamated with the other three. And since in Border tradition the sorrel mare is as much a convention as the honey-colored horse, the mare becomes a sorrel, as indeed two of the four mares she represents actually were.

The legend's insistence that Cortez went to prison not for the killings of Morris and Glover but for stealing the little sorrel mare also has an echo in fact. Throughout the court proceedings against him, the prosecution attempted to show Cortez as a horse thief and thus to prove that he was not, as the defense argued, acting in self-defense when he shot Morris. He was even taken to Pleasanton and hastily convicted of horse theft so the prosecution could refer to him in court as a convicted horse thief, though the Court of Criminal Appeals later threw out the horse-theft charge. And, as we have seen, the English-speaking legend has Cortez die a horse thief after all.

Román Cortez in the horse-trade episode is pictured as loud, foulmouthed, and a trickster. There is no factual evidence to support this legendary view of Gregorio Cortez's brother, but again one finds a clue for it in actual fact. Román, or Romaldo as was really his name, was hit in the mouth by Morris' bullet. The legend seems to have worked back from this bit of fact, taking it as punishment fitting some crime of Román's, and spinning out a whole character sketch to go with it. The changing of Romaldo's name to Román appears to be merely a corruption, perhaps occurring in the *corrido* for the sake of meter. Yet the father of the Cortezes actually was named Román and like his son Romaldo was known for his size and strength, again pointing to a basis in fact for a detail in the legend.

When Cortez was captured, many Texas-Mexicans believed he had surrendered. The belief received support from a statement made by Cortez soon after his capture. After the brown mare gave out at Cotulla, he had lost heart for a couple of hours and had thought of surrendering. The *corrido* maker (who seems to have gone to work immediately after Cortez's capture) explained the supposed surrender as the result of Cortez's concern over the killings of innocent people by the *rinches*.

It soon became known that Cortez had been handed over to

the Rangers without his consent. The betrayal of the hero was a more established and a much more fitting theme for the *corrido* than the hero's surrender without a fight. But no change was made in the ballad. It may have been too late for the original author to make any changes. Or it may have been that the Border people found in the concept of the hero who gives himself up to save his people a novel but an extremely satisfying twist. The legend, however, did attempt to reconcile both views, the surrender and the betrayal. The result is an oddly Christ-like situation, in which Cortez recognizes his betrayer but willingly goes to his own betrayal in order that his people be saved.

Cortez's personal surrender to the governor seems to be a late addition to the legend. He will surrender only to the governor, and he comes all the way to Austin to do so. Cortez did come to Austin to see the governor, after his release from prison in 1913. Evidently the story about his personal surrender to the governor developed after his visit to Colquitt to thank the governor for the pardon. It seems that the older parts of the legend continued to develop while newer ones were being added.

A comparison of some of the folkloric elements in the Cortez legend with their connecting points of fact tells us something about the age and the method of development of the legend. It must have begun during Cortez's flight; and as his capture, trial, and imprisonment were noised about, the legend took them up, following Cortez all the way up to the time of his release and his death.

Under the influence of tradition, the facts were transformed into folklore, often by the blending of similar elements, as in the case of the four mares, or by an interweaving of conflicting ones, as with the surrender and the betrayal views about Cortez's capture. The Cortez legend shows evidence of continuous growth from the time that Cortez first attracted the notice of the Border folk until very recent times, a growth that has added not only to the number of events but to the complexity and the wealth of detail in the narrative.

In the legend the character of Cortez is more fully developed than it is in the *corrido,* but he shares interest with others, who represent folk-hero types too. This is especially true of Román and the little sorrel mare. Román plays a dual role. On the one hand he is the loudmouth; on the other he is the clever hero who gets what he wants through trickery. It is Román's loud mouth that gets him into trouble rather than the trick he plays on the owner of the sorrel mare. Fittingly enough, it is in the mouth that Morris shoots him.

In this character Román plays the part of the anti-hero. He is what men should not be: loud, boisterous, disrespectful, an eternal joker. Men should be quiet and hardworking, excellent vaqueros and good farmers. They should be respectful to their elders, peaceful in manner, and ready to defend their right. In other words, they should be like Gregorio Cortez, who is not only a projection of the Border Mexican's reaction to border conflict but a pattern of behavior as well.

In the horse-trading episode Román appears as another kind of hero, a favorite in the Mexican folk tale. He is the clever rogue of the Coyote type, who triumphs over his enemy not by force but by guile, taking advantage of his enemy's fancied superiority to trick him. The clever hero is common in Border tales. He is the smuggler who feigns deafness in court, the Texas-Mexican who pretends an ignorance of the English language in order to get the best of the American who is trying to swindle him. He is also found in more universal tales, from Spanish and Indian tradition. The cry of the turtle about to be executed by the other animals, "Don't throw me in the water or I'll drown!" has come to stand for the rogue who gets what he wants by pretending not to want it.

The little sorrel mare is a character in her own right, partaking of the attributes of human folk heroes. As a heroine the mare has something in common with those human heroes who begin their careers in obscure or even despised status, men of hidden talents, which come out in an emergency. The mare begins the story in a despised status. Neither her owner nor Román thinks much of her. But Gregorio Cortez recognizes her worth, and she proves herself by outrunning many a better-regarded horse.

She is the youngest son who makes good after his elder brothers fail, the prince who comes disguised as a peasant, the little shepherd who fells the giant warrior with a stone. In short, she is Cinderella herself. The theme is a universal one, but the mare descends directly from the horses celebrated in the ballad form preceding the *corrido,* the sung *décima,* in which the sorry-looking mustang beats the blooded horse when the big stakes are down.

Cortez as a folk hero

Gregorio Cortez remains the chief figure of the legend, appearing in it in three different phases: before the killing of Morris, during the flight, and during his captivity. In each phase Cortez is given different characteristics, though the main outlines are maintained throughout: he continues to be the peaceful man driven to violence and finally brought to bay.

Before the killing of Morris, Cortez is the hero in disguise. His talent for violence, flight, and escape is for the most part unknown to his enemies, hidden as it is behind a peaceful disposition. He is the unknown and unproved hero.

There is just a slight hint of the supernatural in the fact that Cortez is the seventh son of a seventh son, thus destined for great things, and that he has premonitions about future events. Cortez is also, though incidentally, a workman hero, somewhat akin to the work heroes of Anglo-American folklore. He can pick more cotton, plant more corn, and clear more land than any other man. He is a better vaquero and tracker than anybody else. Unlike John Henry and Paul Bunyan, however, Cortez is not a prodigy. His feats are due to industry rather than to superhuman powers. He is a hero who works rather than a worker hero. His excellence as a workman serves to emphasize his character as a peaceful man in his disguised period.

In the killing of Morris and in his subsequent flight, Cortez becomes the warrior hero. It is in this phase of the legend that he resembles most closely the hero of the *corridos.* He becomes the typical guerrilla, the border raider fighting and fleeing, and using warrior's tricks to throw the enemy off. He discourages a group of *rinches* who have "made him a corral" by talking to himself and pretending that he has a large body of men with him. This is a motif that is also found in popular literature. A boys' story about the American Revolution had an American soldier and a little drummer boy capture a whole troop of redcoats by shouting commands at each other, as if they were officers of a large contingent. The same trick is sometimes attributed to Davy Crockett. In the *romances* the besieged garrison throws out its last crust of bread to the enemy, who raise the siege because they think the garrison is too well-provisioned to be starved out. In Chinese tales, the general of the besieged garrison throws open the gates, and the besiegers withdraw.

In some of his feats, the Cortez of the legend resembles folk heroes like Robin Hood. Like Robin he surprises his enemy and provisions himself from them, taking food, arms, and other necessaries and letting them go unharmed. In a way reminiscent of Robin Hood, Pancho Villa, and the Saxon king Alfred, Cortez comes into town in disguise while the chase after him is on, mingles with the townspeople and listens to the tales told about him. He sits among the crowd at the station and listens to them talk about the deeds of Gregorio Cortez, and no one knows that Cortez is sitting there with them.

The hero is recognized and aided by a pretty girl. Again one is reminded, among others, of Robin Hood, whose chief protector is the queen herself. In *Robin Hood's Chase* [Child 146][3] the king goes out hunting for Robin.

> But when that Robin Hood he did hear
>   The king had him in chase,
> Then said Little John, 'Tis time to be gone
>   And go to some other place.

The "other place" turns out to be Queen Katherine's palace. There Robin is safe from pursuit, while the king hunts him in the wood for three weeks.

[3] A number in brackets after a British ballad indicates its position in Francis J. Child's *English and Scottish Popular Ballads*, Boston, 1904.

In the part of the legend dealing with Cortez's captivity, some elements of the warrior-hero pattern remain. The hero escapes all major risks, but he is finally imprisoned by a trick of his enemies, who dare not fight him. And it is a woman, a woman of the enemy, who procures his release. The castle warden's daughter who steals the keys and the princess who intercedes with her father the emperor are represented by President Lincoln's daughter.

In the absence of an emperor, the President of the United States did just as well. Lincoln is chosen because his is the most familiar name, that of the good president. Before Franklin D. Roosevelt's name was added on the "good" side of the list, the most familiar presidential names were Lincoln, Wilson, and Teddy Roosevelt. Both Wilson and Teddy Roosevelt were disliked. Lincoln, the champion of liberty and the friend of Juárez, was admired.

The girl is not President Lincoln's daughter in all variants, but she is always a "Gringo girl," always a daughter of the enemy. The situation between Cortez and President Lincoln's daughter is especially close to that found in some British ballads. In *The Fair Flower of Northumberland* [Child 9] the English girl falls in love with the captive Scottish knight and sets him free, after which he abandons her. The Scottish knight had promised to marry the girl.

> If curteously you will set me free,
> I vow that I will marrie thee,
> So soone as I come in faire Scotland.

He abandons her, telling her he has a wife and children, once she helps him escape.

Because the ballad comes from the English side of that border it shows the Scotsman as false. Had it been Scottish the knight would have promised nothing, in the manner of Cortez. Such is the case in a ballad of Scottish provenience, *James Hatley* [Child 244].

Young James Hatley is accused of stealing the king's jewels and is sentenced to be hanged. The identity of the court is not revealed, but it is one in which English lords have a great deal of influence. The English want to see Hatley hanged. The king's daughter steals into prison, talks to Hatley, and is convinced that he is innocent. She gets the king to spare his life and arranges a trial by combat with Hatley's accuser, Sir Fenwick, who seems to be an Englishman. Hatley wounds Fenwick three times and Fenwick confesses. The English lords still want Hatley to hang, but they do not get their wish. The ballad ends with the king's daughter's speech.

> Up and spake the king's daughter,
> "Come hame, James Hatley, and dine wi' me
> For I've made a vow, I'll keep it true,
> I'll never marry a man but thee."

These might have been the very words of President Lincoln's daughter, though the British ballad leads us to believe that James Hatley accepted the invitation, while Gregorio Cortez does not.

When Cortez leaves his pursuers looking for him in the brush and walks into town, travel-stained and weary and armed with his pistols, he wanders among the people at the station who are retelling the deeds he has done, and no one recognizes him. A short while later, after he has washed, changed clothes, and put his pistols inside a *morral*, he walks along the road toward the river, and everyone who meets him knows him, though no one will tell the *rinches*.

There is no inconsistency here, because when Cortez starts walking along the road to the river he has entered into a different phase of his legend and has become a hero of a different type. When he walks into town, armed but unrecognized, and listens to people tell of his exploits, he is still the pursued hero, the border raider or the Robin Hood. When he begins walking down the road he begins to walk toward captivity.

It is in this last phase that the legend of Gregorio Cortez most closely approaches myth. There are some pagan elements in this part, but it is the Christian influence that is the strongest. Cortez becomes the type of hero who sacrifices his liberty, and even-

122

tually his life, in the interests of his people. This motif is not common in Border tradition, which usually takes too personal, too individual a view to admit concepts of this sort. It appears as far as I know only in the legend and in the longer variants of *El Corrido de Gregorio Cortez.*

It has been mentioned that the combination of the surrender theme with that of the betrayal, both being believed true, has given the captivity of Cortez a strongly Christian tone. El Teco is openly called a Judas, and his fate is somewhat similar to Judas'. He does not hang himself, but neither does he enjoy his money, the thousand *pesos plata* or silver dollars that he receives for his treachery. Like Judas he is reviled, feels remorse, and finally dies. He is shown as acting like a friend to his victim, and if he does not kiss Cortez on the cheek he does put out his hand, a corresponding custom.

The necessity of making Cortez both surrender and be betrayed has led the folk to show Cortez as understanding that he is being betrayed but accepting the betrayal as part of the things he has to undergo, thus making the Christian parallel even closer than may have been originally intended. Twelve years later, when Huerta betrayed and murdered President Madero, a Greater Mexican *corrido* maker was to use the same situation. Madero is shown putting Huerta in control of the army, with the knowledge that Huerta will betray him.[4]

Finally taken, Cortez faces his accusers in court and talks them out of countenance, also like the pre-Christian figure of Socrates at his trial. Unlike Christ and Socrates, however, Cortez convinces his judges and they set him free, but his enemies pursue him still and find another excuse for putting him in prison. The legendary Texas custom which President Lincoln's daughter invokes to free Cortez also echoes the Jewish-Christian tradition. It was supposed to be a Jewish custom at the time of Christ to release a prisoner on the feast of Passover, and it was according to this custom that the insurrectionist Barrabas was released instead of Christ.

[4] *El Cuartelazo Felicista* in Vicente T. Mendoza, *El corrido mexicano,* Mexico, 1954, p. 30.

The legends that accompany many Border *corridos* have their own pattern, one that embraces the narrative of the *corrido* and goes beyond it. Knowing the *corrido* alone, one would hardly guess that the same people that produced it had the turn of mind that could create the legend too. The pattern of the legend is repeated in some details with each hero. The betrayed hero is often found; Cortina is said to have died by poison. The pattern may be so well established that it influences fact. Esther Martínez, who wrote to Governor Colquitt pleading for Cortez's release, sounds as if she believed that the governor gave girls a convict each for Christmas if they asked for them. The wording of her letter reflects tradition, while her action in writing the governor on the other hand reinforced the same traditional beliefs.

Louise Pound once said that most medieval ballads have aristocratic rather than peasant or rural origins because the heroes are kings, princes, and noblemen rather than farmers, tanners, weavers, and tinkers.[5] By the same token Greater Mexican Revolutionary *corridos* should be the product of the officers because their heroes are generals for the most part. There were no kings or princes within the ken of the Border folk, or they would have made the legendary Gregorio Cortez a prince and set him out in a corral or a cotton patch, in disguise of course.

It is significant that Cortez in fact is in disguise when his story begins. He is the warrior passing for a peaceful man. One sees the identification of the average folk member with something he admires as better than himself. The medieval peasant had his prince disguised as a peasant, or at least talking and acting like one. The inoffensive Border Mexican had his warrior hero, disguised—until the proper moment arrived—as an inoffensive man.

Coming half a century after the beginning of border conflict, Gregorio Cortez epitomized the ideal type of hero of the Rio Grande people, the man who defends his right with his pistol in his hand, and who either escapes at the end or goes down before superior odds—in a sense a victor even in defeat. He was

[5] Louise Pound, *Poetic Origins and the Ballad*, New York, 1921, pp. 95ff.

124

an incarnation of a Border legend whose first model forty years before had been Juan Nepomuceno Cortina.

For one of the most striking things about Gregorio Cortez is the way the actual facts of his life conformed to pre-existing legend. In his free, careless youth, in the reasons for his going outside the law, in his betrayal, his imprisonment, and release, and even in the somewhat cloudy circumstances surrounding his death—the actual facts about Cortez's life (so far as we know them) follow the Border-hero tradition that was already well established before Cortez made his celebrated ride.

It was as if the Border people had dreamed Gregorio Cortez before producing him, and had sung his life and his deeds before he was born.

PART TWO

El Corrído de Gregorío Cortez,
a Ballad of Border Conflict

V: THE *Corrído* ON THE BORDER

Before the *corrído*

$\mathcal{C}$*he balladry* of the Lower Border is practically unknown as a type in itself, having received to date but
passing attention from the Texas folklorist and almost none at
all from the Mexican ballad student. It is necessary to describe
it—briefly though it be—in order to show the place which *El
Corrido de Gregorio Cortez* occupies in the Border ballad corpus.

The Mexican ballad form known as the *corrído* dates no
farther back than the middle of the nineteenth century.[1] During
their first century on the Lower Rio Grande, the Nuevo Santander people must have sung their folksongs in forms other
than the *corrído*. These forms evidently were the *romance*, the
décima, and the *copla* or *verso*.

The Spanish *romance* was a preserved ballad form, as the
British ballad has been in the Appalachians. It must have been
brought to the Border by the first settlers in 1749. Other *romances*, already Mexicanized, evidently came in from Greater
Mexico (as we will call the area now comprising the Republic

---

[1] See Mendoza, *El corrido mexicano*, pp. vii–xliv, for an authoritative
history of the Mexican *corrido*. For an English-language discussion see my
own "The Mexican *Corrido*: Its Rise and Fall," in *Madstones and Twisters*,
Texas Folklore Society, Publication XXVIII, Dallas, 1958, pp. 91–105.

129

of Mexico, with the exception of the border regions), most probably during the century of border conflict. Some may have been received during the first century of settlement from New Mexico, already an old and established colony by the time that Nuevo Santander was founded. Some Border *romances* show similarities to New Mexican variants, suggesting that during the Spanish colonial period there may have been a related ballad tradition in the frontier colonies of California, Nuevo Mexico, and Nuevo Santander.

There is reason to believe that the *romance* is as old on the Lower Rio Grande as the first settlements. The predominantly Spanish character of the first settlers would make one think so. There are *romances* whose variants seem peculiar to the Border, apparently not being found among other Mexican groups. These would indicate a native development over a long period of time. Those variants that appear to be native are few indeed, and are on novelesque themes. That they should be novelesque is not surprising; Nuevo Santander was settled in the eighteenth century, when *romances* like *La Isla de Jauja* were the most popular. There may have been a time, however, when more of the old *romances* were known on the Lower Border. This would have been before the *corrido* era.

The *copla* or *verso*, a short lyrical stanza, was also cultivated on the Lower Rio Grande before the rise of the *corrido*. Most of the Border *versos* must have dealt with fugitive local events, and no one with bookish interests was present at the time to record them. A few have survived, and these appear to be related to the *versos* of New Mexico.

Fights with the Indians must have produced their songs, but these too were for the most part lost. I know of only one such song, also in *verso* or *canción* form, and I have heard it on the Border only within my family. We know it as a children's song, but it appears to have been something more serious in other times. *Ahi Vienen Los Inditos* [TFA P1–7][2] is a Border variant

[2] TFA P1–7: Texas Folklore Archive, Paredes Collection, Reel No. 1, Item No. 7. Subsequent references to material in the Texas Folklore Archive at the University of Texas will be made in the same manner.

of the New Mexican *El Comanchito.* Greater Mexican variants, such as *Los Mecos,* appear to have been borrowed from the frontier tradition.

The ten-line stanza known as the *décima* was a well-established folk form by the time that Nuevo Santander was settled. Already in that century there were *decimeros,* folk singers and makers of *décimas.* In 1830, when the first period of Lower Rio Grande history was coming to an end, the *décima* was reaching its height of influence in Mexico. From the very old men one learns how important the *décima* was on the Border until relatively recent times. Men born in the 1860's and 1870's learned this form from their grandfathers, and their fathers preferred the *décima* to the *corrido.*

The Border *décima* must have come in with the first settlers, like the *romance.* It had the same origins as the *décima* in Mexico and must have entered New Mexico at about the same time. It is doubtful, however, that the *décima* came to the Border in the form of broadsides printed in Mexico. Its form must have been the sung *décima,* belonging to an oral tradition transcending the present borders of Mexico both north and south. And it must have been the *decimeros,* the ballad singers, who brought it. One finds no correspondence between the *décimas* of Border tradition and those collected by Professor Mendoza,[3] which come from printed sources and represent the broadside production from the populous and relatively sophisticated areas of central Mexico. But even a superficial study reveals relationships with the *décimas* of New Mexico and Panama, which come from oral tradition. No complete *décimas* seem to have traveled from one place to another, as have the *romances* and some *corridos;* but the same subjects are treated, and sometimes identical *plantas* (the four-line stanza which is glossed in *décimas*) are glossed in much the same language. The favorite form is the simple *décimas con planta* (four ten-line stanzas glossing a quatrain, the *planta*), and it is preferably sung and almost never printed. This would indicate that the Border *décima* is part of a single tradition that at one time extended from the isthmus to the Great Plains.

[3] Vicente T. Mendoza, *La décima en México,* Buenos Aires, 1947.

On the Border the sung *décima* was used as a narrative vehicle as well as for other subjects; and in the nineteenth century it still competed with the *corrido* as a narrative form. The narrative *décima* is far from extinct. In December 1951 I collected a series of six *décima* stanzas, without a *planta,* composed in 1945 by Fulgencio Cisneros, who lives downriver from Matamoros. They relate a wonder, the collision of two American airforce planes, which fell on the Mexican side near Fulgencio's home.

Most narrative *décimas* are of older vintage. They rarely deal with violence, the domestic affairs of the community furnishing the most important narrative themes. Coexistent with the narrative *décimas* are the satiric, humorous, and didactic, and those which memorialize a person and lament his death.

The *corrido* century

The period from 1836 to the late 1930's embraces the life span of the *corrido* of the Lower Border. These hundred years were a time of profound and violent changes for the old Spanish province of Nuevo Santander.

About 1836 there began a three-pronged attack on the Rio Grande settlements: civil war, Indian raids, and the English-speaking invasion. In that year Santa Anna overthrew the Federalist constitution of 1824, which had given Tamaulipas, formerly Nuevo Santander, a great deal of autonomy. The year before, Santa Anna had ordered the disarming of local militias, a decree that caused serious resentment on the frontier. Texas revolted, and though the official government of Tamaulipas declared in favor of Santa Anna, the Rio Grande people favored Texas rather than Mexico. The rebellion in Texas brought thousands of central Mexican troops to the Rio Grande, where they were provisioned for the campaign; and after San Jacinto these troops returned, exhausted and provisionless, to live off the Rio Grande country until 1846. They were a tremendous drain on the Rio Grande economy.

Like the Texans the Rio Grande people revolted. As early as

January 1836 Centralist troops had to return from Texas to put down a Federalist uprising at Mier. By 1838 the Federalist movement had become a scheme for a Republic of the Rio Grande, under the leadership of Antonio Canales, a Monterrey lawyer. Battles between rancheros and Santa Anna's troops went on intermittently until 1840, when Canales surrendered. The Republic of Texas appears to have played a Machiavellian role in the Rio Grande movement. Officially it remained neutral, but unofficially it gave the Federalists just enough aid to keep them in the field, with the frank intention of weakening Mexico through internal strife.[4]

The five years of civil war imposed an additional burden on the Rio Grande settlements, leaving them too weak to defend themselves from savage Indian attacks which also began in 1836 and which succeeded in wrecking the Rio Grande economy. Indians descended on the whole Mexican frontier, armed and supplied by American traders who accepted their booty in exchange for arms, whiskey, and other articles. The fact that the Indian raids began in 1836, when Americans seriously began to think of taking over large sections of northern Mexico, speaks for itself.

Raids and skirmishes between Texans and Mexicans went on during the period between the battles of San Jacinto and Palo Alto. With Taylor's advance across the Nueces the Lower Rio Grande became even more of a battleground. Rio Grande rancheros formed part of the Mexican cavalry at Palo Alto and Resaca. After these American victories the rancheros neither surrendered nor retreated, as did the Mexican regulars. They remained on Taylor's flanks as guerrillas all the way to Monterrey, often causing more trouble than Santa Anna's armies. Consequently, the Rio Grande ranchero did not endear himself to Taylor's men, many of whom later settled along the Rio Grande.

[4] David Martell Vigness, *The Republic of the Rio Grande: An Example of Separatism in Northern Mexico,* Doctoral dissertation, University of Texas, 1951, pp. 207ff.

After 1848 the Nueces–Rio Grande area—the northern half of the former province of Nuevo Santander—became part of the United States. A pre-Civil War type of carpetbagger moved into the territory to make his fortune, using the Texas legend as his excuse for preying on the newly created Americans of Mexican descent. The Mexican's cattle were killed or stolen. The Mexican was forced to sell his land; and if he did not, his widow usually did after her husband was "executed" for alleged cattle rustling. Thus did the great Texas ranches and the American cattle industry begin.

Different aims called for different methods in what is now known as the Lower Rio Grande Valley. There the fortune-makers organized political machines and acquired large blocks of land for later development projects. The foundations of the "magic valley" boom of the 1920's were being laid. Since labor and amenable votes were part of the scheme, no concerted effort was made to drive the Mexican out of the country. He was merely dispossessed.

Then, in 1859, came Juan Nepomuceno Cortina's revolt. Cortina, whose family once owned much of the land on which Brownsville is now located, was the first Border Mexican to "fight for his right with his pistol in his hand." He was forced into open conflict with American authority after he shot the Brownsville city marshal, who was mistreating a servant of Cortina's mother. Cortina and his rancheros briefly occupied Brownsville, won a few engagements, and finally gave way to superior force. The people who sympathized with him were subjected to reprisals; others suffered merely because they were of the same origins as he. Cortina, meanwhile, escaped across the newly created border, establishing a pattern that would be followed by others during the next three-quarters of a century.

The American Civil War and the French invasion of Mexico, coming shortly after Cortina's uprising, complicated the clash of peoples along the Lower Border. Most Borderers, including Cortina himself, sided with the Union and the Liberal party of Juárez. Union agents operated on the Mexican side of the Border, taking advantage of the resentment against the American fortune-makers to incite guerrilla raids against the Confederates. Cortina was perhaps the best known of these *enganchados* or Union-inspired guerrillas, who fought the Confederacy on one bank of the Rio Grande and Maximilian's empire on the other. The Confederates also had their Border allies, among them Captain Benavides, whose best-known exploit was the slaying of Union guerrilla chieftain Octaviano Zapata.

After the Civil War a new element of adventure came to the Border in the cattle drives to Kansas, in which the Rio Grande vaqueros participated. The trail to Kansas had its dangers, not the least of which—to the Mexican vaquero—was the traversing of territory where people often thought the best Mexican was a dead one.

In Mexico Porfirio Díaz became dictator in 1877, to rule the country for some thirty years. Díaz began his career from Brownsville, receiving assistance from people on both sides of the Border, and when he attained power he proceeded to hold it through a force of rural police patterned closely on the Texas Rangers. The *rurales* kept the peon in subjection while investors made their fortunes through the exploitation of Mexican men and Mexican resources.

The Mexican part of the Lower Border—a land of small rancheros rather than of *hacendados*—remained comparatively unaffected by the Díaz type of economy. But Don Porfirio was committed to co-operation with the United States, from whose southern borders would come any successful uprising against his power. He was, therefore, eager to help pacify the Border. He withdrew Cortina to Mexico City and kept him a prisoner for the rest of Cortina's life. He pursued smuggling and other lawlessness along the Rio Grande.

But the action most resented on the Border was Díaz's extradition agreement with the United States. Under this agreement any Borderer who got into trouble in Texas and fled across the river was to be handed over to American authorities. In return, Díaz would get his hands on any men who revolted against his authority and fled into Texas. The function of the border line as a refuge for the man up in arms "defending his right" was seriously threatened. This, the Border people felt, was extremely unfair. Illustrative of their state of mind was the Rio Grande City affair of August 1877. Two Border men charged with murder were released from the Rio Grande City jail by a band that "broke open the jail by force and arms"[5] in the style of *Jock o the Side*. Deliverers and delivered were pursued across the border, and Rangers demanded their extradition. Tamaulipas Governor Servando Canales, a staunch Díaz supporter but a Border man, refused to obey Díaz's orders to comply with the demand for extradition. Three of the men were somehow turned over to the Rangers, and Border sentiment against Díaz grew bitter. Díaz sent regular troops against Canales, but these joined Canales' forces when they reached the Border. For a while Díaz's months-old dictatorship was in danger. In the end things were smoothed over, and no more of the culprits were handed over to American authorities.

In later years, when Díaz was more firmly in power, things were different. A man who fled across the border into Mexico might find refuge in outlying districts with friends or relatives. If he fell in the hands of the central government's authorities, he would be handed over to the United States. This helped keep alive on the south bank the old feelings of particularism that had never died out on the Texas side.

Extradition agreements notwithstanding, the Border continued to be much the same. Díaz had received his first popular support among the Lower Border rancheros. It was among these same rancheros that the first rebellions against him came. Catarino Garza, native of the Brownsville-Matamoros area, led what was probably the first rebellion against Díaz in 1890, according to Pierce because of "some alleged indignity" Garza had suffered from Díaz officials.[6] Garza organized his force in Texas and crossed into Mexico from Zapata County. After some initial successes he was defeated and forced back into Texas, where Ranger Captain Hall and a posse unsuccessfully attempted to arrest and

[5] Cecil Bernard Smith, *Diplomatic Relations Between the United States and Mexico*, Master's thesis, University of Texas, 1928, pp. 54ff.
[6] Pierce, *A Brief History*, p. 72.

disarm the remnants of his men. Later a Border sheriff, Robert Haynes of Zapata County, succeeded by persuasion where Hall had failed by force.

Border conflict continued through the Díaz period, though on a more limited and personal scale for the most part than during the fifties and sixties. Most fortune-makers on the Texas side had made their piles and become more conservative. But the slow dispossession of small rancheros went on.

Meanwhile the Mexican and his culture were reasserting themselves on the north bank. The area south of the great ranches remained isolated, and many old American families became Mexicanized. By the 1890's Cameron County (with Brownsville, the center of fortune-making activity, as its seat) had a Texas-Mexican sheriff. In other towns on the Texas side Mexicans occupied city and county posts. By 1915 a Texas-Mexican and relative of Cortina, José Tomás Canales, sat in the state House of Representatives, representing the Border area.

But by 1915 things had taken another turn. In 1910 Díaz fell from power, and half the Border was soon engaged in civil war. Officially only the Mexican side was involved. In truth, Mexicans on both sides were active in the Revolution. Much of the scheming was done in Texas, while many Borderers who were legally Americans crossed into Mexico to take part in the fighting.

By 1915 the unrest in Mexico had spread to the Texas side. An uprising broke out on the north bank. Bands of Border men under the leadership of Aniceto Pizaña and Luis de la Rosa raided as far as King Ranch, burning ranches, killing American civilians, and attacking army detachments. A plan for a Spanish-speaking republic of the Southwest was discovered, reminiscent of the Republic of the Rio Grande of the 1830's. Historians have called the Pizaña uprising a German plot. Others have blamed Carranza or the I.W.W. "Eyewitnesses" went on official record as having seen not only Germans but Japanese among the seditionists. The beginning of a new "boom" on the Texas side of the Border, exacerbating cultural conflicts, and the success of the Revolution on the Mexican side were factors which have not been given the importance they deserve in the 1915 uprising.

World War I anti-German feeling did give an additional excuse for outrages on innocent Mexicans. Estimates of the Mexicans killed are put as high as five thousand. In a legislative investigation initiated by Representative Canales, at risk of his own life, Rangers were charged with murder, wanton killing, flogging and torture of prisoners, drunkenness, and assault.[7] Canales was twice threatened with death by Texas Rangers, once in Brownsville and once on Congress Avenue in Austin, two blocks from the Capitol, where Canales was a Representative in the Texas Legislature.[8]

The results of the Pizaña uprising were very much the same as were those of Cortina's blow for equal rights. "Development" of the country was accelerated. Pierce ends an account of Ranger operations on the Border with the following paragraph.

The author cannot let pass this opportunity to say that during the bandit raids of 1915 many evil influences were brought to bear to clear the country of the Mexicans. To his knowledge more than one was forced to flee and to convey his chattels before going.[9]

The Pizaña affair helped perpetuate a state of mind conducive to the *corrido* of border conflict until the beginning of World War II in Europe.

The earliest Border *corridos*

Whatever ballads and ballad-like songs were composed on the Lower Rio Grande in the first two decades of border conflict have been lost, but that such songs were composed is fairly certain. One may safely assume that the border-conflict ballad tradition was several decades old before it began to produce songs that were memorable enough to survive. Keeping song books or commonplace books was not a widespread Border custom; so it is unlikely that much of the older ballad production will ever be recovered, though some of it un-

[7] Webb, *The Texas Rangers*, p. 514.
[8] Letter from Mr. J. T. Canales to the author, dated March 6, 1953, and subsequent interview with Mr. Canales in December 1953.
[9] Pierce, *A Brief History*, p. 115.

doubtedly awaits discovery. The favorite ballad subjects must have been the Indian raids, the struggle to establish a Republic of the Rio Grande, and the guerrilla warfare against Zachary Taylor's troops. It is not too much to assume that the people of the town of Guerrero sang ballads about their famed Indian fighter Antonio Zapata after he was captured and executed by Santa Anna's troops in 1840. And one can imagine that Antonio Canales, the old Federalist and guerrilla against Taylor, had ballads made about him, which helped perpetuate his memory so that in 1916, when Pershing entered Mexico to pursue Villa, a Canales brigade was formed on the Lower Border. Prominent ranchers like Blas Falcón, not to mention Juan Nepomuceno Seguín, the disillusioned Texas patriot, also fought Taylor's troops during the Mexican War and probably were ballad heroes. Such ballads may have been *décimas, coplas,* or songs in miscellaneous forms, the first gropings toward the *corrido.*

A great-aunt of mine, María del Jesús Cisneros, who was born in 1850 used to tell that as a young girl she heard *corridos* about Cortina's exploits of the late 1850's. What form these *corridos* took, whether they were in what we know as the *corrido* form or in some other pattern, it is impossible to tell. However, in the summer of 1954 I collected a three-stanza fragment [TFA P21–7] from Zeferino González, 75, who assured me that there were several *corridos* sung about Don Juan Nepomuceno when González was a boy. The fragment, in the form recorded, is a late *corrido.* One stanza tells of Cortina's death and the joy it caused among Americans on the Border. Since Cortina died in 1892, this particular stanza belongs to the 1890's.

The other two stanzas, though, are not closely related to the one about Cortina's death and seem to be from two other ballads. One expresses joy because Cortina has left his imprisonment and come to visit his friends on the Border, and apparently refers to Cortina's visit to Matamoros in 1890, after Díaz had kept him prisoner in Mexico City for fourteen years. The third stanza seems to go farther back.

Ese general Cortina	That general Cortina
es muy libre y soberano,	Is very sovereign and free;

139

han subido sus honores	His honor has increased
porque salvó a un mexicano.	Because he has saved a Mexican.

This evidently refers to Cortina's first exploit, his defense of his mother's servant. The stanza could have been composed at any time after 1859. The tune to which Zeferino González sang the ballad is not like the *corrido* tunes of the 1880's and 1890's but sounds more like those of the songs of the 1860's, some of which will be mentioned shortly.

Cortina definitely is the earliest Border *corrido* hero that we know of, whether his exploits were put into *corridos* in 1860 or later. Border people usually distinguish quite clearly among *décimas, danzas,* lyric songs, and *corridos*. Reports that there were early *corridos* about Cortina deserve credence, especially in view of the fragments collected from Zeferino González. The Cortina ballads apparently were the first ballads of border conflict as well as the first *corridos* of the Border.

One would expect ballads of the 1860's to sing about battles against the French and of the exploits of the *enganchados* or Union-inspired guerrillas against the Confederates. No *enganchado* ballads have been discovered, as far as I know. In 1954 I collected several songs of the period, which give one some idea of the type of ballad being sung by the Border people at that time. One of them, *El Corrido de los Franceses* [TFA P17–3, sung by Petra Longoria de Flores], is almost but not quite a true *corrido.*

Entraron los franceses,	The French came in,
entraron como bala,	Like a cannon ball,
un paso à la frontera,	One step to the Border
dos a Guadalajara.	And two back to Guadalajara.

Pero Juárez, pero Juárez,	Juárez, Juárez,
viva la libertad.	Long live liberty.

Entraron los franceses	The French came in,
entraron como locos	They came in like mad;
son muchos los que entraron,	Those that came in were many,
los que salieron pocos.	Those that went out were few.

140

The line is heptasyllabic, but the *corrido* spirit is there, especially in the boast that the French may take all of Mexico but that they cannot hold the Border. The second stanza reminds one of *El Corrido de Gregorio Cortez:*

Decían los americanos:	The Americans said,
—Si lo encontramos ¿qué haremos?	"If we find him, what shall we
Si le entramos por derecho	do?
muy poquitos volveremos.	If we fight him man to man
	Very few of us will return."

The oldest Border *corrido* that has come down in complete form is *El Corrido de Kiansis,* which records the novelty of the first cattle drives to Kansas in the late 1860's and early 1870's. Nicanor Torres, one of those from whom I have collected the ballad [TFA P13–1], was five years old when the Kansas Trail opened in 1867. Some of his cousins and his older brothers made the trip to Kansas. Hilario Cisneros, born in 1867, also gave me the ballad. He learned it from one of the men who made the trip. From their accounts it seems definite that *El Corrido de Kiansis* was being sung in the Brownsville-Matamoros area by 1870. Under the name of *El Corrido de los Quinientos Novillos* (The Corrido of the Five Hundred Steers), it has been collected as far south as the state of Hidalgo in central Mexico.[10] It is the oldest true *corrido* that I know of, not only on the Border but in the Greater Mexican corpus as well.

The meeting of the two cultures gives rise to *El Corrido de Kiansis,* with the members of the English-speaking culture already controlling the purse strings. The theme is not border conflict but conflict with the elements and with the hardships of the trail. Death appears on the horns of a bull rather than in the muzzle of a revolver. The *caporal,* who is the hero, is shown on the *caballo melado,* the honey-colored horse that is so often the sign of the hero in the border conflict *corridos.* Some fifty years later *El Corrido de Kiansis* was to serve as the model for *El Corrido de la Pensilvania.* By that time the Border men were no longer cowboys. They went to Pennsylvania by rail instead of on

[10] Mendoza, *El corrido mexicano,* p. 451.

horseback, to work on the railroad instead of on the cattle trail. These two ballads enclose a significant period in the history of the Border *corrido*.

Ballads borrowed from Greater Mexico

In Greater Mexico, meanwhile, a *corrido* tradition was also developing, which would replace the *décima* as the most important ballad form. In the 1850's, when the border conflict tradition was taking shape on the Rio Grande, one hears of *corrido*-like songs in Mexico; but it is not until the late 1870's, after Porfirio Díaz was in power, that the Mexican *corrido* takes its definite form.

A number of ballads came to the Border from Greater Mexico during the *corrido* century. Most of them were *corridos*, with an occasional *danza*, a type much like the *habanera*, used primarily for lyric themes but sometimes given narrative form. The Border people sang these songs but appear to have made little use of the same themes in their own balladry. Among the Greater Mexican importations were ballad subjects dealing with personal or family relationships, such as the love tragedy and the ballad of filial disobedience. Especially popular was the theme of the girl who is killed at a dance by a jealous suitor. Usually the girl is killed because she goes out against her mother's wishes.

The community dance was one of the few occasions on which Border women had much to do with outsiders, with the usual jealousies and quarrels. Filial obedience was extremely important to the Borderer's way of life, and has been pointed out in the discussion of the Border community as a patriarchal society. It is significant, then, that the Lower Border communities seem to have originated no dance-and-brawl or disobedient-son ballads. Ballads of this sort, borrowed from the Greater Mexican stock, were widely sung and must have been useful in regulating conduct in the community. But the interest of the Border ballad makers seems to have been on matters other than these.

The Corrido *on the Border*

The lyrical ballad, moody and dark, is also an importation from Greater Mexico. The somber, weird strain and the introduction of revenants and of supernatural signs of fatality (absent in the *romance*) are characteristic of such Mexican ballads as *El Hijo Desobediente, A Las Tres de la Mañana,* and *La Tísica.* Combined with the border conflict tradition, they give the balladry of the Lower Border a close resemblance to Scottish balladry. But the dark ballad is not native to the Border. It was an importation which the native ballad makers did not imitate. The lyrical folksong also seems to be exclusively of Greater Mexican provenience. The genius of the Border ballad makers does not seem to have tended toward lyric songs, or toward the beautiful, sad type of melody that is most generally associated with Mexican music.

Other ballad importations are more frankly sentimental. Some of these are Mexican *danzas,* such as *Preguntas Niña,* in which a man tells a little girl that he is single because his true love died at a dance. *Después de un Baile* (After a Ball), a waltz, is a very close translation of Charles K. Harris' *After the Ball* and a rare example of American influence on Border balladry [TFA P10–5, sung by Manuel Hinojosa]. I am told that *Después de un Baile* has been in oral tradition for at least fifty years.

Border outlaw *corridos*

The outlaws against the Díaz regime were the first important *corrido* heroes of Greater Mexico. But since these men symbolized a struggle between classes rather than cultural strife or civil war, the ballads about them were of a proletarian cast: the ballad heroes rob the rich to give to the poor and the ballad style is definitely sentimental.

Many of the Greater Mexican outlaw *corridos* were sung on the Border, and some of their commonplaces were borrowed for the heroic Border *corrido.* What was not borrowed was the concept of the *corrido* hero. The Border *corridos* make a very definite distinction between the hero of border conflict and the mere outlaw. Border robbers are not Robin Hoods. Neither do they repent on the scaffold in moralizing verses. They are quite frankly rogues—realistic, selfish, and usually unrepentant. *El Automóvil Gris* [TFA P38–6, sung by Cornelio Varela], for example celebrates the deeds of a group of young Matamoros men of "good" family, officers in a Carrancista division raised in the Matamoros area, who are supposed to have organized a robber band known as the Grey Automobile Band. They operated in Mexico City and went home to Matamoros and to cities in the United States—and even to Europe, it is said—to enjoy their loot. Their ballad is a rollicking song, showing one of the leaders in his cups at Matamoros.

En Matamoros me verán	In Matamoros you can see me,
borracho y fumando buenos puros,	Drunk and smoking fine cigars,
tomando cerveza y coñac	Drinking beer and cognac
y gozando a la voz de la alegría.	Enjoying life to the sound of merrymaking;
Y estos pendientes que tengo	I have things I must do,
los tengo en San Antonio,	They'll be done in San Antonio,
en Nuevo Orleáns	In New Orleans
y allá en Berlín.	And over in Berlin.
Yo soy la mano que aprieta,	I am the hand with the death grip,
que asalta y asesina,	That murders and surprises;
me llamo Higinio de Anda	My name is Higinio de Anda,
y me he paseado en París.	And I have seen Paris.

If the ballad maker wants to justify the deeds of his robber hero, he will transform him into a border raider fighting against the outside group, the Americans.

The smuggler occupied in the Borderer's scale of values a much higher place than the robber, a place very close to that of the Border hero fighting for his right. This is not surprising if one remembers the average Borderer's hostile attitude toward the Rio Grande as an international boundary. Up until recent years, when enforcement has been more stringent, violation of the international line and small-scale smuggling were the general custom. The type of men involved in the earlier days gave smuggling an almost respectable character. Scarcely had Texas become independent when prominent Texans were engaged in smuggling with the Rio Grande settlements. Some of the Brownsville fortune-makers are said to have engaged in smuggling in a large way after 1848. Toward the close of the century, a smuggler so well known that he was called *El Contrabandista* (The Smuggler) operated in the Brownsville-Matamoros area. He was Don Mariano Reséndez, celebrated in *corridos*. A landowner on the Mexican side, and well-to-do, Don Mariano was no small-time operator. His band is said to have been large and well-organized and engaged in pitched battles with guards and soldiers when intercepted. Textiles were the chief item smuggled. *El Corrido de Mariano Reséndez* [TFA P1–2, P1–3, P15–4, and P39–1, sung by Jesús Gómez, Nicanor Torres, and Juan and Alfredo Guajardo] is intermediate between the *corrido* of border conflict and the outlaw ballad. Some of its language is reminiscent of the Greater Mexican outlaw *corridos*. In other parts it sounds like the *corridos* of border conflict.

Later smuggling ballads have to do mostly with fights with customs guards on the American side, who are almost invariably identified not as *guardas* (guards) but as *rinches* (rangers). In *El Corrido de Laredo* [TFA P38–2, sung by Cornelio Varela] the ballad maker lauds his native city, telling of its brave men who make the "agents of the law walk with care." It is not only in World War I that the Laredoans have proved their valor, the singer says. In many fights between smugglers and *rinches* they have shown what they can do. That is why the American law treats Laredo men with respect.

Lower Border smuggling ballads are not about the details of smuggling or its consequences. The heroes are not taken prisoners. They either shoot their way out or die fighting, and it is the battle with the *rinches* and not the smuggling that forms the subject of the *corrido*.

El día tres de diciembre,	On the third day of December,
qué día tan señalado,	What a well-remembered day,
mataron tres gallos finos	Three cocks of the fighting breed
esos rinches desgraciados.	Were killed by those wretched rangers.

The Mexican charge that the *rinche* shot preferably from ambush is brought out in the smuggling *corrido,* as it is in the *corrido* of border conflict proper.

Los rinches son muy valientes,	The rangers are very brave,
no se les puede quitar;	That cannot be denied;
nos cazan como venados	They have to stalk us like deer
para podernos matar.	In order to kill us.

The Borderer against the *fuereño*

Even on the Border the Díaz rural policeman was an overbearing man, and he often clashed with the Borderer, who did not feel that he should let his right be violated. *El Corrido de Arnulfo González* [TFA P19–10, sung by Luis and Lisandro Flores] is about a clash between a Border man and a *rural.* Arnulfo is sitting down when a *rural* lieutenant passes by. Arnulfo stares, offending the *rural.* They fight and both are killed, and the ballad comments.

Qué bonitos son los hombres	How beautiful to see two men
que se matan pecho a pecho,	Fight to the death face to face,
cada uno con su pistola,	Each one of them with his pistol,
defendiendo su derecho.	Each one defending his right.

The *rural,* it appears, also had a "right" to defend, the right to object to being stared at.

Catarino Garza, the rebel against Díaz, has the distinction of appearing in Border balladry as a raider both on the north and the south banks. *El Corrido de Catarino Garza* [TFA P43–4, sung by Mercurio Martínez] is about the exploits of Garza's men on the south bank, while *El Corrido del Capitán Hall* [TFA P44–2, sung by Mercurio Martínez] deals with the brush that the remnants of the Garcistas had with the Ranger captain.

With the outbreak of the Revolution in 1910 there arose the Greater Mexican heroic *corrido.* Some Greater Mexican Revolutionary *corridos* were widely sung, but the Border produced its own Revolutionary ballads, such as *La Toma de Matamoros* [TFA P5–1, sung by Nacho Montelongo], about the capture of

Matamoros by the Carrancista general Lucio Blanco. Most of the Lower Border became Carrancista, and perhaps because of that the Pancho Villa ballad cycle found little favor. Villa is an important figure only as a border raider against the Americans, and not as a general against the Carrancistas. The favorite Villa *corrido* is *La Persecución de Villa* (The Pursuit of Villa) [TFA P4–8, sung by Nacho Montelongo]. In some variants Pershing's soldiers are called *rinches* too.

The Revolution was never as important a theme as border conflict. *El Corrido de Alonso* [TFA P21–5, sung by Pedro and Raúl Salazar] continues the latter theme on the south bank into the 1920's. General Margarito, a Revolutionary chieftain who is not only a *fuereño* according to the legend but a Villista as well, takes over a small Border town, killing one of the town council in the process. The dead man's son, Alonso, flees across the Border with his mother, grows up in Brownsville, and then goes back to avenge his father. Alonso rids the town of the oppressive authority of Margarito, though his primary purpose is personal vengeance. He tells the townspeople:

Pues ahora sí, comerciantes,	And now is the time, you merchants,
a trabajar con esmero,	Attend to your work with care;
ya les maté a Margarito	I have killed you Margarito
que les quitaba el dinero.	Who took the money you made.

Then he rides back to Texas, saying that he has knocked over the hive but that others must take care of the bees.

The Border Mexican against the *rinches*

The *corrido* of border conflict assumes its most characteristic form when its subject deals with the conflict between Border Mexican and Anglo-Texan, with the Mexican—outnumbered and pistol in hand—defending his "right" against the *rinches*. The *corrido* of border conflict follows a general pattern, out of which emerges the Border concept of the hero. It is a concept that is reflected in other *corrido* themes as well, because border conflict dominated Border balladry for

147

almost a century. Basically the pattern is that established with Cortina in 1859. It is always expressed in the *corrido* form.

Pablo González is walking past the Rio Grande City courthouse with his wife when she is insulted by the Anglo-American law. He shoots a *rinche* and takes to the brush with his rifle and his pistol, where he fights off numbers of *rinches* who come after him. Finally another Border Mexican, who he thinks is his friend, visits Pablo and unloads his rifle when Pablo is not looking. A little while later Pablo is attacked and shot down by the *rinches* while he is trying to load his rifle.

Rito García rides home one afternoon, at peace with the world. He hears screams as he nears his ranch at El Cenizal. The *rinches* are there, searching his house, manhandling his womenfolk, shooting his young son. Rito meets them on the road and shoots several of them. He crosses the river and feels safe, but a scoundrelly Díaz official turns him over to the Americans. In one version of the story he is executed; in another he is sent to prison and later given to a pretty girl as a Christmas present.

Jacinto Treviño is in Matamoros when the news comes to him that an American on the north bank has beaten Jacinto's brother to death with a piece of iron pipe. Jacinto crosses into Texas, kills the American and makes his way back to the river, carrying his brother's body and fighting off the *rinches* at the same time. Later he hears that the *rinches* have offered a reward for him; so he again crosses the river, engages them in a gunbattle, kills several and returns to the south bank.

Ignacio Treviño is quietly drinking off a whiskey at the White Elephant Saloon in Brownsville when a whole army of Texas Rangers and deputies ride into town. They have come to wipe out the Brownsville police force, which is made up of Mexicans. One particular Ranger has come down with the special job of shooting police chief Joe Crixell in the back. Ignacio fights them all at the White Elephant and drives them away, but his victory is temporary. In the end he and other survivors of Crixell's force have to seek refuge across the river.

And so the pattern has been put together, that same pattern which finds expression in the ballads and stories about Gregorio

Cortez. It is never the same in all its details, nor does it always correspond to fact, but it carries the real man along with it and transforms him into the hero. The hero is always the peaceful man, finally goaded into violence by the *rinches* and rising in his wrath to kill great numbers of his enemy. His defeat is assured; at the best he can escape across the border, and often he is killed or captured. But whatever his fate, he has stood up for his right.

The *corrido* of border conflict as a dominant form

The period of border conflict resulted in the gradual emergence of the *corrido* as the dominant form of Lower Border balladry. The conflict period was shorter than similar ones in medieval Europe. The Border *corrido,* by the time it entered its decadent period in the 1930's, had not assumed total hegemony over Border balladry, as did the *romance* in Spain. But the process is clearly evident, and because it was not completed it is easier to see in action. One can see the balladry of the Lower Border working toward a single type: toward one form, the *corrido;* toward one theme, border conflict; toward one concept of the hero, the man fighting for his right with his pistol in his hand.

Border balladry begins the century of conflict in diverse forms. As the *corrido* emerges, it assimilates the *romance* survivals that had come from Spain. Novelesque romances become definitely *corridos,* adapted to local conditions. One presumes the existence of some remnants of heroic *romances* in the echoes found in the language of the *corrido.* These, if they did exist, also were assimilated into the *corrido.* The *verso* almost completely disappears. The *décima* holds its own for some time, but toward the latter part of the period it is in neglect. Some *décimas* are remembered as *corridos* and their fragments are given the *corrido* form. The same thing that happens to the *décima* occurs to the newly arrived *danza.*

Border conflict dominates as a theme. The old ballad subjects, dealing mostly with the everyday activities of the Rio Grande folk, lose much of their interest. Ballads are received from Greater Mexico, from Cuba, and even from the United States, but their themes, mostly proletarian, are not imitated. The local ballads all take on the complexion of conflict. The term *rinche* (Texas Ranger) is extended not only to possemen but to border patrolmen, immigration officers, prison guards, and even to Pershing's soldiers when they are in pursuit of the border raider Pancho Villa. In some cases, such as in *El Corrido de José Mosqueda,* a ballad with a purely outlaw background is transformed into a ballad of border conflict.

The concept of the hero as a man fighting for his right also becomes dominant. The proletarian ballad's concept of the hero as an outlaw who robs the rich to give to the poor does not gain acceptance, though Greater Mexican ballads containing it are sung and enjoyed. Nor does the Border outlaw repent, to furnish a moral for the crowd. The outlaw is either seen frankly as an outlaw, without sentimentalizing, or he is made an actor in border conflict. The hero, however, is not the highwayman or the smuggler, but the peaceful man who defends his right. The Border ballads that have been most widely accepted are those containing the three factors mentioned: *corrido* form, border-conflict theme, and a hero that defends his right.

In 1901 border conflict was sixty-five years old. It had been more than forty years since Cortina. On a June day in 1901 Gregorio Cortez sat peacefully at home, far from the Border, relaxing after the noonday meal and watching his corn grow. Sheriff Brack Morris of Karnes County drew up beside Gregorio's gate in a surrey with fringe on top. The events that followed were told in legend and ballad. Gregorio Cortez came to epitomize the Border *corrido* hero, and his ballad brought the elements of the heroic Border *corrido* to a focus. *El Corrido de Gregorio Cortez* set the model for the twentieth-century heroic *corrido* of the Lower Border. It is not too much to suggest that it had an influence on the Greater Mexican heroic *corrido,* which began ten years after Cortez rode his famous ride.

VI: VARIANTS OF *Gregorío Cortez*

The Mexico City Broadside

1

Como decimos, así es,
en mil novecientos uno,
el día veintidós de junio
fue capturado Cortés.

As we say, so it is;
In nineteen hundred and one,
On the twenty-second of June
Cortez was captured.

2

En junio día veintidós
por telégrafo supieron
que a Cortés lo aprehendieron
entre el Sauz y Palafox.

In June, on the twenty-second,
By telegraph it was known
That Cortez had been apprehended
Between El Sauz and Palafox.

3

Se aprehendió en Campo de
   Oveja,
de don Abraham de la Garza,
él perdió toda esperanza,
ya en la frontera de Texas.

He was captured in Sheep Camp,
Of Don Abraham de la Garza,
He lost all hope
When he was already on the Texas
   border.

4

Que viva nuestra nación,
aunque sufriendo revés,
Viva, Gregorio Cortés,
que ha honrado su pabellón.

Long live our country
Although suffering setback,
Long live Gregorio Cortez,
Who has honored his flag.

5

Murieron tres aprehensores,
por falta en determinar,
y así han podido pagar
los justos por pecadores.

Three captors died
For lack of discernment,
And thus there have paid
The just for the sinners.

6

Todito el Río Grande estaba,
resguardando el litoral,
parece que se esperaba,
conflicto internacional.

All the Rio Grande
Was guarding the shore;
It seemed that they were expecting
An international conflict.

7

La madre patria es hogar,
que hijo e hija ama,
pues México tiene fama,
disciplina militar.

The mother country is a home
That loves both daughter and son,
For Mexico has fame,
Military discipline.

8

Cortés a Morris mató,
la pistola que sirvió,
por otra luego cambió
a un amigo que encontró.

Cortez killed Morris;
The pistol that was used
He exchanged for another
With a friend that he met.

9

Su coche a tiro tomó,
toda esta advertencia tuvo,
tres millas y media anduvo
y allí se apeó y amarró.

His coach and team [?] he took,
He was careful to do all this;
He rode three miles and a half
And then got down and tied up.

10

De América su nación,
ha sufrido este revés,
pues nuestro hermano Cortés
ha honrado su pabellón.

Of America her nation
Has suffered this setback,
For our brother Cortez
Has honored his flag.

11

Se oyen de Cortés querellas
lamentándose al Creador,
el pabellón tricolor
idéntico a las estrellas.

From Cortez are heard complaints,
Lamenting to the Creator,
The tricolor flag,
Identical to the stars.

12

Gregorio Cortés venía
de incógnito y lo entregaron,

Gregorio Cortez was coming
In disguise and he was betrayed;

y así lo determinaron,
porque así les convenía.

Thus it was arranged,
Because it was to their interest.

13

La grande alarma que hoy pasa
en San Antonio, Laredo,
por el gran furor y miedo,
querían acabar la raza.

The great alarm that now happens,
In San Antonio, Laredo,
From the great fury and fear
They wanted to exterminate our
    people.

14

Llegó a casa de Robledo,
allí con él conversó,
nada de esto les contó,
porque no tuvieran miedo.

He got to Robledo's house,
There he conversed with him;
He told them nothing of this,
So they wouldn't be afraid.

15

Glover aquí lo asaltó,
descalzo salió de aquí,
volvió por calzado ahí,
y a Glover muerto encontró.

Glover surprised him here,
Barefoot he went out of here;
He returned for his shoes
And found Glover dead.

16

A Cortés llegan con fallos,
siendo íntegro mexicano.
Diciendo:—¿Cortés y hermano
son ladrones de a caballo?

To Cortez they come with
    judgments,
Being an upright Mexican,
Saying, "Cortez and brother
Are thieves on horseback?"

17

¡Dios de mí tenga clemencia
adiós, esposa, ay de mí!
por cincuenta años salí
sentenciado, a penitencia.

May God on me have mercy,
Farewell, wife, woe is me!
For fifty years I departed,
Sentenced to the penitentiary.

18

Así difundió su amor,
nuestro Redentor Jesús.
Gracias mil, don Pablo Cruz,
Editor "DEL REGIDOR."

Thus did he diffuse His love,
Jesus, our Redeemer;
A thousand thanks, Don Pablo Cruz,
Editor of *El Regidor*.

19

Pablo Cruz se distinguió
como íntegro mexicano,
este prominente hermano
que su ayuda me impartió.

Pablo Cruz distinguished himself
As an upright Mexican,
This prominent brother
Who gave me his help.

20

Su indulgente Redacción
y su unión confraternal,
con su luz intelectual,
él abrió una suscripción.

His indulgent Staff
And his confraternal union,
With his intellectual light,
He began a subscription.

21

Participo esta noticia,
a gente culta y honrada . . .
los de lista enumerada,
la suerte le sea propicia.

I make this news known
To cultured and honest people;
Those on the numbered list—
May fortune be propitious to them.

22

¡Y aquí acaba de una vez,
la desgracia lamentando! . . .
Aquí se acaba cantando
el Corrido de Cortés.

And here ends at once,
The misfortune lamenting! . . .
This is the end of the singing
Of the ballad of Cortez.

Variant X

1

En el condado de Carnes
miren lo que ha sucedido,
murió el Cherife Mayor
quedando Román herido.

In the county of Karnes,
Look what has happened;
The Major Sheriff died,
Leaving Román badly wounded.

2

Serían las dos de la tarde
cuando la gente llegó,
unos a los otros dicen:
—No saben quién lo mató.

It must have been two in the
    afternoon
When people arrived;
They said to one another,
"It is not known who killed him."

3

Se anduvieron informando
como media hora después,
supieron que el malhechor
era Gregorio Cortez

They went around asking questions,
About half an hour afterward,
They found that the wrongdoer
Had been Gregorio Cortez.

4

Ya insortaron a Cortez
por toditito el estado,
que vivo o muerto se aprehenda
porque a varios ha matado.

Now they have outlawed Cortez,
Throughout the whole state;
Let him be taken, dead or alive;
He has killed several men.

Variants of Gregorio Cortez

5

Decía Gregorio Cortez
con su pistola en la mano:
—No siento haberlo matado,
lo que siento es a mi hermano.

Then said Gregorio Cortez,
With his pistol in his hand,
"I don't regret that I killed him;
I regret my brother's death."

6

Decía Gregorio Cortez
con su alma muy encendida:
—No siento haberlo matado,
la defensa es permitida.

Then said Gregorio Cortez,
And his soul was all aflame,
"I don't regret that I killed him;
A man must defend himself."

7

Venían los americanos
más blancos que una paloma,
de miedo que le tenían
a Cortez y a su pistola.

The Americans were coming,
They were whiter than a dove,
From the fear that they had
Of Cortez and of his pistol.

8

Decían los americanos,
decían con timidez:
—Vamos a seguir la huella
que el malhechor es Cortez.

Then the Americans said,
Then they said fearfully,
"Come, let us follow the trail;
The wrongdoer is Cortez."

9

Le echaron los perros jaunes
pa' que siguieran la huella,
pero alcanzar a Cortez
era seguir a una estrella.

They set the bloodhounds on him,
So they could follow his trail,
But trying to overtake Cortez
Was like following a star.

10

Tiró con rumbo a Gonzales
sin ninguna timidez:
—Síganme rinches cobardes,
yo soy Gregorio Cortez.

He struck out for Gonzales
Without showing any fear,
"Follow me, cowardly rangers,
I am Gregorio Cortez."

11

Se fué de Belmont al rancho,
lo alcanzaron a rodear,
poquitos más de trescientos,
y allí les brincó el corral.

From Belmont he went to the
  ranch,
They succeeded in surrounding
  him,
Quite a few more than three hundred,
But there he jumped their corral.

12

Cuando les brincó el corral,
según lo que aquí se dice,
se agarraron a balazos
y les mató otro cherife.

When he jumped their corral,
According to what we hear,
They got into a gunfight,
And he killed them another sheriff.

13

Decía Gregorio Cortez
con su pistola en la mano:
—No corran, rinches cobardes,
con un solo mexicano.

Then said Gregorio Cortez,
With his pistol in his hand,
"Don't run, you cowardly rangers,
From just one Mexican."

14

Salió Gregorio Cortez,
salió con rumbo a Laredo,
no lo quisieron seguir
porque le tuvieron miedo.

Gregorio Cortez went out,
He went toward Laredo
They decided not to follow
Because they were afraid of him.

15

Decía Gregorio Cortez:
—¿Pa' qué se valen de planes?
No me pueden agarrar
ni con esos perros jaunes.

Then said Gregorio Cortez,
"What is the use of your scheming?
You cannot catch me,
Even with those bloodhounds."

16

Decían los americanos:
—Si lo alcanzamos ¿qué
    haremos?
Si le entramos por derecho
muy poquitos volveremos.

Then the Americans said,
"If we catch up with him, what
    shall we do?
If we fight him man to man,
Very few of us will return."

17

Allá por El Encinal,
según lo que aquí se dice,
le formaron un corral
y les mató otro cherife.

Over by El Encinal,
According to what we hear,
They made him a corral,
And he killed them another sheriff.

18

Decía Gregorio Cortez
echando muchos balazos:
—Me he escapado de agua-
    ceros,
contimás de nublinazos.

Then said Gregorio Cortez,
Shooting out a lot of bullets,
"I have weathered thunderstorms;
This little mist doesn't bother me."

19

Ya se encontró a un mexicano,

Now he has met a Mexican;

Variants of Gregorio Cortez

le dice con altivez:
—Platícame qué hay de nuevo,
yo soy Gregorio Cortez.

He says to him haughtily,
"Tell me the news;
I am Gregorio Cortez."

20

—Dicen que por culpa mía
han matado mucha gente,
ya me voy a presentar
porque eso no es conveniente.

"It is said that because of me
Many people have been killed;
I will surrender now
Because such things are not right."

21

Cortez le dice a Jesús:
—Ora sí lo vas a ver,
anda diles a los rinches
que me vengan a aprehender.

Cortez says to Jesús,
"At last you are going to see it;
Go tell the rangers
To come and arrest me."

22

Venían todos los rinches,
venían que hasta volaban
porque se iban a ganar
los mil pesos que les daban.

All the rangers were coming,
Coming so fast they even flew,
For they wanted to get
The thousand dollars they were
offered.

23

Cuando rodearon la casa
Cortez se les presentó:
—Por la buena sí me llevan
porque de otro modo no.

When they surrounded the house,
Cortez suddenly appeared before
them,
"You will take me if I'm willing,
But not any other way."

24

Decía el Cherife Mayor
como queriendo llorar:
—Cortez entrega tus armas,
no te vamos a matar.

Then the Major Sheriff said,
As if he was going to cry,
"Cortez, hand over your weapons;
We are not going to kill you."

25

Decía Gregorio Cortez,
les gritaba en alta voz:
—Mis armas no las entrego
hasta estar en calaboz'.

Then said Gregorio Cortez,
Shouting to them in a loud voice,
"I won't surrender my arms
Until I am in a cell."

26

Decía Gregorio Cortez,

Then said Gregorio Cortez,

decía en su voz divina,
—Mis armas no las entrego
hasta estar en bartolina.

27
Ya agarraron a Cortez,
ya terminó la cuestión,
la pobre de su familia
lo lleva en el corazón.

28
Ya con ésta me despido
a la sombra de un ciprés,
aquí se acaba cantando
el corrido de Cortez.

He said in his godly voice,
"I won't surrender my arms
Until I'm inside a jail."

Now they have taken Cortez,
Now matters are at an end;
His poor family
Are suffering in their hearts.

Now with this I say farewell,
In the shade of a cypress tree;
This is the end of the singing
Of the ballad of Cortez.

Variant A

1
En el condado del Carmen
miren lo que ha sucedido,
murió el Cherife Mayor,
quedando Román herido.

2
Otro día por la mañana,
cuando la gente llegó,
unos a los otros dicen:
—No saben quién lo mató.

3
Se anduvieron informando
como tres horas después,
supieron que el malhechor
era Gregorio Cortez.

4
Ya insortaron a Cortez
por toditito el estado,
que vivo o muerto lo aprehendan
porque a varios ha matado.

5
Decía Gregorio Cortez

In the county of El Carmen
Look what has happened;
The Major Sheriff died,
Leaving Román badly wounded.

The next day, in the morning,
When people arrived,
They said to one another,
"It is not known who killed him."

They went around asking questions,
About three hours afterward;
They found that the wrongdoer
Had been Gregorio Cortez.

Now they have outlawed Cortez,
Throughout the whole state;
Let him be taken, dead or alive;
He has killed several men.

Then said Gregorio Cortez,

con su pistola en la mano:
—No siento haberlo matado,
al que siento es a mi hermano.

With his pistol in his hand,
"I don't regret that I killed him;
I regret my brother's death."

6

Decía Gregorio Cortez
con su alma muy encendida:
—No siento haberlo matado,
la defensa es permitida.

Then said Gregorio Cortez,
And his soul was all aflame,
"I don't regret that I killed him;
A man must defend himself."

7

Venían los americanos
que por el viento volaban
porque se iban a ganar
tres mil pesos que les daban.

The Americans were coming;
They seemed to fly through the air;
Because they were going to get
Three thousand dollars they were
offered.

8

Tiró con rumbo a Gonzales,
varios cherifes lo vieron,
no lo quisieron seguir
porque le tuvieron miedo.

He struck out for Gonzales;
Several sheriffs saw him;
They decided not to follow
Because they were afraid of him.

9

Venían los perros jaunes,
venían sobre la huella,
pero alcanzar a Cortez
era seguir a una estrella.

The bloodhounds were coming,
They were coming on the trail,
But overtaking Cortez
Was like following a star.

10

Decía Gregorio Cortez:
—¿Pa' qué se valen de planes?
Si no pueden agarrarme
ni con esos perros jaunes.

Then said Gregorio Cortez,
"What is the use of your scheming?
You cannot catch me,
Even with those bloodhounds."

11

Decían los americanos:
—Si lo alcanzamos ¿qué
    haremos?
Si le entramos por derecho
muy poquitos volveremos.

Then the Americans said,
"If we catch up with him, what shall
    we do?
If we fight him man to man,
Very few of us will return."

12

Se fué de Brownsville al
    rancho,

From Brownsville he went to the
    ranch,

lo alcanzaron a rodear,
poquitos más de trescientos,
y allí les brincó el corral.

They succeeded in surrounding
  him;
Quite a few more than three hundred,
But there he jumped their corral.

13

Allá por El Encinal,
según lo que aquí se dice,
se agarraron a balazos
y les mató otro cherife.

Over by El Encinal,
According to what we hear,
They got into a gunfight,
And he killed them another sheriff.

14

Decía Gregorio Cortez
con su pistola en la mano:
—No corran, rinches cobardes,
con un solo mexicano.

Then said Gregorio Cortez,
With his pistol in his hand,
"Don't run, you cowardly rangers,
From just one Mexican."

15

Tiró con rumbo a Laredo
sin ninguna timidez:
—Síganme, rinches cobardes,
yo soy Gregorio Cortez.

He struck out for Laredo
Without showing any fear,
"Follow me, cowardly rangers,
I am Gregorio Cortez."

16

Gregorio le dice a Juan
en el rancho del Ciprés:
—Platícame qué hay de nuevo,
yo soy Gregorio Cortez.

Gregorio says to Juan,
At the Cypress Ranch,
"Tell me the news;
I am Gregorio Cortez."

17

Gregorio le dice a Juan:
—Muy pronto lo vas a ver,
anda y dile a los cherifes
que me vengan a aprehender.

Gregorio says to Juan,
"You will see it happen soon;
Go call the sheriffs
So they can come and arrest me."

18

Cuando llegan los cherifes
Gregorio se presentó:
—Por la buena sí me llevan,
porque de otro modo no.

When the sheriffs arrive,
Gregorio gave himself up,
"You take me because I'm willing,
But not any other way."

19

Ya agarraron a Cortez,
ya terminó la cuestión,

Now they have taken Cortez,
Now matters are at an end;

Variants of Gregorio Cortez

la pobre de su familia	His poor family
la lleva en el corazón.	Are suffering in their hearts.

20

Ya con ésta me despido	Now with this I say farewell,
a la sombra de un ciprés,	In the shade of a cypress,
aquí se acaba cantando	This is the end of the singing
la tragedia de Cortez.	Of the ballad about Cortez.

Variant B

1

Pongan cuidado, señores,	Gentlemen, give your attention,
la desgracia ha sucedido,	The misfortune has occurred;
murió el Cherife Mayor	The Major Sheriff died,
quedando Román herido.	Leaving Román badly wounded.

2

Otro día por la mañana	The next day, in the morning,
cuando la gente se juntó,	When people arrived;
unos a los otros se dicen:	They said to one another,
—No saben quién lo mató.	"It is not known who killed him."

3

Decía Gregorio Cortez	Then said Gregorio Cortez,
con su pistola en la mano:	With his pistol in his hand,
—No siento haberte matado,	"I don't regret that I killed you;
lo que siento es a mi hermano.	I regret my brother's death."

4

Decía Gregorio Cortez	Then said Gregorio Cortez,
con su alma muy encendida:	And his soul was all aflame,
—No siento haberte matado,	"I don't regret that I killed you;
la defensa es permetida.	A man must defend himself."

5

Decían los americanos	Then the Americans said,
con muchísima timidez:	With a lot of fear,
—Vamos a seguir la huella	"Come, let us follow the trail;
que el malhechor es Cortez.	The wrongdoer is Cortez."

6

—Si lo alcanzamos ¿qué le haremos,	"If we catch up with him, what shall we do to him?

si le hablamos por derecho,
si le hablamos por derecho
muy pocos arrendaremos.

If we talk to him man to man,
If we talk to him man to man
Very few of us will return."

7

Tiró rumbo a Piedras Negras
sin ninguna temidez:
—Síganme, no sean cobardes,
yo soy Gregorio Cortez.

He struck out toward Piedras
Negras,
Without showing any fear,
"Follow me, don't be cowards;
I am Gregorio Cortez."

8

Llegando ya a Palo Alto
lo volvieron a alcanzar,
poquitos más de trescientos,
y allí les brincó el corral.

When he had reached Palo Alto
They caught up with him again;
Quite a few more than three hundred,
And there he jumped their corral.

9

Decía Gregorio Cortez
echando muchos balazos:
—Me he escapado de aguaceros,
contimás de nublinazos.

Then said Gregorio Cortez,
Shooting out a lot of bullets,
"I have weathered thunderstorms;
This little mist doesn't bother me."

10

En el conda'o de Consiri,
a según como se dice,
lo volvieron a alcanzar
y allí mató otro cherife.

In the county of Karnes City,
According to what we hear,
They caught up with him again,
And there he killed another sheriff.

11

Ya se encontró un mexicano,
sin ninguna temidez:
—Platícame qué hay de nuevo,
yo soy Gregorio Cortez.

Now he has met a Mexican,
Without showing any fear,
"Tell me the news;
I am Gregorio Cortez."

12

—Dicen que por causa mía
han matado mucha gente,
ya me voy a presentar
porque· eso no es conviniente.

"It is said that because of me
Many people have been killed;
I will surrender now
Because such things are not right."

162

13

Cortez le dice a Jesús:
—Orita lo vas a ver,
anda dile a los cherifes
que me vengan a aprehender.

Cortez says to Jesús,
"Now you are going to see it;
Go tell the sheriffs
To come and arrest me."

14

Venían todos los cherifes,
venían que hasta volaban,
porque se iban a ganar
diez mil pesos que les daban.

The sheriffs were coming,
Coming so fast they even flew,
For they wanted to get
The ten thousand dollars they were
    offered.

15

Cuando rodearon la casa
Cortez se les presentó:
—Por la buena sí me llevan,
porque por la mala no.

When they surrounded the house,
Cortez suddenly appeared before
    them,
"You will take me if I'm willing,
But not any other way."

16

Decía el Cherife Mayor
como queriendo llorar:
—Gregorio, entrega tus armas,
no te vamos a matar.

Then the Major Sheriff said,
As if he was going to cry,
"Cortez, hand over your weapons;
We are not going to kill you."

17

Decía Gregorio Cortez,
decía y en alta voz:
—Mis armas no las entrego
hasta no estar en calaboz'.

Then said Gregorio Cortez,
He said and in a loud voice,
"I won't surrender my arms
Until I am in a cell."

18

Decía Gregorio Cortez
en voces altas y finas:
—Mis armas no las entrego
hasta no estar en bartolina.

Then said Gregorio Cortez,
In a loud and fine voice,
"I won't surrender my arms
Until I am inside a jail."

19

Ya con ésta me despido
con las hojas de un ciprés
aquí se acaba cantando
el corrido de Cortez.

Now with this I say farewell,
With the leaves of a cypress tree,
This is the end of the singing
Of the ballad about Cortez.

1

En el condado del Carmen
la desgracia ha sucedido,
murió el Cherife Mayor
quedando Román herido.

In the county of El Carmen
The misfortune has occurred;
The Major Sheriff died,
Leaving Román badly wounded.

2

En el condado del Carmen
la desgracia sucedió,
murió el Cherife Mayor,
no saben quién lo mató.

In the county of El Carmen,
The misfortune occurred;
The Major Sheriff died;
It is not known who killed him.

3

Salió con rumbo a Laredo
sin ninguna timidez:
—Síganme rinches cobardes,
yo soy Gregorio Cortez.

He went out toward Laredo,
Without showing any fear,
"Follow me, cowardly rangers,
I am Gregorio Cortez."

4

Decía Gregorio Cortez,
con su alma muy encendida:
—No siento haberlo matado,
la defensa es permitida.

Then said Gregorio Cortez,
And his soul was all aflame,
"I don't regret that I killed him;
A man must defend himself."

5

Decía Gregorio Cortez
con su pistola en la mano:
—No corran rinches cobardes
con un puro mexicano.

Then said Gregorio Cortez,
With his pistol in his hand,
"Don't run, you cowardly rangers,
From a real Mexican."

6

Como a las ocho serían,
como tres horas después,
supieron que el malhechor
era Gregorio Cortez.

It must have been about eight
  o'clock,
About three hours afterward,
They found out that the wrong-
  doer
Had been Gregorio Cortez.

7

Iban los americanos
por el viento que volaban
porque se iban a ganar
dos mil pesos que les daban.

The Americans were riding
Through the air as if they flew;
Because they wanted to get
Two thousand dollars they were
  offered.

164

8

Decían los americanos:
—Si lo hallamos ¿ qué le
  haremos?
Si le entramos por derecho
Muy poquitos volveremos.

Then the Americans said,
"If we find him, what shall we do?
If we fight him man to man
Very few of us will return."

9

Iban los americanos
iban siguiendo la huella,
porque alcanzar a Cortez
era alcanzar a una estrella.

The Americans were riding,
They were following the trail;
Because trying to overtake Cortez
Was like overtaking a star.

10

Decía Gregorio Cortez:
—¿Pa' qué se valen de planes?
No me pueden agarrar
ni con esos perros jaunes.

Then said Gregorio Cortez,
"What is the use of your scheming?
You cannot catch me,
Even with those bloodhounds."

11

Gregorio le dice a Juan:
—Muy pronto lo vas a ver;
anda diles a los rinches
que me vengan a aprehender.

Gregorio says to Juan,
"You will see it very soon;
Go tell the rangers
To come and arrest me."

12

Allá por el Encinal
lo alcanzaron a rodear,
poquitos más de trescientos
y allí les brincó el corral.

Over by El Encinal
They succeeded in surrounding
  him;
Quite a few more than three hun-
  dred,
But there he jumped their corral.

13

Salió Gregorio Cortez,
salió con rumbo a Laredo,
no lo quisieron seguir[1]
porque le tuvieron miedo.

Gregorio Cortez went out,
He went out toward Laredo,
They decided not to follow
Because they were afraid of him.

14

Venían todos los rinches,
venían buscando a Cortez,
les preguntaban a muchos:

All the rangers were coming,
They were looking for Cortez;
They asked of many people,

[1] Lines in italics were forgotten by singer during actual recording and supplied later to the collector.

—¿Dónde está el Rancho 'e El Ciprés?

"Where is the ranch of El Ciprés?"

15

Cuando llegaron los rinches
Gregorio se presentó:
—Por la buena sí me llevan,
porque de otro modo no.

When the rangers arrived,
Gregorio gave himself up,
"You will take me if I'm willing,
But not any other way."

16

Ya mataron a Cortez,
ya se acabó la cuestión,
la pobre de su familia,
la lleva en el corazón.

Now they have killed Cortez,
Now matters are at an end;
His poor family
Are suffering in their hearts.

17

Ya con ésta me despido
con las hojas del ciprés,
aquí termina el corrido
de don Gregorio Cortez.

Now with this I say farewell,
With the leaves of the cypress,
This is the end of the ballad
Of Don Gregorio Cortez.

Variant D

1

En el condado del Carmen
tal desgracia sucedió,
murió el Cherife Mayor,
no saben quién lo mató.

In the county of El Carmen,
What a misfortune has occurred;
The Major Sheriff died,
It is not known who killed him.

2

Otro día por la mañana,
cuando la gente llegó,
unos a otros se decían:
—Cortez fué el que lo mató.

The next day, in the morning,
When people arrived,
They said to one another,
"Cortez was the one who killed him."

3

Decía Gregorio Cortez
con su alma muy encendida:
—No siento haberlo matado,
la defensa es permetida.

Then said Gregorio Cortez,
And his soul was all aflame,
"I don't regret that I killed him;
A man must defend himself."

4

Decían los americanos:
—Si lo hallamos ¿qué le haremos?

Then the Americans said,
"If we find him what shall we do to him?

Variants of Gregorio Cortez

Si le entramos por derecha	If we fight him man to man,
muy poquitos volveremos.	Very few of us will return."

5

Se encontró y un mexicano,	He met a Mexican,
le dice con altivez:	He says to him haughtily,
—Platícame qué hay de nuevo,	"Tell me the news;
yo soy Gregorio Cortez.	I am Gregorio Cortez."

6

Decía Gregorio Cortez	Then said Gregorio Cortez
con su pistola en la mano:	With his pistol in his hand,
—No siento haberlo matado,	"I don't regret that I killed him;
lo que siento es a mi hermano.	I regret my brother's death."

7

Corrían los americanos,	The Americans were galloping,
corrían mas que volaban,	They more than galloped, they flew,
porque se iban a ganar	Because they wanted to get
tres mil pesos que les daban.	Three thousand dollars they were
	offered.

8

No sabemos la verdad,	We do not know the truth,
según lo que aquí se dice	According to what we hear
lo volvieron a alcanzar	They caught up with him again
y les mató otro cherife.	And he killed them another sheriff.

9

Decía Gregorio Cortez	Then said Gregorio Cortez,
con su pistola en la mano:	With his pistol in his hand,
—No siento haberlo matado,	"I don't regret that I killed him;
lo que siento es a mi hermano.	I regret my brother's death."

10

No sabemos la verdad,	We do not know the truth,
según lo que aquí se dice	According to what we hear,
lo volvieron a alcanzar	They caught up with him again
y les mató otro cherife.	And he killed them another sheriff.

11

Venían los americanos	The Americans were coming,
más blancos que una amapola,	They were whiter than a poppy,
porque le tenían miedo	Because they were afraid
a Cortez y a su pistola.	Of Cortez and of his pistol.

12

Ya con ésta me despido
a la sombra de un ciprés,
aquí se acaba el corrido
de don Gregorio Cortez.

Now with this I say farewell,
In the shade of a cypress tree,
This is the end of the ballad
Of Don Gregorio Cortez.

Variant E

1

En el condado del Carmen
miren lo que ha sucedido,
murió el Cherife Mayor
quedando Román herido.

In the county of El Carmen
Look what has happened;
The Major Sheriff died,
Leaving Román badly wounded.

2

Se anduvieron informando
como tres horas después,
no hallaron quién lo mató
y el malhechor es Cortez.

They went around asking questions
About half an hour afterward,
They didn't find out who killed him,
And the wrongdoer is Cortez.

3

Le echaron los perros jaunes
para alcanzarle la huella,
pero alcanzar a Cortez
era alcanzar una estrella.

They set the bloodhounds on him,
To overtake his trail,
But overtaking Cortez
Was like reaching a star.

4

Gregorio le dice a Juan
en el rancho del Ciprés:
—Platícame qué hay de nuevo,
yo soy Gregorio Cortez.

Gregorio says to Juan
At the ranch of El Ciprés,
"Tell me the news,
I am Gregorio Cortez."

5

Venían los americanos
que por el viento volaban,
a ver si podían ganar
tres mil pesos que les daban.

The Americans were coming
Almost flying through the air,
They were hoping to get
Three thousand dollars they were
    offered.

6

Decían los americanos:
—Si lo hallamos ¿qué le
    hacemos?
Si le entramos por derecho
muy poquitos volveremos.

Then the Americans said,
"If we find him, what shall we
    do to him?
If we fight him man to man
Very few of us will return."

7

Y en el punto de Los Fresnos	And at the place called Los Fresnos
lo alcanzaron a rodear,	They succeeded in surrounding him,
como unos trescientos hombres,	About three hundred men,
y allí les brincó el corral.	And there he jumped their corral.

8

Cuando les brincó el corral	When he jumped their corral
varios cherifes lo vieron,	Several sheriffs saw him;
no lo quisieron seguir	They decided not to follow
porque le tuvieron miedo.	Because they were afraid of him.

9

Decía Gregorio Cortez	Then said Gregorio Cortez,
abrochándose un zapato:	As he was tying his shoe,
—Aquí traigo más cartuchos	"I have more cartridges here
pa' divertirlos un rato.	To entertain you a while."

10

Decía Gregorio Cortez	Then said Gregorio Cortez
con su pistola en la mano:	With his pistol in his hand,
—¡Ah, cuánto rinche cobarde	"Ah, how many cowardly rangers,
para un solo mexicano!	Against one lone Mexican!"

11

Ya con ésta me despido	Now with this I say farewell
a las hojas de un ciprés,	By the leaves of a cypress tree,
aquí se acaba el corrido	This is the end of the ballad
de ese Gregorio Cortez.	Of that man called Gregorio Cortez.

Variant F

1

En el condado del Carmen	In the county of El Carmen
este caso ha sucedido,	This occurrence has taken place;
murió el Cherife Mayor	The Major Sheriff died,
quedando Román herido.	Leaving Román badly wounded.

2

Decía Gregorio Cortez	Then said Gregorio Cortez,
con su pistola en la mano:	With his pistol in his hand,

—No siento haberlo matado,
al que siento es a mi hermano.

3
Venían todos los rinches,
venían que se mataban
porque se iban a ganar
diez mil pesos que les daban.

4
Venían los americanos
que se daban con la gorra,
porque le tuvieron miedo
a Cortez con su pistola.

5
Gregorio le dice a Juan
En el rancho del Ciprés:
—Platícame que hay de nuevo,
que soy Gregorio Cortez.

6
En el condado del Carmen
lo volvieron a alcanzar,
poquitos más de trescientos
y allí les brincó el corral.

7
Decía el Cherife Mayor
como queriendo llorar:
—Cortez, entrega tus armas,
no te vamos a matar.

8
Decía Gregorio Cortez,
les gritaba en alta voz:
—Mis armas no las entrego
ha' no estar en calaboz'.

9
Ya con ésta me despido
a la sombra de un ciprés

"With His Pistol in His Hand"

"I don't regret that I killed him;
I regret my brother's death."

All the rangers were coming,
They were coming at breakneck
        speed,
Because they were going to get
Ten thousand dollars they were
        offered.

The Americans were coming
And they were very annoyed
Because they had been afraid
Of Cortez and of his pistol.

Gregorio says to Juan
In the ranch of El Ciprés,
"Tell me the news,
For I am Gregorio Cortez."

In the county of El Carmen
They caught up with him again,
Quite a few more than three hun-
        dred,
And there he jumped their corral.

Then the Major Sheriff said,
As if he was going to cry,
"Cortez, hand over your weapons,
We are not going to kill you."

Then said Gregorio Cortez,
Shouting to them in a loud voice,
"I won't surrender my arms
Until I am in a cell."

Now with this I say farewell
In the shade of a cypress tree,

170

aquí se acaba cantando
el corrido de Cortez.

This is the end of the singing
Of the ballad of Cortez.

1

En el condado del Carmen
tal desgracia sucedió,
murió el Cherife Mayor,
no saben quién lo mató.

In the county of El Carmen
What a misfortune occurred,
The Major Sheriff died,
It is not known who killed him.

2

Serían las dos de la tarde,
como media hora después,
supieron que el malhechor
era Gregorio Cortez.

It must have been two in the
    afternoon,
About half an hour afterward,
They found that the wrongdoer
Had been Gregorio Cortez.

3

Soltaron los perros jaunes
pa' que siguieran la juella
pero alcanzar a Cortez
era seguir a una estrella.

They let loose the bloodhounds
So they could follow the trail,
But trying to overtake Cortez
Was like following a star.

4

Esos rinches del condado
iban que casi volaban
porque se querían ganar
tres mil pesos que les daban.

Those rangers of the county
Rode so fast they almost flew,
Because they wanted to get
Three thousand dollars they were
    offered.

5

En el condado de Kiancer
lo llegaron a alcanzar,
a poco más de trescientos
y allí les brincó el corral.

In the county of Kansas
They succeeded in overtaking him,
Something more than three hundred,
And there he jumped their corral.

6

Decía el Cherife Mayor
como queriendo llorar:
—Cortez, entrega tus armas,
no te vamos a matar.

Then the Major Sheriff said,
As if he was going to cry,
"Cortez, hand over your weapons;
We are not going to kill you."

7

Decía Gregorio Cortez

Then said Gregorio Cortez,

con su pistola en la mano:
—¡Ah, cuánto rinche montado
para un solo mexicano!

With his pistol in his hand,
"Ah, how many mounted rangers
Against one lone Mexican!"

8
Ya con ésta me despido
a la sombra de un ciprés,
aquí se acaba el corrido
de don Gregorio Cortez.

Now with this I say farewell,
In the shade of a cypress tree,
This is the end of the ballad
Of Don Gregorio Cortez.

Variant H

1
En el condado de Kansas
tal desgracia sucedió,
mataron el Cherife Mayor,
dejando a Román herido.

In the county of Kansas
What a misfortune occurred;
They killed the Major Sheriff,
Leaving Román badly wounded.

2
Decía Gregorio Cortez
con su pistola en la mano:
—Síganme rinches cobardes,
yo soy Gregorio Cortez.

Then said Gregorio Cortez,
With his pistol in his hand,
"Follow me, cowardly rangers,
I am Gregorio Cortez."

3
En el ranchito en Isbel
lo alcanzaron a rodear;
poquito más de trescientos,
y allí les brincó el corral.

In the little ranch at Isbel
They succeeded in overtaking him;
Quite a few more than three hundred,
And there he jumped their corral.

4
Iban los americanos
más blancos que una paloma,
de miedo que le tenían
a Cortez con su pistola.

The Americans were riding,
They were whiter than a dove,
From the fear that they had
Of Cortez and of his pistol.

5
Decían los americanos:
—Si lo alcanzamos ¿qué
haremos?
Si lo pezcamos por derecha
muy poquitos volveremos.

The Americans said,
"If we catch up with him, what
shall we do?
If we fight him man to man
Very few of us will return."

172

Variants of Gregorio Cortez

6

Decía Gregorio Cortez	Then said Gregorio Cortez,
con su pistola en la mano:	With his pistol in his hand,
—Síganme rinches cobardes,	"Follow me, cowardly rangers,
yo soy Gregorio Cortez.	I am Gregorio Cortez."

7

En el rancho del Ciprés	In the ranch of El Ciprés
Gregorio le dice a Juan:	Gregorio says to Juan,
—Vé avísale a los cherifes	"Go let the sheriffs know,
que me vengan a aprehender.	So they can come arrest me."

8

Aquí va la despedida	Here goes the *despedida*,
a la sombra de un ciprés,	In the shade of a cypress tree,
aquí se acaba cantando	This is the end of the singing
el corrido de Cortez.	Of the ballad of Cortez.

Variant I

1

Iba Gregorio Cortez	Gregorio Cortez was riding
con su pistola en la mano:	With his pistol in his hand,
—No siento haberlos matado,	"I don't regret having killed them;
lo que siento es a mi hermano.	I regret my brother's death."

2

Tomó rumbo a Piedras Negras	He struck out for Piedras Negras,
sin ninguna timidez:	Without showing any fear,
—Síganme rinches cobardes,	"Follow me, cowardly rangers,
yo soy Gregorio Cortez.	I am Gregorio Cortez."

3

Iban los americanos	The Americans were riding
que parecía que volaban,	So fast that they seemed to fly,
también se iban a ganar	For they wanted to get
diez mil pesos que les daban.	Ten thousand dollars they were offered.

4

Decían los americanos:	The Americans were saying,
—¿Si lo alcanzamos qué haremos?	"If we catch up with him, what shall we do?
Si le hablamos por la buena	If we come to him with soft words,
muy poquitos quedaremos.	Very few of us will be left."

5

Decía Gregorio Cortez
con su alma muy encendida:
—Pues yo no entrego mis armas
hasta estar en bartolina.

Then said Gregorio Cortez,
And his soul was all aflame,
"I won't surrender my arms
Until I am in a cell."

6

Otro día por la mañana
él solo se presentó:
—Por la buena sí me llevan,
lo que es de otro modo no.

On the next day, in the morning,
He surrendered of his own accord,
"You can take me if I'm willing,
But not any other way."

VII: *Gregorio Cortez,* A STUDY

The variants

*J*n *the* textual study of *El Corrido de Gregorio Cortez* use will be made of the eleven variants which make up Chapter VI. One, referred to as the Mexico City broadside, is a *corrido* of Mexican provenience, representing a different ballad from the other variants. It is included for purposes of comparison. The other variants, A, B, C, D, E, F, G, H, I, and X, are all of the Border *corrido*.

The Mexico City broadside appears in Vázquez Santa Ana's *Canciones, cantares y corridos mexicanos.*[1] Vázquez publishes it without comment and without music. In *El romance español y el corrido mexicano*, Mendoza publishes a list of *corridos* which he did not include in his work because he could not find any music for them. Among them is *El Corrido de Gregorio Cortez.*[2] Since Mendoza has drawn liberally from Vázquez Santa Ana's works, his *Corrido de Gregorio Cortez* very probably is the one published without music by the latter. The Greater Mexican

[1] Higinio Vázquez Santa Ana, *Canciones, cantares y corridos mexicanos*, Mexico, 1925, pp. 173–176.
[2] Vicente T. Mendoza, *El romance español y el corrido mexicano*, Mexico, 1939, pp. 786ff.

Gregorio Cortez is obviously a broadside, and it is doubtful that it was widely sung. It was followed immediately afterward by *El Corrido de León Gzolgosz*, which Vázquez publishes a few pages before that of Cortez.[3] Vázquez says that the Gzolgosz *corrido* "became popular in Mexico during the month of October 1901. Since the press of Mexico at that time commented in different forms on the death of President McKinley, the people would repair to the public plazas to hear this *corrido* sung."[4] It is very probable that *El Corrido de León Gzolgosz* superseded *El Corrido de Gregorio Cortez* as the Mexico City sensation of the day, and that the professional *ciegos* or blind minstrels stopped singing the latter after October 1901. It is extremely doubtful that the Greater Mexican *Gregorio Cortez* was ever sung by the people in general, even in Mexico City. It is even more doubtful that it found its way into the rural areas. At least, no other variants except the Vázquez Santa Ana broadside have come to my attention.

The Mexico City broadside's detailed reporting of fact makes it easy to establish its approximate date. One may assume with almost no probability of error that the broadside was made between August 4 and September 15, 1901. The *corrido* tells what Mexico City knew about Cortez up to the time when he was sentenced to fifty years for the murder of Schnabel.

¡Dios de mí tenga clemencia,	May God on me have mercy;
adiós, esposa, ay de mí!	Farewell, wife; woe is me.
por cincuenta años salí	For fifty years I departed,
sentenciado, a penitencia.	Sentenced to the penitentiary.

The sentence for the death of Schnabel was reported in *El Popular* on August 4; so that date would be the earliest on which the Mexico City broadside could have been produced.[5] The more sensational death sentence, given Cortez on October 11, is not mentioned in the broadside. McKinley had died on September

[3] Vázquez Santa Ana, *Canciones, cantares y corridos,* pp. 168–170.
[4] *Ibid.,* p. 170.
[5] *El Popular de Mexico,* August 4, 1901, p. 1.

176

14, and the ballad about Gzolgosz became popular in October. It is most probable that the Cortez broadside was produced soon after news of his fifty-year conviction got to Mexico City, about mid-August, and that it ceased to be sung during October, when the *ciegos* turned to Leon Gzolgosz as a newer and more sensational subject. This would make the popular life of the Mexico City broadside about six weeks.

Variants A to I are versions of the Border *Corrido de Gregorio Cortez* collected from traditional sources. They are arranged according to length, Variant A having twenty quatrains and Variant I six. All except Variant A are the result of my own collecting in relatively recent years. Six of the variants were recorded on tape in 1954 and now are part of the Texas Folklore Archive at the University of Texas.

Variant A is not only the longest but the earliest collected variant of the group. It occupies both sides of a phonograph record, Vocalion number SA 283 8351, lent to me by Mr. Valeriano Cortez, who tells me that he has owned the record since 1920. Austin record shops say that the Vocalion company no longer exists, and that the recording is a collector's item as far as they know. There is no doubt about the authenticity of the singers, who are called "Los Trovadores Regionales" on the record. From their style they are very definitely Border *corrido* singers, and their version of the events, especially the place names, makes one think that they came from Brownsville or the vicinity.

Variant B is the longest of the variants that I have collected, and it comes from the oldest singer to record for me. It is nineteen quatrains long, one less than Variant A, and was recorded on August 2, 1954 [TFA P14–6]. The singer is Nicanor Torres, 92, of Brownsville. Torres says that he sings the *corrido* "as it was originally." The tune to which he sings the ballad is different from the one used in the other variants and is evidently the "old tune" referred to by some *guitarreros*. Torres was born on the Border and has lived in the vicinity of Matamoros and Brownsville all his life. Though some of his brothers were vaqueros, he was a farm laborer during his younger years. He is a reservoir of folk knowledge. Interesting is his sense of geography. He knows that Cortez "comes from a place called Consiri [Karnes City]" but believes that the place is a little town not very far from the river, on the Border.

Variant C, seventeen quatrains long, was collected at Valle Hermoso, Tamaulipas, a new boom town a few miles south of Matamoros. Félix Orozco Martínez and his *mariachi* sang Variant C on August 6, 1954 [TFA P20–5]. Orozco is not a native Borderer, having been born in San Luis Potosí. He makes his living playing at Valle Hermoso *cantinas* with his *mariachi* band, and is the most professional of the singers who gave me variants of *Gregorio Cortez*.

Variant D, twelve quatrains long, was recorded in Brownsville on August 21, 1954 [TFA P35–3]. The singers are Alberto and Fernando Garza, Fernando Rodríguez, and Pioquinto Medina, their ages being between 60 and 30. Alberto Garza was in his time a well-known *guitarrero*, though now he lives in town and does not sing the old ballads much. All the others are amateur musicians and singers.

Variant E is eleven quatrains. Only the text of this variant was collected. It was obtained from Gil González Cisneros, 25, at Las Comas, Tamaulipas, downriver from Matamoros, in December 1951. Gil González is one of the young men who have preserved a great deal of the *corrido* tradition. He is known in his area as a man with a good memory. Gil does not play the guitar and sings in small gatherings of relatives and friends purely for the fun of singing.

Variant E, nine quatrains, was sung for me by Ignacio (Nacho) Montelongo at Brownsville on July 25, 1954 [TFA P4–4]. Nacho Montelongo is one of the best known of the downriver *guitarreros*. He is forty-eight years old and has been playing and singing for about the last forty years. He does not sing for pay. He has a small farm on the south bank of the river, but since he was born on the American side at Port Isabel, he comes and goes freely. During the summer of 1954 he was working on the American side because the drouth had ruined his crop. In spite of his visits to town, Nacho is one of those *guitarreros* who have resisted the influence of the radio and the movies. He does not play the modern popular pieces, as do many other singers.

For Variant G, eight stanzas long, only the text is available. I collected it sometime during 1941 from two *guitarreros* at a *cantina* in Matamoros which was patronized by rancheros. In 1941 I was just beginning to get interested in the study of the *corrido,* and I did not get the exact date when the variant was collected, nor the names and background of the two singers who gave me the text. They were two guitar players of the kind that go from *cantina* to *cantina* making at least part of their living by their songs.

Variant H, also eight stanzas, was collected from Raquel Ocáñez de Guerrero, 40, at Brownsville on August 17, 1954 [TFA P31–5]. Mrs. Guerrero is one of the few *corrido*-singing women of the Border (except for the newcomers, either street singers from the interior or local aspirants to radio fame). She is a housewife and sings for her own enjoyment only. Her father was a well-known amateur ballad singer, and she learned her *corridos* from him.

Variant I, only six quatrains, was collected from Luis Flores Cisneros, 48, and was recorded at Matamoros on August 20, 1954 [TFA P34–4]. Luis Flores, though perhaps not as widely known as other *guitarreros,* has a reputation as an amateur singer and guitar player. He is also a *corrido* maker. *El Corrido de Juan Peña* [TFA P20–3] is one of his own compositions.

My search for the earliest variant of the Border *Corrido de Gregorio Cortez* (or of any other Border *corrido,* for that matter) has been up to the present time entirely fruitless. There is a possibility that some of the Border *corridos* appeared in an early form as broadsides. There were small printing presses and Spanish-language newspapers in almost every Border town. The evidence seems to be against it, however. The Border *Gregorio Cortez* shows no signs of having been written for the broadside press. It appears to be the product of the *guitarreros,* composed with the aid of the guitar and circulated orally.

Variants A to I, collected from different stages of oral tradi-

179

tion, are none of them in any way complete. What the original *Corrido de Gregorio Cortez* looked like one can only guess. Variant X is offered as my guess. It is a reconstruction, something on the order of those done by paleontologists, except that I had more to go on than most paleontologists do. I have not assumed a single line of Variant X, every line that appears there coming from oral tradition. X is made up entirely of quatrains from Variants A to I, with the exception of a few variations within lines, coming from other versions with which I have been familiar for thirty-five years or so. The elements that make up Variant X have been selected and put together in accordance with definite and consistent rules, based on the assumption (which the traditional variants support) that the original ballad was intended to inform and that it was therefore more detailed and factual than its later variants.

I did not begin by attempting to set a limit on the number of stanzas for Variant X. I took as my general outline the story of Cortez and chose from the variants available to me those quatrains that told the story most fully and most accurately. This, I believe, corresponds with the Border singer's own views about the ideal *corrido*, one that tells all the story. I ended up with a ballad of twenty-eight quatrains. Full-length *corridos* have between twenty and thirty quatrains, though some go as high as forty. The Mexico City *Corrido de Gregorio Cortez* has twenty-two quatrains. The original Border *corrido* may have been about thirty quatrains long.

As variants developed in *El Corrido de Gregorio Cortez* and the purely factual elements lost their importance, quatrains were arranged more with an eye toward dramatic effect than toward chronology. In Variant X, I have followed chronological order. The main problem was in the selection of the quatrains, since not all of them are pure narrative. All stanzas which embody widely known conventions have been left out of Variant X. It is possible that the original maker may have included some of them in his ballad, but such conventional stanzas, which become attached to most *corridos* in some variant or other may well be considered separately. Repetitions have been avoided for the most part, since they are usually the result of variations made by different singers. But such repetition as that found in quatrains 5 and 6 of Variant X seems to be too organic to the narrative to be either accidental or the result of separate development. It is repetition of an incremental sort. Furthermore, in the traditional variants in which they appear, these two quatrains are found together, one after the other.

As the ballad singer gets farther and farther away from the events of which he sings, he loses all interest in dates, and he tends to corrupt place names or to replace them with those of nearby and familiar places. For Variant X, I have chosen those quatrains which preserve original place names, as being more probably in their original form. Verifiable place names like Gonzales, Laredo, and El Encinal are often found. In some variants even Karnes County has survived as *Carnes,* pronounced in two syllables like the Spanish plural of "meat." In one instance I have substituted a place name. One variant of the *corrido* has Cortez leave Gonzales for Brownsville and then to "the ranch." Cortez was never near Brownsville during his flight. According to factual sources, he left Gonzales for Belmont, and from Belmont went to the Schnabel ranch, where Glover and his posse surprised him; so I have substituted Belmont for Brownsville, in the belief that the *corrido* originally said "Belmont."

I believe that I can offer Variant X without too many apologies as a point of departure for the study of other variants, and that it gives a fairly accurate idea of *El Corrido de Gregorio Cortez* before singers began to develop their own variants.

Narrative style

One can get a good idea of the narrative style of the original *Corrido de Gregorio Cortez* from a study of Variant X. Also, one more fully appreciates the traditional excellence of Border *corridos* like that of Cortez by comparing Variant X, the longest and most circumstantial Border variant, with the Mexico City broadside. We are given the opportunity of seeing one and the same ballad theme treated simultaneously, in two distinct manners and according to widely different ballad traditions.

The Border *corrido* was composed for a predominantly rural folk, to whom the theme had immediate interest—an immediacy that was far more than geographical. From its language it is evident that the Border *corrido* was composed by one of the Border folk themselves, a *guitarrero* presumably. The Mexico City broadside was composed for the populace of a large city, to whom the subject had only a passing interest of a sensational nature, for whom Gregorio Cortez was a remote figure, neither idea nor man. It was composed by a broadside balladeer, with some pretensions to learning perhaps, rather than by one of the people for whom it was made.

The Mexico City broadside was composed and sung ostensibly for the collection of funds to be used in Cortez's defense. The Border people made and sang their ballad in response to an inner need, whose sources have been fully discussed in the first part of this book. To his hearers the broadsider offers the kind of attraction that they were used to getting, a sensational crime, because though the broadside treats Cortez as a hero and says that he has "honored his flag," it is evident that the interest is not on Cortez defending his right but on Cortez the poor prisoner in the toils of the law. The ballad which apparently pushed the Cortez broadside out of favor concerns the assassination of President McKinley, but it is called "The Ballad of Leon Gzolgosz." The focus of interest is not on the event but on the criminal. On the other hand, the Border *corrido* is interested in the man and his deeds, and the ballad maker's object is—above all—to tell a good story.

The style of the broadside is pseudoliterary. The *corrido* stanza—already well established by 1901—is abandoned in favor of the literary *redondilla*. The more rigid rhyme scheme—*abba*—imposes an additional burden on the weak talents of the versifier, who has to resort to extremely awkward phrasing and sometimes to completely obscure or irrelevant statements to be able to work in his rhyme. Awkwardness and dullness of style are sometimes as difficult to translate as felicity of phrase, and the reader who knows no Spanish may not appreciate to the full the scantiness of inspiration of the broadside. The author is very careful about his facts, especially in the matter of names and dates, showing that he was working with the written record of the case before him. Even Morris' name is given correctly. The meticulous assembly of facts is used as the basis for commentary of a general nature about Mexican-American relations. The point of view is national, and Cortez is shown as a son of Mexico, who honors his flag by his actions and discomfits the American nation, which suffers a setback in the matter.

The maker of the Border *corrido* makes no effort to be original or literary, and by staying within the ballad traditions of his people he succeeds in composing in a natural and often a forceful style. Using the comparatively free *corrido* stanza, *abcb*, and drawing liberally from previous *corrido* conventions, he makes his task of composing a relatively easy one, and he can concentrate on telling his story. He is not interested in facts per se. Action is more important to him. He mentions only the most important place names and ignores dates altogether. Morris ceases to be Morris and becomes the Major Sheriff, since it is in that function that he is important to the story. The point of view is local rather than national. There is no flag-waving, no generalizations about international relations or nationalities. Cortez is Cortez, a man fighting for his life because he has defended his right. He refers to himself as a Mexican, but the word has no national connotations. Its meaning is cultural; it is a word that describes Cortez and his kind of people, and to him it is almost equivalent to man, just as to most people of Spanish background *cristiano* (Christian) has come to mean "person." The strong distinction between Spaniard and native Mexican so often found in Greater Mexican folklore is not common on the Border. All people of Spanish culture are seen as *mexicanos*.

But perhaps the most significant difference between the Mexico City broadside and Variant X is in the way the narrative elements are developed. All the stylistic defects of the broadside could be overlooked if it only contained a good story—a story at least. The twenty-two quatrains of the broadside, however, are a loose commentary in which bits of narrative are mixed up with invocations, exhortations, huzzas, and moralizing. The broadside begins with the capture of Cortez, where the Border *corrido* ends, showing the ballad maker's main point of interest. Three quatrains are devoted to the minute details of the capture and to the way the news came to Mexico City. The fourth quatrain is a cheer for Mexico and for Cortez.

Two quatrains follow, summarizing some narrative matter. We are told that three "captors" have died, and thus in one line all the action narrated in Variant X is dismissed. In pretty muddled language, the ballad maker manages to convey the idea that innocent people have been killed and that there were so many people guarding the border that it appeared as if an "international conflict" was about to begin. The mention of war makes the author patriotic again, and he devotes the seventh stanza to another huzza.

From the end of the story he then hops back to the beginning, giving two quatrains (8–9) that truly have the appearance of narrative, though the narrative details are particularly unexciting: Cortez's exchange of pistols with a friend and his getting off the buggy and tying it to a tree after going three and one-half miles. This is all the narrative that the broadside apparently can sustain, and with quatrain 10 it turns for the third time to a patriotic aside. Cortez is again said to have honored his flag. He is shown lamenting before God the injustices he has suffered. There is more talk about the American and the Mexican flags. Stanza 12 begins as narrative, a jump back to the capture of Cortez, and for two lines we are told how Cortez was in disguise and how he was betrayed. But the first two lines merely serve as the basis for commentary in the last two. Stanza 13 is also commentary, on the rumor that the Americans were trying to exterminate all Mexicans in Texas.

In quatrains 14 to 17 the ballad maker gets back to narrative of an extremely disconnected sort. Quatrain 14 is probably the best one in the broadside, telling in an economical style about Cortez's arrival at the Robledo house after his flight from Karnes County. Quatrain 15 colorlessly tells of Glover's attack on the

Robledo house and Glover's death. Quatrain 16 jumps all the way back to the time before Morris' death and shows Cortez being accused of horse theft. And in quatrain 17 Cortez calls on God to have pity on him, something very characteristic of the Greater Mexican *corrido* but foreign to the heroes of the Border *corrido*.[6] With quatrains 18 through 21 the broadside maker finally gets down to his point, the soliciting of funds. And with quatrain 22 he brings in the formal close, the *despedida*, and ends his song.

The twenty-eight quatrains of Variant X are easily divided into eight sections, which are actually eight little "scenes," covering twenty-six stanzas, followed by a pair of conventional stanzas in the form of the *despedida* or farewell.[7] The first scene opens with the hero offstage, and he is kept there for four quatrains, one seventh of the total length of the *corrido*. This beginning with the hero offstage, while his name and his actions are discussed, is a familiar as well as an effective device in the theater. When the action opens, Cortez has left the scene of the killing of Morris. "In the county of Karnes, look you what has happened," says the ballad singer, lifting the curtain on a scene in which the Major Sheriff lies dead and Román is badly wounded. People arrive and wonder who killed the Major Sheriff. Finally Cortez is identified, and the word goes out to get him dead or alive.

It is only after these final lines, "Let him be taken, dead or alive, because he has killed several men," that the scene shifts to Cortez, riding along in his flight. He speaks, and in his speech

---

[6] The Border hero may call on God to aid his arms, but he does not call for help to get out of a tight spot. Mariano Reséndez remarks, "I have no hope left but God and my rifle." The Greater Mexican *corrido* hero, Tolentino, driven by enemy soldiers against a lagoon, shouts to the Holy Child, "Get me out of this lagoon!"

[7] Since Variant X is a reconstructed variant, certain things must be noted. The structure of X is that of traditional variants like A and B, except that in X other quatrains have been added to some "scenes." Variant X is compared to the Mexico City broadside because X is the longest and most detailed variant presented in this study—six quatrains longer than the Mexico City broadside—and by broadside standards should be the slowest and the dullest.

there is an answer to the argument of his pursuers, an answer understood by the hearers of the ballad but of which Cortez himself is not aware. The focus rests on Cortez for two stanzas, during which we find out, through his own mouth, why he killed Morris and what his feelings are.

The scene shifts rapidly again, back to the shooting, where the possemen are mounting and setting off in pursuit. The confusion of the first moments and the natural reluctance to be the first on the trail of a desperate man are well described in the stanzas in which the possemen tell each other, "Well, let's get on his trail; we know who he is." They set the bloodhounds loose, but trying to catch Cortez is like following a star.

The scene changes back to Cortez with quatrain 10; and as his pursuers get on his trail he is followed through the different stages of his journey. Stanzas 10 to 13 describe his flight to Gonzales, the "corral" which Glover set up for him, and the death of Glover. The scene ends in quatrain 13 with another picture of Cortez, standing pistol in hand and shouting out his boast to the *rinches*, whom he has defeated and put to flight. Stanzas 14 to 18 describe the flight to Laredo, with the focus shifting from Cortez to his pursuers and returning with them back to Cortez, who is again cornered. Cortez kills another sheriff and again speaks his boast. With stanzas 19 to 21 the story moves toward its resolution. Cortez meets "a Mexican," apparently not Jesús González, who tells him about the killings of innocent people. The Mexican's answer to Cortez's question is not given; it is implied in Cortez's "tell me the news" and in his reaction to the supposed answer he receives, "If people are being killed because of me, then I'm going to give myself up." Not only is there economy of style in this passage but a dramatization of what might have been exposition.

Cortez then asks Jesús González to get the *rinches*. In stanzas 22 and 23 the point of view changes to the possemen, who have been told—offstage—about Cortez's desire to surrender. They hurry to the place where Cortez is waiting for them, eager for the reward, and Cortez comes out to meet them, still defiant. The narrative proper ends with "scene" number eight, which is an exchange between the Major Sheriff who leads the posse and Gregorio Cortez, covering stanzas 24 through 26. The Major Sheriff assures Cortez, in a tearful voice, that the posse wants to arrest him, not to kill him. Cortez, wise to the ways of posses, refuses to hand over his weapons until he is inside a jail cell.

The story ends with Cortez and the Major Sheriff facing each other, Cortez still refusing to give up his arms. The last two quatrains form the *despedida* or formal close, both beginning with *ya*, most closely translated in this context as "now." "Now they have taken Cortez; now matters are at an end." "Now with this I say farewell." In other words, "This is the end of the story." In the days before curtains a player came to the front of the stage and said much the same thing when the play was ended.

The scenic structure of Variant X is typical of the Border heroic *corrido*. The setting in motion of the action in a few swift lines, the introduction of the hero speaking out his boast in the second scene, after his first exploit, thus giving the whole narrative a middle-of-things feeling, the tendency to tell the story not in a long, continuous, and detailed narrative but in a series of shifting scenes and by means of action and dialogue—all these are stylistic devices typical of the Border *corrido*. In ballads about Jacinto Treviño, about Alonso Flores, and even about José Mosqueda, the train robber, a couple of stanzas get the story going and then the hero appears, shouting out his boast or his defiance. From that moment on, the story moves swiftly to its conclusion, with the point of view shifting rapidly from the hero to his adversaries and back again, and from one position in space to another if the action covers a great deal of ground. This is not the style of the proletarian broadside, an extreme example of which is found in the Mexico City ballad about Cortez.

Change and development

The theory that ballads go through a process of reshaping and paring away in the hands of the folk is generally accepted by ballad students. It is through the development of variants that the folk transform a ballad into something different from what they receive from the ballad maker.

Variant X is offered as a close approximation of the original form of *Gregorio Cortez*. In it the principal intention is to narrate. The variant focuses on the exploits of Cortez, beginning with the killing of Morris and ending with Cortez's capture. Though it avoids for the most part comments from the narrator and all unnecessary detail, the *corrido* gives a fairly complete account of the facts, as the facts were then known to the Border people. One might also note the following: the narrative style is swift and compact; it is composed into scenes; there is a liberal amount of dialogue; no names of the American participants are given, the major ones being identified by the same title, the Major Sheriff. With these points in mind, and using Variant X for reference, one may study Variants A through I to see what changes have taken place as different singers have modified the *corrido* in accordance with their own memory of it, as well as with their own tastes and inclinations.

The information that we have about the singers of Variant A is mostly internal. From oral sources (from Valeriano Cortez, who lent me the record on which Variant A appears) we learn that it dates from about 1920, about midway during the period of development of *Gregorio Cortez*, some twenty years after its composition. We know nothing about the age of the singers at the time of recording, or how long they knew the song and where they learned it.

Internal evidence indicates that the "Trovadores Regionales" who recorded Variant A were folksingers, *guitarreros* from the Brownsville-Matamoros area. Their style of singing is not that of the smooth professional. The *regional* indicates that the "Trovadores Regionales" were conscious of their own section of the country. And the appearance of Brownsville as one of the stops in the flight of Cortez suggests that the "regional troubadours" were from the Brownsville-Matamoros region.

Variant A has eight stanzas less than Variant X. In its twenty stanzas it leaves out some of the events recorded in X and introduces changes of its own. Some place names are changed, but of all the variants A comes the closest to conserving the original names. Karnes County has become El Carmen, as in most variants, and Belmont has become Brownsville. But Gonzales, Laredo, and El Encinal, important points along Cortez's route to the Border, are still found in A. Of the nine traditional variants, only A mentions Gonzales, though El Encinal and Laredo appear in others.[8] Variant A makes two other important changes in names. Jesús, the betrayer of Cortez, has become Juan, and he is identified with the first Mexican whom Cortez meets on the way and who gives him information about the innocent people that have been killed. When Cortez identifies himself, instead of speaking haughtily as in other variants, he speaks at a ranch called El Ciprés. The word *altivez*, "pride" or "haughtiness," has been dropped, and *ciprés* is borrowed from the *despedida* to rhyme with *Cortez*.

Variant A maintains interest and force throughout the part which deals with struggle, flight, and pursuit. The first "scene" has a well-balanced four-quatrain structure; the flight is told in a series of rapid quatrains beginning with *decía, venía, decía, venían*. It is in the last part that Variant A shows less taste and imagination than do other variants. Gregorio Cortez meets Juan at the Rancho del Ciprés, asks him the news, and sends him to get the *rinches*. The *rinches* come and Cortez is taken. The stanza in which Cortez gives the reasons for his decision to surrender has been dropped. This weakens the whole narrative, as well as the character of Cortez. The hearer must conclude that Cortez is some sort of bravo who wants to show the law what a rough fellow he is, and who surrenders after having proved his point. Or one may conclude that Cortez, in giving up the fight, wants to keep up a boastful front. The sheriffs arrive and Cortez surrenders, shouting all the while that they are taking him because he wants to be taken. For Variant A has also dropped the last scene showing the *rinches* riding eagerly to the point where Cortez awaits them and then cautiously approaching him, as well as Cortez's last speech, in which he capitulates but keeps his arms until he is safe in a cell. The comment about Cortez's

[8] The reason for the persistence of Encinal and Laredo is that they appear at the ends of lines and are easily rhymed, while Gonzales is not.

poor family has been kept, and together with the lack of the stanzas mentioned, it gives the ending of Variant A the tone of the broadside ballads about bandits and bravos. In sum, one can see that Variant A represents a shortening of the original ballad. One also sees that the stanzas that have been left out of A have not improved it but weakened it instead.

Variant B was recorded late in the summer of 1954, but its source, Nicanor Torres, was already fifty-eight years old in 1920, when Variant A is believed to have been recorded. Torres was about forty when the ballad first appeared. He is a bit hazy about dates and places. He says that he knows the song as it originally came out, back in 1915 or 1912 when Cortez killed the sheriffs. He also places Karnes City in the vicinity of San Benito, about twenty miles from the Rio Grande. In any event Torres was singing the *corrido* before 1920. He has retained a fairly long version, in spite of his years (he was ninety-two in 1954), but there is little doubt that time has made changes in his variant.

B is nineteen quatrains—but one shorter than Variant A. B is not A minus one quatrain, however. In general one can say that while A emphasizes the beginning of the *corrido*, B emphasizes the ending. In B the "county of El Carmen" disappears entirely. No place name is given; the formal opening, instead of being an integral part of the narrative as in most other variants, becomes purely a convention, in the style of the broadside *corrido*. Instead of "In the county of El Carmen/ Look what has taken place!" we have "Listen now, gentlemen,/ A tragedy has taken place." The pointing effect of the *look* is lost; Variant B has the narrator talking to his listeners and obstructing their view of the events by his intrusion. El Carmen is not the only place name that disappears in Variant B. So do El Encinal and Laredo, both original place names, while Gonzales becomes Piedras Negras. Brownsville is not mentioned, but Palo Alto, a few miles from Brownsville, takes its place. Karnes City, as Consiri, appears as another place where Cortez was overtaken and where he killed another sheriff in shooting his way out.

While A takes fifteen of its twenty stanzas to tell of the events from the killing of Morris to Cortez's reaching the Border, B does it in the first ten of its nineteen, including the formal opening. B does a good job of excision, and though some well-known stanzas are left out, the flight-and-pursuit-and-fight pattern is well developed. The scenes are shorter but they are well balanced; the same pattern as in A is followed in this first part, except that about one-third of the quatrains are left out.

It is in the surrender part, from the meeting of Cortez with the Mexican who gives him news to the *despedida*, that Variants A and B differ the most. Variant A does the job in three quatrains. Two quatrains are given to the meeting between Cortez and "Juan," who is both the news-giving Mexican and Jesús, the betrayer. In the third stanza (A-18) the posse arrives and Cortez gives up, all the while saying that they can arrest him the proper way or not at all. Variant B gives eight quatrains to this last scene; it shows not Cortez surrendering meekly while talking big, but Cortez at bay. The meeting with the first Mexican and the reason for Cortez's decision to surrender are fully given. Cortez sends for the posse; the posse's eagerness to get to Cortez and their reticence once they are on the spot are described. They surround the house, and Cortez suddenly appears before them. The same line in Variant A, "Gregorio se presentó," comes to mean something entirely different by the adding of a pronoun, "Cortez se les presentó." The first means "Gregorio surrendered to them," while the second is "Cortez suddenly appeared before them."

Cortez appears before the posse, with his weapons in his hands. The words he speaks then have meaning. He has not surrendered; he is bargaining and still ready to fight if he cannot get his own terms. The "you can take me only the proper way" is apropos here, as can be seen from the exchange that follows between Cortez and the Major Sheriff, who asks him to give up his weapons, stating that the posse is not going to kill him. In other words, the Major Sheriff promises that he will arrest Cortez in "the proper way." But Cortez does not trust the sheriff. He answers in a loud voice that he will not give up his arms until he is safe in a cell. This last picture of Cortez, standing before the posse and refusing to hand over his arms, is reinforced by repetition. Stanzas 17 and 18 tell the same thing in different words. Then Variant B ends with the last half of the *despedida* as it appears in A, leaving out the stanza of commentary beginning, "Now they have taken Cortez." This makes B end abruptly. The hearer already knows that Cortez was taken, but B does not show him the capture. It leaves the hearer with a picture of Cortez with his weapons in his hands, still refusing to surrender. By dropping the quatrain of commentary Variant B makes up for what it does with the formal opening. If it introduces the narrator unduly in the opening stanza, it eliminates him at the close, except for the "Ya con ésta me despido," which is as purely conventional as the phrase "I have ended" or "I have served you," spoken at the end of a song.

In Variant B we already note the tendency, found in some of the shorter variants, to see the hero at bay, defiant to the last. Variant B is still full of detail; we know quite well why Cortez has decided to surrender and why he insists on keeping his weapons. But already in it the typical concept of the hero is beginning to emerge.

B has its defects. If it improves on the ending, it fails with the formal opening. There are other minor blemishes, such as quatrain 6, in which the singer's memory seems to have failed him. Some lines have nine instead of eight syllables. However, it is by means of slips like that of quatrain 6 that new stanzas are developed, combining elements of two or three old quatrains. It just happens that the singer's recasting of this particular quatrain was not a happy one. The presence of nine and sometimes even ten syllables in the usually octosyllabic *corrido* line is not entirely unknown. The singer follows the accent furnished by the melody instead of the syllable count of the verse form. Other singers, perhaps more conscious of form, would abbreviate words or leave them out, relying on implication to convey their full meaning. For example, the line which in B is nine syllables, "hasta no estar en bartolina" is often sung as "hasta estar en bartolina" or "ha' no estar en bartolina." An occasional nine-syllable line among octosyllables, though it does not read well, does not sound out of place in singing.

The dropping of the first part of the *despedida*, with its comment on the taking of Cortez and its effects on his family, was an important step in the development of other variants of *Gregorio Cortez*. In Variant B it may have been done by Torres himself, since he probably knew a longer version many years ago. Perhaps the important thing to establish is not that Torres himself did it but that men of his type would be the ones likely to make the change. Torres, like almost every other singer of repute, is a ballad maker himself, having made some *décimas* as well as some *corridos*. Both the defects and the merits of Variant B show the merits and the defects of Torres as a folk poet. The broadside *corrido* opening of B may be explained by the fact that Torres knows a great many Greater Mexican *corridos* of the broadside type. Blemishes such as quatrain 6 are due to the slight lapses of a memory that is extremely good at ninety-two. As for the way that Variant B ends, it may be that Torres learned the *corrido* in that form, that it was already in the process of change when he first heard it early in the century. Again, he may have consciously made the change many years ago and then forgot about it. Or he may have learned it imperfectly, thus making the change unconsciously. But the important point is that in 1954, though his memory was beginning to grow shaky, and though he faltered a bit in the beginning, Torres gave the last scene in much detail. Evidently the picture of Cortez facing the *rinches* and refusing to surrender his arms appealed to Torres, in 1954 and in previous years as well.

Variants C through I, as will be seen, are all developments of the two tendencies represented by Variants A and B.[9] One tendency is toward the showing of Cortez as surrendering to the *rinches* while saying, "You must arrest me the proper way." The other shows him either still in flight at the end or at bay and defiant.

Variant C is related to A, but its seventeen quatrains have

[9] It is understood, of course, that most of these variants are being sung today; so that all exist at the same time.

peculiarities of their own. C is not, as are A and B, a "Browns-ville" variant. There are no Brownsville-area place names, and what original names are left are much changed. Cortez is shown striking out for Laredo immediately after killing Morris. Besides Laredo, El Encinal has been conserved, as well as the mythical Rancho del Ciprés. The details of the chase are much more blurred than in either A or B, though eleven quatrains are given to this part of the narrative. The ending is much like A, except that more details are given. The *rinches* are shown asking the way to the Rancho del Ciprés, where Cortez is awaiting them. No reason is given for Cortez's surrender, and when the posse arrives, Cortez gives up as in A, saying that he must be arrested in the proper manner. There is no dialogue between Cortez and the Major Sheriff, while the commentary on the taking of Cortez and on the effects on his family is preserved. The *despedida* begins, however, with "Ya mataron a Cortez" (Now they have killed Cortez). This may have been merely forgetfulness; the singer did forget a few lines while singing. Or the killing may be a reference to later events, when Cortez was released from prison and was said to have been poisoned. The most probable explana-tion is that singer Orozco Martínez, not being from the Border, is not familiar with the legend and thinks that the chase ended with Cortez's death rather than with his capture.

There are two details in Variant C that are significantly de-veloped in other variants. Variant A shows Cortez with his pistol in his hand twice, once when Cortez first speaks in the ballad, saying that he killed Morris because of his brother, and another time when he calls the rangers cowards and tells them not to run. Variant C has dropped the quatrain about the brother and moved up the "don't run cowardly rangers" quatrain where the one about Román appears in A. The quatrain showing Cortez with his pistol in his hand, shouting taunts at the fleeing rangers became a favorite, as is seen by its presence in other, later Border *corridos*, such as those of the two Treviños.

Variant C has a double formal opening. Both quatrains 1 and 2 begin with "In the county of El Carmen," quatrain 2 having taken its last line from quatrains like the second in A: "no saben quién lo mató." The result is incremental repetition in the formal opening. Other, shorter variants have taken the second of these quatrains and used it alone as a formal opening, eliminating Román from the narrative.

Variant D though collected in Brownsville is not a "Brownsville" variant. No Brownsville place names are brought in; in fact, all place names are eliminated except El Carmen. D is one of those variants that have replaced the "Look what has happened" opening with the second quatrain of C. Román's name is thus left out, and two stanzas are telescoped into one. Román is mentioned in later quatrains, not by name but merely as Cortez's brother, in the "pistola en la mano" quatrain, which is given twice.

The most interesting thing about D is that the surrender is entirely eliminated. Cortez meets the Mexican who gives him the news in quatrain 5, before the middle of the ballad. He then says that he is not sorry that he killed the Major Sheriff, that he is sorry for his brother. Then the *rinches* are shown after him. He stands, fights, and runs, and is shown killing two other sheriffs. Then the *corrido* ends with the stanza about the Americans being white-faced with fear. As Variant D stands, Cortez seems to have got away, and in this variant he belongs with the heroes who cross the border and escape.

Variant E's eleven quatrains follow the general structure of D. E is a "Brownsville" variant, though it was collected on the Mexican side of the river. Three place names survive: El Carmen as usual, the Rancho del Ciprés, and Los Fresnos, a small town north of Brownsville. After the formal opening, the next two stanzas are pretty weak, weaker than those of most other variants. Then Cortez meets the news-giving Mexican in the fourth quatrain, very much as in D. The pattern that follows is better balanced than in D, with chase, fight, and breakthrough being related very compactly. The fighting proper is over with the eighth quatrain. Then the singer brings in, in the ninth quatrain, the "tying his shoe" convention which Border balladry has borrowed from the Greater Mexican *corrido*, probably from *El Corrido de Demetrio Jaúregui*. Cortez is shown tying his shoe and telling the rangers he still has a lot of ammunition to play with them awhile.

It is the tenth stanza of Variant E, the last one except for the formal ending, that introduces a significant change. The quatrain showing Cortez taunting the rangers and calling them cowards is one of the most popular ones in Border balladry.

Decía Gregorio Cortez	Then said Gregorio Cortez,
con su pistola en la mano:	With his pistol in his hand,
—No corran rinches cobardes	"Don't run, you cowardly rangers,
con un solo mexicano.	From just one Mexican."

Variant E has used this for the next to the last stanza, but with a difference.

Decía Gregorio Cortez	Then said Gregorio Cortez,
con su pistola en la mano:	With his pistol in his hand,
—¡Ah, cuánto rinche cobarde	"Ah, how many cowardly rangers,
para un solo mexicano!	Against one lone Mexican."

From the narrative it seems that Cortez is free and is making it to the border as he did in D. But by implication this quatrain shows him at bay, and there is a note of sadness in his defiance. Emerging from a merely boastful quatrain is the concept of the Border hero hopelessly outnumbered by his enemies. All that would be needed in other variants would be to adapt the new quatrain to the situation in which the Major Sheriff asks Cortez to surrender, and the Cortez ballad would express what Cortez had come to represent for the Border Mexican.

Variant F represents one of the final stages in the development of that end, though it in itself does not include the "so many of them against one of me" quatrain that is found in E. Only nine quatrains in length, F was collected in 1954 from Nacho Montelongo, who stated that he had learned it in 1916, when he was about ten years old. The text of F is closely related to that of B and seems to be a shortening of it. Of F's nine stanzas, eight appear in B. Six also appear in A, but the resemblance to B is stronger. Stanza 4 of F appears neither in A nor B, but it does appear in other variants, such as D (11) and H (4). F may be divided into three parts: quatrains 1–2, 3–5, and 6–9. F's quatrains 1 and 2 are B's 1 and 3. F's 6, 7, 8, and 9 are B's 8, 16, 17, and 19. Quatrains 3 and 5 in F are 14 and 11 in B.

Variant F has condensed into quatrains 1 and 2 the narrative which covers six quatrains in A and four in B. The flight-pursuit-fight part, which covers nine quatrains in A and six in B, is condensed into three quatrains (3–5). The decision to surrender, the sending for the posse, and the surrender itself are all left out. Immediately after his "jumping the corral" Cortez is seen again at bay, and the Major Sheriff speaks, telling Cortez to hand over his weapons. Cortez answers, as in Variant B, that he will not give them up until he is safe in a cell, and the *corrido* ends abruptly with the *despedida*. The tendency begun in Variant B, which dropped the last stanza of comment and focused on Cortez still defiant in defeat, has been developed in Variant F as far as could be done without the addition of new elements. The addition of a different element, taken over from variants such as E, does occur in Variant G.

Variant G, eight quatrains in length or one less than F, was collected in 1941, thirteen years before Variant F, but it has all signs of being a later version. It appears to be a recasting of F or of a variant very much like it. Like F, G is divided into three main parts: quatrains 1–2, 3–5, and 6–8, with quatrain 8 being the *despedida* or formal close. Five of G's eight stanzas correspond to five of F's, and they are found in the same order. The last four quatrains of each variant correspond to each other, and the first quatrain in both is very much the same.

In the use of place names Variants F and G are also similar. F begins quatrains 1 and 6 with "In the county of El Carmen," giving the same place for the killing of the Major Sheriff and for the later encirclement of Cortez. G begins quatrain 1 with "In the county of El Carmen" and quatrain 5, which corresponds to F's 6, with "In the county of Kiancer." Like *El Carmen, Kiancer* is one of the corruptions of *Karnes*. No other place names are used except the Rancho del Ciprés, used in F in a quatrain which does not appear in G.

It is in its beginning and in the next-to-last quatrain that G makes changes not found in F, changes which bring in material found in other variants and which result in one of the best variants of the Cortez *corrido* that one can find. G's first quatrain, like F's, tells that the Major Sheriff has been killed in the county of El Carmen, but G's quatrain is much like that found in Variant D. It compresses the killing and the search all into four lines, leaving out the wounding of Román. G continues the story of the search for the killer of Morris for four more lines, ending with the naming of Cortez. Then its third quatrain shifts suddenly to action with the words "Soltaron los perros jaunes/ pa' que siguieran la juella." There is an unexpected widening of horizon, a sudden jumping into life after the slow second quatrain. The remaining five stanzas follow those found in F pretty closely. Missing are F's 2, in which Cortez justifies his killing of Morris, and 4, in which the Americans are shown scared to death of Cortez and his pistol. The pattern of flight-pursuit-encirclement-fight is covered in three swift quatrains. Cortez is encircled, jumps the corral, and is encircled again, when the Major Sheriff speaks to him, offering him his life. The Cortez of G, however, does not answer as does the Cortez of F, saying that he will hand over his weapons when he is safe in a cell. Instead we have a modification of the quatrain found in Variant E.

Decía Gregorio Cortez	Then said Gregorio Cortez
con su pistola en la mano:	With his pistol in his hand,
—¡Ah, cuánto rinche montado	"Ah, how many mounted rangers
para un solo mexicano!	Against one lone Mexican!"

The word "cowardly" is changed into "mounted," removing the last element of boastfulness from the *corrido*, and thus the tragic tone of the variant is affirmed. The narrative has been cut to the bone; just enough has been left to lead as swiftly as possible to the main point, the picture of the hero going down, but going down defiant, before great odds. All the preceding lines lead toward this scene, which illuminates the hero for a brief moment, and shows him as the projection of the ballad people who created him. Román has disappeared, and with him all the background concerning the killing of the Major Sheriff.

The details of the chase, the route with its place names and its skirmishes between Cortez and his pursuers have been condensed into twelve lines. The boastful elements—the cowardly rangers, the white-faced pursuers who run when they see Cortez—are also gone. Everything that is left is told in a plain sober style, and leads directly toward the short dialogue between the Major Sheriff and Cortez, which was to the hearers of the ballad symbolic of themselves.

The emergence of variants like G shows a shift of interest from the story of Gregorio Cortez, which had become familiar, to the drama in Cortez's situation, a situation which the Border Mexican identified with his own. From a ballad-story hero, Cortez became a symbol of the Borderer himself, the prototype of the hero of border conflict, not only on a physical but on a cultural plane. The physical elements of border conflict are preserved, but the pattern of violence, pursuit, temporary encirclement, swift pursuit, and final encirclement is developed in a rapid, economical style. This series of quick narrative strokes leads inevitably to the final situation. The action stops, and the Major Sheriff speaks, promising Cortez his life. Cortez answers bitterly, showing his realization of defeat, but with his pistol still in his hand. Since the final stanza is a mere convention, the ballad really ends with Cortez's short, two-line speech, expressing the Border Mexican's realization that he too is outnumbered and that he must lose his struggle to keep his own way of life.

Variants like G carry the process of ballad transformation about as far as it can go in their particular direction. Variants H and I are developments in other directions. Variant H, like Variant G, is eight stanzas in length, but it lacks the compactness and dramatic qualities of G. In it one notices a slackening of the *corrido* quatrain form. Quatrain 2 is much like a *redondilla,* while quatrain 1 rhymes *abbc*. This variant seems to be one in transition. Quatrain 2, for example, is made up of the first half of A5 (B3) and the last two lines of A15 (B7). Karnes appears as Kansas, and another place name is added, Isbel. Since this is a "Brownsville" variant, perhaps Point Isabel is the original of "El ranchito de Isbel." Variant H is a further development, though not a very happy one, of the tendency found in Variant A, in which the surrender of Cortez rather than his defiance is emphasized.

Variant I is another example of the development of *El Corrido de Gregorio Cortez* in a direction other than the heroic-dramatic form that is exemplified by Variant G. Variant I also arises from the longer variants which have narration as their main purpose. It is the shortest variant that I have collected, being only six quatrains long. One of the most interesting things about Variant I is that it has dropped both the formal opening and the *despedida*, something that is very rare in the *corrido*. Few *corridos* do this and remain complete entities, but in Variant I we have a *corrido* that has dropped both these formal devices and yet remains a unit. Even Variant H, one might note, in which the stanzaic form itself has declined, has kept both formal opening and close, and all other variants that I am familiar with include these two conventions.

The amount of dialogue is greater in Variant I than in other variants, there being direct discourse in five of its six quatrains. Variant G, which emphasizes action leading up to one dramatic scene at the last, has dialogue in only two of its eight quatrains, the last two before the formal close. Variants A and B have a good proportion of dialogue, never showing conversations by means of indirect discourse, as is often the case in the Greater Mexican *corrido*. In A there are twenty-two lines of dialogue out of eighty, and in B thirty-three out of seventy-six. This is a high proportion of dialogue; many medieval ballads have less. In Variant I, however, almost one-half of the *corrido*, eleven out of twenty-four lines, is dialogue.

Another *corrido* convention that is almost abandoned in Variant I is the use of the introductory phrase before direct discourse, in the form of *decía*. The *decía* phrase is not in itself objectionable. It functions as a sort of stage direction, and to some hearers at least it adds a sort of bare tenseness to the tone of the narrative. In Variant G, we find the *decía* convention in both of the two speeches made. In A, eight of the ten speeches are in-

Gregorio Cortez, A *Study*

troduced by *decía*, and in B nine of the fourteen. In Variant I the *decía* phrase is found in two out of five speeches. The three lines thus economized are used for straight narration, enhancing the effectiveness of the variant's few lines. Thus, out of the thirteen lines that are not dialogue, ten are used for narrative. If the *decía* convention had been strictly adhered to, nine of the thirteen lines would have been used to introduce the speaker and only four would have been narrative. The substitution of narrative for the introductory phrase, which in some cases is done simply by removing the *decía* and replacing it with another verb, is most impressive in the opening stanza, the familiar one showing Cortez with his pistol in his hand. The substitution of *ir* (to go) for *decir* (to say) gives an entirely different feeling to the quatrain and changes the kind of picture given the hearer as the ballad opens.

Iba Gregorio Cortez   Gregorio Cortez was riding
con su pistola en la mano: With his pistol in his hand,
—No siento haberlos matado,   "I don't regret having killed them;
lo que siento es a mi hermano.   I regret my brother's death."

One cannot help feeling that the old heroic *romance* tradition submerged in the native *corrido*, has here reasserted itself. One of the ballads about the Cid immediately comes to mind.

Cabalga Diego Laínez   Diego Laínez rides
al buen rey besar la mano . . . To kiss the good king's hand . . .

Variant I again uses *ir*, this time instead of *venir*, at the beginning of the third quatrain. This use of *to go* instead of *to come*, as in the more vividly narrative or dramatic variants, gives Variant I a sense of remoteness that complements the bareness of detail. Not only has the chase disappeared, but even the county of El Carmen and the Major Sheriff are gone. Cortez is seen going, or riding along with his pistol in his hand. He speaks, saying he has killed someone and that he is grieving for his brother. He leaves for Piedras Negras, the only place name given, daring the rangers to follow him. Posses are said to be on

201

his trail, though the ballad does not make it appear that they have caught sight of him or that pursuer and pursued have made any sort of contact. Then Cortez is shown giving himself up.

There is an enigmatical, suggestive air about Variant I. It does not tell us who or where Cortez is, and it merely suggests why he is a fugitive. The killing of the sheriff, the bloodhounds, the challenges, and the fights have all disappeared. Pursuit is mentioned, but it has a remote quality, as if it were happening off stage. There is no true beginning and no true end, so that the variant has an unreal tableau-like quality. It approaches the style of such British ballads as *The Three Ravens* and *The Twa Corbies*, which imply rather than tell a story. Of all the variants of *Gregorio Cortez*, it is Variant I that most closely resembles British ballads of the kind that Professor Child liked best, and which he considered could be found only on the lips of the very old, after having passed through many generations of singers. In the case of Variant I, both the singer, Luis Flores, and the ballad are about half a century old. And instead of rocking the cradle, the hand of Luis Flores swings the lasso and strums the guitar.

These variants show how *El Corrido de Gregorio Cortez*, a typical Border *corrido*, developed as it traveled from singer to singer, sometimes changing for the better and sometimes for the worse. At least three types of ballads have resulted from the variations of the original *corrido*. In Variants A and B we have the ballad of the narrative type, in which heroic action is described by means of scenic, graphic narrative. The scope is episodic in that it covers a fairly short period of the hero's life, no intention existing of telling what went before and after the action described. As in the best ballads of the medieval period in Europe, these variants eschew lengthy details and commentary, giving only narrative and dialogue. A second type of ballad is found in Variant G. Here the narrative, already episodic, has been narrowed down to a point. It is made to converge on a brief moment, moving swiftly forward to a revealing and dramatic scene, an illuminated moment in which the hero is seen as symbolic of the folk themselves. Variant I has developed in still a different direction. It is a suggestive ballad with a high proportion of dialogue, without beginning or end, seen remotely and almost mysteriously, reminding one (in an often-used figure) of those scenes that one looks into through a lighted window from a passing vehicle. In these variants of *El Corrido de Gregorio Cortez*, one has a contemporary example of the process through which ballads go in developing from comparatively long and detailed originals into shorter works which are sometimes true works of art, and which continue to live after the events that gave them birth are forgotten or have been turned into legend.

It would appear that the original Border *corrido* was composed soon after Cortez's capture on June 22, 1901, about a month or six weeks before the composition of the Mexico City broadside. No variant that I have ever heard mentions anything beyond the capture of Cortez. The longer ones make it obvious that the end of the story is reached with Cortez's capture.

Ya agarraron a Cortez,	Now they have taken Cortez,
ya terminó la cuestión . . .	Now matters are at an end . . .

It is not probable that the Border ballad maker would have stopped with Cortez's capture if he could have added details about his imprisonment, about the Gonzales trial, and about attempts to lynch Cortez on August 11 of the same year. The legend has incorporated all this, and has followed Cortez up to the time of his death. The *corrido* maker would more than likely have done the same, if he had had the material at hand. The Border *Gregorio Cortez* shows all evidence of having been struck off immediately, while the excitement of the chase was still stirring the Border.

No sabemos la verdad,	We do not know the truth,
según lo que aquí se dice . . .	According to what's said here.

This gives the impression of narration which is taking place before fast-breaking events have had time to take shape and order. Even the newspapers in San Antonio, who had trained men working for them, published confused reports during Cortez's flight and did not straighten out most of the facts until several days after his capture. The Border ranchero, getting his news by word of mouth, must have heard conflicting reports, so that two men on meeting and exchanging the latest reports about Cortez would be likely to say, "I don't know if it's true, but this is what people are saying." It was under those conditions that the *corrido* maker must have composed *Gregorio Cortez*.

Though the ballad has been in continuous favor with Border singers for more than fifty years, there have been periods when it was more widely sung than at other times. The first such period must have occurred between 1901 and 1905, between the capture of Cortez and his final commitment to the penitentiary. This was the period of "high feeling." Tradition has it that men could get arrested or beaten, or lose their jobs if they sang *El Corrido de Gregorio Cortez*. There may have been some basis of fact to this. The Anglo-American farmer, watching his Mexican laborers at work in the fields, could very well have felt that they were contemplating sedition or murder if they suddenly burst out singing about Cortez. And it would irk the farmer to think that part of the money he was to pay his help might end up in the fund for Cortez's defense. The mocking verses about the white-faced Americans, scared to death of Cortez and his pistol, certainly would not seem amusing to most Anglo-Americans of the time. Also, the very fact that the ballad was taboo on the north bank of the Rio Grande would make it even more widely sung there. The court battles had their influence too. Though the Border *corrido* makes no mention of a petition for funds, it was probably a much better fund raiser than the Mexico City broadside, with its outright appeal for money.

After Cortez went to prison for the murder of Glover, *El Corrido de Gregorio Cortez* ceased to be a burning issue. It was probably sung less persistently and less often, though the area in which it was sung continued to extend itself. The *corrido* appears to have been widely sung only on the Border during its first period. Cortez's son, Valeriano, who certainly would remember hearing the ballad about his father and to whom people would be likely to sing it if they knew it, says that he never heard *El*

Corrido de Gregorio Cortez until about the time of World War I. Valeriano Cortez has lived all of his life in the vicinity of Austin and Houston. His statement would make one think that *Gregorio Cortez* moved north of the Border country at a very slow pace. Its movement south, aided by the itinerant laborers from central Mexico, must have been more rapid.

The imprisonment of Cortez took the *corrido* from the topical class and placed it in the category of old ballads about past events. It was probably during Cortez's nine years in prison that the *corrido* went through its first development. In 1913, when the Mexican Revolution called forth heroic themes, and when friction along the Lower Border was building up toward the Pizaña uprising of 1915, Cortez was released from prison. His release made the *corrido* a thing of the moment again. At least until 1920, when the Border again quieted down, *El Corrido de Gregorio Cortez* enjoyed a second birth. The 1913–1920 period was an important one in its development. For, although the release of Cortez and the growing border conflict again made the ballad of immediate interest, enough time had passed since the events treated in the *corrido* so that the details became less important than they had been originally, while Gregorio Cortez continued to develop as a symbol, as a personification of the spirit of border strife.

From the 1920's on, the development of *El Corrido de Gregorio Cortez* is a gradually descending one. It was in the 1920's that I remember hearing and learning my first *corridos,* and among the Border heroes of that time the name of Cortez led all the rest. It was about this time, as far as can be ascertained, that the Vocalion recording (Variant A) was made. The beginning of World War II found *Gregorio Cortez* still being sung. In 1941, when I first became interested in ballad study, I found the Cortez *corrido* still a favorite among the *guitarreros.* During World War II and immediately thereafter, another recorded version of the *corrido* was played a great deal in the *cantinas* on both sides of the river. The feelings excited by the war, and the fact that Border Mexicans were again under arms (this time as comrades-in-arms of their old adversaries) gave *El Corrido de Gregorio*

Cortez one last period of vigor before it and the tradition it represents gave way to a new music and a new age.

Versification, rhythm, and structure

In its simplicity of versification, a simplicity that lends itself to strength of expression, *El Corrido de Gregorio Cortez* resembles the *romance*. Like almost all Border *corridos, Gregorio Cortez* has no refrain. There is no repetition to form stanzas of five, six or eight lines. The melody has four members only, corresponding to the four lines of the quatrain. It is repeated, with the usual variations common to folksingers, for each succeeding stanza.

The quatrain is divided into two parts of two lines each, with a very definite pause after the second line, making what is actually a sixteen-syllable line.

Soltaron los perros jaunes / pa' que siguieran la juella,
pero alcanzar a Cortez / era seguir a una estrella.

The half stop at the end of the second line is never violated, and every quatrain ends with a full stop. Each individual line is also end-stopped, there being no run-on lines. Thus the ballad is made up of individually independent quatrains, each made up of two parts of two lines each, which in turn are made up of two equal parts. This balanced structure is carried into the grouping of the quatrains. In Variant A the first four quatrains form a unit, the first "scene" in the narrative. These four quatrains are divided into two subunits of two quatrains each, covering two separate actions, the discovery of the dead sheriff and the discovery of the killer. The next scene introduces Cortez and is made up of two quatrains, both beginning with *decía*, which are an example not only of incremental repetition but of balanced structure as well. The next four quatrains begin respectively with the words *venían, tiró; venían, decía* (they were coming; he struck out; they were coming; he said). Again we have a balanced arrangement of four units which fall into two parts, each part of which effects a rhythmic change in point of view, from pursuers to pursued and back again. One finds the same thing in the *despedida* or formal close. It is made of two quatrains, each beginning with the word *ya* (now). "Now they have taken Cortez. . . . Now with this I say farewell." This high development of structural rhythm must owe something to the balanced structure of the *romance* line.

El Corrido de Gregorio Cortez, like most *corridos,* uses the *abcb* rhyme pattern. Of the twenty-eight stanzas of Variant X only three use assonance instead of rhyme. (The coupling of *jaunes* with *planes* may be considered imperfect rhyme.) Two of these are pairings of *dice* with *cherife,* a foreign word. The other is *rodear* with *corral.* There is a high proportion of *agudos* or masculine endings, which appear for the most part on the rhyming lines. Variant X has twelve out of twenty-eight quatrains with masculine rhymes; A has nine out of twenty, and B eleven out of nineteen. Of a total of 112 lines in Variant X, forty-two or more than one-third have masculine endings. The predominance of *agudo* endings both in the rhyming lines and elsewhere, with their abrupt effect, which the singers emphasize by shouting out the short, explosive last syllable, is one of the things that gives *Gregorio Cortez* the vigor it possesses. Among the shorter variants one might consider G, which has developed the concept of Cortez as the defiant hero, and I, which has gone in another direction. Of G's thirty-two lines sixteen are *agudos.* The first two stanzas, moreover, which not only give the opening scene but set the tone of the whole ballad, have *agudos* on six of their eight endings. A balanced pattern is followed in these two quatrains, each having its first line feminine and the other three masculine. Variant I, on the other hand, has only seven of its twenty-eight lines with stressed final syllables, and they are scattered about in no particular arrangement.

Balanced structure is not carried into the line, as it is in the *romance.* Many traditional *romances* have a trochaic rhythmic pattern, dividing the line, by means of a caesura after the fourth syllable, into four and four syllables. The most common line division in *Gregorio Cortez* is that of five and three or three and five. Sometimes it is two and six: "Miren/ lo que ha sucedido."

207

When sung, however, the rhythm of the tune imposes itself upon that of the text. The lines of each quatrain then take the following division: two-six, two-six, two-six, and four-four, the last line reverting to the ideal *romance* rhythm. The tune-imposed accent remains constant, falling on the second, fourth, and seventh syllables, except that in the last line the accent on the fourth is stronger, because the double beat occurs on the fourth syllable instead of on the second, as in the first three lines.

> En el/ condado del Carmen
> Miren/ lo que ha sucedido,
> Murió el/ Cherife Mayor
> Quedando Ro/ mán herido.

In Spanish song, which usually "springs" the natural rhythm of speech with the rhythm of the tune, it seems important to consider both the rhythm imposed by the tune and that of the spoken or chanted word, since the *corrido* is sung and not recited. The quatrain just quoted could be scanned thus as poetry.

```
                 —u/u—/uu—/u
                 —u/u—/uu—/u
                 u—/u—/uu—/
                 u—/uu—/u—/u
```

The tune, however, would scan thus.

```
              u—‖ u—/uu—/u
              u—‖ u—/uu—/u
              u—‖ u—/uu—/u
              u—/u—‖ uu—/u
```

The extreme regularity of the latter is evident. The change in caesura in the last line gives relief to what would become an exaggerated emphasis otherwise. Variety is also obtained by the superimposition of the freer rhythm of verse accent. The counterpoint of verse against tune is common enough in Spanish song. In *Gregorio Cortez* the effect of syncopation is especially strong. It heightens the abruptness of the masculine endings. Both tunes used in the singing of *Gregorio Cortez*, the present tune and the "old tune" that has almost disappeared, have the same accent pattern, though their melodies are somewhat different.

Gregorio Cortez, A *Study*

Both tunes are in major keys and have a very short range. If one disregards the opening note, the current tune of *Gregorio Cortez* has a range of only six semitones. Even considering the first note, the range is still less than an octave by two semitones. The short range allows the *corrido* to be sung at the top of the singer's voice, an essential part of the *corrido* style. Though the whole melody can be and sometimes is accompanied with the two basic chords on the guitar (the major chord formed on the tonic and the dominant seventh), it is customary to end the second line of the quatrain with the major chord formed on the subdominant, the *tercera* in the language of the *guitarreros*. Together with the high-register singing and the counterpointing of rhythms, this adds a great deal of vigor, almost defiant vigor, to the delivery of the *corrido* when it is sung by a good singer.

The formal opening and the formal close or *despedida* (farewell) are characteristic of the *corrido* form. Very often, however, one finds *corridos*—or late variants of earlier ones—without a formal opening. It is sometimes the first thing to go when the folk set to work on a *corrido* to cut it down to their own size and shape. Because it is so closely woven into the narrative itself, the formal opening of *Gregorio Cortez* has shown great capacity for survival. Only Variant I of those presented in this study has dropped the opening, and it has also dropped the *despedida*, something that is even rarer. Variant I is a good ballad, but it is almost outside the *corrido* classification.

The reason for the vitality of the formal opening in *Gregorio Cortez* is that it not only sets the scene for the narrative but sets the tone as well.

En el condado del Carmen,	In the county of El Carmen,
miren lo que ha sucedido;	Look what has happened;
murió el Cherife Mayor,	The Major Sheriff died,
quedando Román herido.	Leaving Román badly wounded.

The story is already moving; the first act has already taken place by the time one finishes the first quatrain. Even the "miren lo que ha sucedido," which is reminiscent of the "I will now sing" convention, is given a different emphasis. One gets the feeling

that the speaker is not the narrator talking to his audience, but
the spectator viewing the bloody result of the meeting between
the Cortezes and Morris. The line has a pointing effect that
makes an actor of the narrator. It is the same sort of effect obtained in the *romance* about the Cid and the Moorish king.

¡Hélo, hélo por do viene,	See him! See him where he comes,
el moro por la calzada!	The Moor coming down the road!
caballero a la jineta	Mounted in the Arab style
encima una yegua baya . . .	On a bay mare . . .

The formal opening in *Gregorio Cortez* has survived because
it is not a formal opening in the conventional sense. It has resisted the tendency to drop the opening stanza and to begin the
ballad in the middle of things because it already begins in the
middle of the story. Even the place name has survived in almost
all variants. The original opening must have said *Carnes,* pronounced in two syllables. I have heard singers begin the *corrido*
thus, but not in recent years. *El Carmen* has taken the place of
Carnes, though *Kansas* and its derivatives, *Kiansis* and *Kiancer,*
are sometimes found. Evidently singers found "the county of
Meats" a little odd, and substituted familiar names that sounded
something like it.

The formal close is much more set as a form and is more rigidly
observed than is the formal opening. It is recognized by the folk
as a thing in itself and is given a name, *despedida*. The first and
third lines of the *despedida* are a set convention, varying only
on rare occasions, and then according to conventions of their
own. The second and fourth lines are variable, the fourth carrying the name of the *corrido* or saying something about its subject, and the second varying in originality according to the imagination of the ballad maker and the exigencies of the rhyme.

Ya con ésta me despido	Now with this I say farewell
con la flor de la ortiguilla;	With the flower of the nettle;
aquí se acaba el corrido	This is the end of the ballad
de Margarito García.	Of Margarito García.
Ya con ésta me despido	Now with this I say farewell
a la sombra de un ciprés	In the shade of a cypress tree;

aquí se acaba el corrido	This is the end of the ballad
de don Gregorio Cortez.	Of Don Gregorio Cortez.

Some variations may be introduced in the third line, but the "farewell" of the first line is almost invariable.

The *despedida* has an important structural function; it is a formal device for achieving a sense of unity and completeness in a shortened or fragmentary variant. Few *corridos* drop the *despedida* and remain complete entities. In comparing variants of the same *corrido*, one sometimes finds shortened versions that have lost perhaps fifteen or twenty stanzas in their transformation from long ballads into short dramatic ones. But they still conserve the *despedida*.

In *Gregorio Cortez* the convention is observed in its most rigid form in almost all the variants. All except Variant I have the *despedida*. All the remaining variants use the shade, or the leaves of the cypress as the subject for the rhyming line, and all of those, except H, begin with the line "Now with this I say farewell" and end with some form of "This is the ballad about Gregorio Cortez." The *despedida* may be said to be one of the most important identifying marks of the *corrido*. In *Gregorio Cortez*, which is an example of the Border *corrido* tradition at its best, the *despedida* is preserved in its strictest form.

The use of the imperfect and of syllable-supplying devices

One of the *corrido* conventions that descends directly from the *romance* is the use of syllable-supplying devices, ways of adding an extra syllable to a line in order to make it a standard octosyllable. The *romance* makers frequently used the imperfect tense of the verb as a syllable-supplier, since the imperfect in Spanish usually has one more syllable than its corresponding preterite form. The device, like many inventions, must have been born out of necessity. But like many innovations, it later became a convention, one which gave a particular kind of feeling to the action, a feeling of immediacy and rapid movement.

In the *corrido* the use of the imperfect has lost almost completely its syllable-supplying function and has become entirely a device to heighten the action. It is applied most often to the verb *decir* (to say). The form *dijo* is almost nonexistent in the *corrido*. It is always *decía*, "he *or* she was saying." So well established is the convention that *decía* is used even when the extra syllable it supplies makes a total of nine, while *dijo* would give the required eight. *Decía* is then pronounced as two syllables, the second diphthongized: *deciá*.

Deciá Gregorio Cortez . . .	Then said Gregorio Cortez . . .
Deciá el Cherife Mayor . . .	Then the Major Sheriff said . . .

The same is true with other verbs. Sometimes the same verb form, counted first as two and then as three syllables, will appear in successive lines. This happens more than once in *Gregorio Cortez*, especially with the verb *venir*.

Venián los americanos,	The Americans were coming;
venían que se mataban . . .	They were coming at breakneck speed . . .

The use of the imperfect has a great deal to do with the *corrido*'s vivid narration. In *Gregorio Cortez* the effect of flight and pursuit which runs through the earlier part is enhanced by the alternate use of the verbs *decir* and *venir*, both in the imperfect: "Venían todos los rinches; decía Gregorio Cortez." (All the rangers were coming; Gregorio Cortez was saying.) The use of *venir* instead of *ir*, making the movement of the possemen be seen from the point of view of Cortez, also helps in making the action vivid, but the alternation of the two verbs in the imperfect tense imparts a sense of motion, a sense of being not in the past, looking back at something that has happened, but in a fluid present in which both singer, hearers, and events are all identified with each other.

Though the substitution of the imperfect for the preterite is found in the *corrido* mostly with *decir*, it sometimes occurs in verbs of action which in some variants take the preterite. A variant of *Gregorio Cortez* preserved in manuscript by Leonor Cortez, the wife of the ballad hero, uses the imperfect of *ir* where other variants use the preterite.

Iba con rumbo a Laredo . . .	Se fué con rumbo a Laredo
Iba con rumbo a Gonzales . . .	Se fué con rumbo a Gonzales

Most uses of the imperfect aside from *decir* are with other verbs that introduce a speech, such as *contestar, llorar,* and *gritar* (to answer, to cry, and to shout).

The present (after the imperfect) is preferred over the preterite in verbs denoting speech, as seen in the lines in which Cortez asks news of a Mexican he meets.

Ya se encontró a un mexicano,	Now he has met a Mexican;
le dice con altivez . . .	He says to him haughtily . . .

Le dijo could have been used as well, as far as meter is concerned; so in cases like this the matter of adding syllables does not enter at all. The preterite of verbs introducing speech is so little used that when it does appear it seems stiff and awkward to one already used to the *corrido* conventions. Often the use of the preterite, especially with *decir*, is a sign that the *corrido* in question has very weak ties with tradition.

The *corrido* has taken from the *romance* the use of the imperfect for the preterite, but the imperfect has lost most of its function as a supplier of extra syllables. The *corrido*, however, has also inherited from the *romance* the tendency to use syllable-supplying devices of other sorts. The number of the devices that may be used is unlimited, but there are some that are so frequent as to be conventional. Among these are *ese, ya,* and *y. Ese* (that) is used in *Gregorio Cortez* either in place of *el* (the) or with *de* (of) to supply one extra syllable.

"De ese Gregorio Cortez" for "De Gregorio Cortez"

"Esos rinches del condado" for "Los rinches del condado"

As with the imperfect in the *romance, ese* must have become general in the *corrido* only as a space filler at first. But the many shades of meaning of the word *that* soon made the convention more significant. One needs only to consider such expressions as "Oh, that" and "That man" in English, which change their meaning depending on context or tone of voice. *Ese,* depending on context, can express feeling from the admiring, as it does in the first example above, to the contemptuous, as in the second. The first can be translated as "That famous man known as Gregorio Cortez"; the second (with a curl of the lip) as *"Those* rangers of the county."

The use of *ya,* especially at the beginning of the line, is one of the most common devices found in *Gregorio Cortez.* It not only serves to supply an eighth syllable to a seven-syllable line, but it gives the same feeling of being in the middle of events that is often attained in the *romance* by the use of the imperfect. *Ya,* with a meaning somewhere between *now* and *already,* gives the hearer the impression that he is witnessing events taking place so fast that he cannot get them all as they happen.

Ya insortaron a Cortez	Now they have outlawed Cortez
Ya se encontró a un mexicano	Now he has met a Mexican
Ya agarraron a Cortez	Now they have taken Cortez
Ya se acabó la cuestión	Now the matter has ended

This use of *ya* again goes back to the *romance.*

Ya se asienta el Rey Ramiro,	And now King Ramiro sits down,
ya se asienta a sus yantares . . .	Now he sits down to his food.
Ya se salía el rey moro	Now the Moorish king was going
de Granada para Almería . . .	From Granada to Almeria.

Some singers take the *ya* as nothing but a syllable-supplying device, often substituting other fillers, such as *muy* (very) and *y* (and). "Ya se encontró a un mexicano" may become "Y se encontró a un mexicano" or even "Se encontró y a un mexicano." "Ya pronto lo vas a ver" is changed to "Muy pronto lo vas a ver." The use of *muy* as a filler is also found in "Con su alma muy encendida" (With his soul very much aflame).

In the examples above, *y* functions as a syllable-supplying device. This is the case when it is placed between two vowels, to act as a consonant and break the elision of the vowels, making two syllables out of one; or when it begins a line before a consonant and, acting as a vowel, supplies an extra syllable in that fashion. There is a very decided tendency among *corrido* singers, however, to begin lines with a *y* before a vowel. *Y* then functions as a consonant, adding nothing to the syllable count and apparently having no real significance in the line. Nothing of the sense is lost by leaving out these *y*'s. In certain contexts the *y* may change the tone, as does *and* in such expressions as "And what makes you think so?" But the use of what seems a superfluous *y* in the *corrido* line rarely involves this kind of change in tone.

Y en el condado del Carmen	(And) In the county of El Carmen
Y esos rinches del condado	(And) Those rangers of the county
Y iba Gregorio Cortez	(And) Gregorio Cortez was riding
Y otro día por la mañana	(And) The next day in the morning
Y oigan ustedes, señores	(And) Listen now, gentlemen

The examples given above (one could add many more) all are the opening lines of their respective quatrains. Disregarding the consonantal *y*, they all begin with a vowel. The opening line of the quatrain is not the only place where singers insert a consonantal *y*, but they usually put one there if the opening line begins with a vowel. They also repeat the *y* periodically in lines beginning with vowels, though there is no regular pattern. Personally, I have noted that in singing one adds the *y* in these places without being conscious of doing so.

The presence of this apparently superfluous *y* at the beginning of certain lines may be explained. If one produces and holds a very tense consonantal *y*, such as that in a very emphatic *yes*, the lips and throat will be in very much the same position assumed by the *corrido* singer in order to produce the clear, high-pitched, and vibrating tone of voice in which the *corrido* is normally sung. Spanish vowels are relatively open except for the *i*. The *corrido* singer, on beginning a tune with an *a, e, o,* or *u,* instinctively prepares his lips and throat for the tense, high delivery of the *corrido,* and the first sound that comes out of his mouth is a consonantal *y.* From observation of myself and other singers, I have noticed that the *y* sound appears less often when one sings softly or in a key lower than the extremely high one normally used for the *corrido.*

The initial *y* in such cases bears little if any relationship to the conjunction *and.* It is much more closely related to the high, protracted *ay!* with which the sung *décima* is begun. The *y* not only serves to get the vocal apparatus into the right position for song; it also helps get the singer in the proper mood of tense absorption in the ballad, especially when it is a heroic *corrido.* So the initial *y* does have meaning, but it is of the kind that cannot be put down on the printed page. It helps the singer put himself in the right mood and the right physical attitude to sing the *corrido* as it should be sung: high and loud and tense and clear, with a great deal of seriousness complemented by the tenseness of the voice, since it tells in a serious and emphatic way a serious and dramatic story to an audience which is interested in the drama of the tale rather than in lyric beauty.

Corrido imagery in *Gregorio Cortez*

The Border *corrido* is not given to detailed description or to a great deal of embroidery in language. Its main object is narrative, and it keeps adjectives and figures of speech to a bare minimum, being in this respect very much like its parent, the *romance.* But the *corrido* is not entirely bare of imagery. In *Gregorio Cortez* one finds a handful of instances in which the ballad maker has used figurative language. The imagery used in these instances may be divided into two kinds: that which though conventional has its basis in the actual life of the Border and that which is purely conventional and unsupported—in fact, often contradicted—by observation of things that the Borderer knows.

Olrik, in his book on Danish balladry, says that imagery in the

Danish ballad leans toward agricultural interests, since the people who sang the ballads were mostly farmers. Arrows fly "as thick as hay," and the Swedes are overthrown "as a farmer reaps his corn."[10] The Border *corrido* also uses familiar things in its few figures of speech, but the figures are drawn from the life of the vaquero rather than from that of the farmer. Horseracing and cockfighting were the Border ranchero's principal entertainments, and both appear in the Border Mexican's imagery. A man will boast that he can do something *sin vara*, without the need of the quirt. And brave men, as in the popular speech of all Mexicans, are fighting cocks.

Gregorio Cortez has none of the conventional images based on horseracing and cockfighting, but it has taken some others from the everyday working life of the vaquero. When a posse of three hundred men surround Cortez, they "make him a corral," as vaqueros very often did with a mustang or a wild bull, by stopping up the trails in the brush. But getting Cortez inside the corral is the easy step. Going in after him is the trick, and like a wild bull Cortez "leaps out of their corral," leaving dead and wounded in his path.

At another point in his flight, Cortez is overtaken and fights off an attack by his pursuers. After he puts them to flight he boasts that he has had harder fights than the one they gave him.

Decía Gregorio Cortez,	Then said Gregorio Cortez,
echando muchos balazos:	Shooting out a lot of bullets,
—Me he escapado de aguaceros,	"I have weathered thunderstorms;
contimás de nublinazos.	This little mist doesn't bother me."

The memory of trips up the Kansas Trail with bunches of nervous steers that were likely to stampede in thunderstorms seems to be behind this figure. There is a quatrain in *El Corrido de Kiansis* which commemorates the stampedes begun by thunderstorms.

Al llegar al Foro West	On reaching Fort Worth
se vino un fuerte aguacero,	A big thunderstorm came up;

---

[10] Axel Olrik, *A Book of Danish Ballads,* translated by E. M. Smith-Dampier, Princeton, 1939, p. 13.

| pa' poderlos detener | In order to hold them back |
| les formamos tiroteo. | We did a lot of shooting. |

Such figures are directly connected with the Border Mexican's way of life. More numerous are the figures of speech that are entirely conventional, that are contradicted rather than supported by the Borderer's experience, indicating that they have been inherited from older traditions. When Cortez's pursuers start out on his trail, their faces are said to be "whiter than a dove." It is doubtful that the *corrido* maker or any of the people that have sung the ballad ever saw a white dove. That they saw many dark-colored doves is more than merely probable, since the Border is full of the local drab-colored bird. The dove here, of course, is the white dove of religious paintings, the Holy Spirit and the bird that Noah set loose after the flood. The white dove is universal among peoples of European culture. The Border Mexican had as his models lyric songs from Greater Mexico, in which the dove is either blue or white. Here observation did not enter at all into the *corrido* imagery.

Other singers, perhaps seeking to get rid of the assonance in *paloma-pistola* (since assonance is often considered a blemish by *corrido* singers) have made the figure "más blancos que una amapola" (whiter than a poppy.) The opium poppy, common in the interior of Mexico, is said to be white; so the figure apparently has been made to conform to actual experience. This would be so except for the fact that the Borderer does not call the poppy *amapola*. To him the *amapola* is the pink primrose that grows wild in the chaparral in February and March after a damp winter. The poppy is very aptly called *adormidera,* apparently a local word which could be translated as "soporific." The "white as a poppy" comparison could probably be traced to the lyric songs imported from Greater Mexico.

In variants such as F the figure has been completely changed, and the Americans are shown "striking themselves with their caps" because of their fear of Cortez. The meaning of "que se daban con la gorra" is harder to unravel. It is obviously a figure of speech, since the last item of apparel that either the Mexican vaquero or his Texas neighbors would wear would be a cap. *Gorra* on the Border is used to mean "ridicule," though in the interior of Mexico it seems to mean "panhandling" or "mooching." (On the Border the equivalent word is *corba*.) Perhaps in "que se daban con la gorra" the idea that the Americans were striking themselves with their hats in frustration is combined with the implication that they were ridiculing each other because they could not catch Cortez.

When the pursuit after Cortez is begun, the bloodhounds are let loose to follow the trail, but trying to catch Cortez, the *corrido* says, is like following a star, a shooting star that one would follow with his eyes. This again is an old convention, and the idea that following a star in this way is useless and unlucky is found in Border tales. The use of the star as a measure of the impossibility of a task brings to mind John Donne's line.

There are few other passages in *Gregorio Cortez* that might be considered as instances of the use of figurative language. The *rinches* are said to be coming to the spot where Cortez is to give up so fast "that they almost fly," a common figure. Some variants change this to "they almost broke their necks" (que se mataban), perhaps a more vivid twist for a horseback people. The passages with figurative language are few, however. The main object of the *corrido* is to narrate in as concrete a language as possible, and to create its vivid effects through simplicity of diction and a dramatic style rather than through verbal adornments.

The *corrído* language

The *corrido* language for the most part is simple and direct. The influence of the pseudoliterary broadside, with its preference for the highest-sounding word, has been negligible on the Border, where ballads are composed in the language that the rancheros use every day.

The reminiscences of former Spanish usage are much the same as those found in other parts of Spanish America: such things as the use of *fierro* for *hierro* (iron), *ora* for *ahora* (now), *entenado* for *hijastro* (stepson), *contino* for *contínuo* (continuous), *debda* and *cibdad* for *deuda* and *ciudad* (debt and city). In *Gregorio Cortez* the use of *calabozo* (dungeon) for "jail" is a slightly medieval touch. The English word "calaboose" shows the currency of *calabozo* for "jail" in the Southwest. *Bartolina*, also meaning "dungeon," is another word used for "jail" in *Gregorio Cortez*. *Querer* (to want, wish) is used in at least one conventional line in the old Spanish sense of "on the point of." *Como queriendo llorar* is most accurately translated as "on the point of tears," just as *los gallos querían cantar* in the *romance* meant "the cocks were beginning to crow."

Metathesis, assimilation, and dissimilation, especially the confusion of *i* and *e*, are too common wherever Spanish is spoken to require special comment. Such constructions as *permetida, temidez,* and *conviniente* are probably much the same everywhere. From Mexico comes the habit of using the diminutive *ito,* and sometimes *itito,* not always as a diminutive but sometimes as an intensive, *ito* corresponding to "very" and *itito* to "very very." *Limpio* (clean) is declined *limpiecito* (very clean) and *limpiecitito* (very very clean). *Igualito,* from *igual* (the same), is "exactly the same"; *bastantito,* from *bastante* (enough), becomes "quite a lot." In *Gregorio Cortez* there are two uses of this intensive diminutive, one with *todo* (all) in *toditito el estado* and the other with *pocos* (few) in *poquitos más de trescientos. Toditito el estado* is a very emphatic way of saying "the whole state." *Poquitos más de trescientos* means "quite a few more than three hundred."

The Border people have their native words, usually coined under the influence of the English-speaking counterculture. The enemies of the hero are the *cherifes* and the *rinches.* "Sheriff" easily gives *cherife* because of the lack of the *sh* sound and the tendency to end words with an unaccented vowel, the masculine nouns with either *o* or *e. Cherife* means not "sheriff" but "deputy." The sheriff himself is *El Cherife Mayor,* the high or major sheriff, a term reminiscent of the Robin Hood ballads.

Any American armed and mounted and out to kill Mexicans is

a *rinche* to the *corrido* folk. *Rinche* is a rendering into Spanish of "ranger." The English *a* [e] is usually rendered into the Spanish *e* [ɛ], so that "Baker" becomes *Beker*, then by dissimilation *Bekar* and finally *Becas*. "Scraper," the roadgrading machine, becomes *escrepa*. This seems to follow a historical tendency in the Spanish language, according to which *queiso* has become *queso; seipa, sepa; primeiro, primero*. One would expect "ranger" to become *renche* instead of *rinche*. Perhaps the introduction of the *i* is an instance of dissimilation, or the influence of the *n* may be the cause. There is a good chance, though, that the *i* in the accented syllable of *rinche* owes something to the same tendency that results in the *y* before vowels at the beginning of important lines. It could be a sign of tenseness, both in execution and in the attitude of the singer. Whatever the reasons for its development, *rinche* is not a pleasant-sounding word, and the words which most closely approximate it in sound, such as *chinche, hinche, linche,* and *pinche* in its obscene sense all have unpleasant associations.

The Border Mexican has a way of taking the English equivalent of a Spanish noun and making an adjective out of it, in order to give a more precise meaning to the Spanish word. The best example of this tendency in *Gregorio Cortez* is found in *perros jaunes. Jaun,* except for the dropping of the *d,* is a very close rendition of "hound," and thus *perros jaunes* may be translated as "dogs called hounds," something pretty close to the "houndog" of the South. However, the *perro jaun* refers to the bloodhound specifically. Whatever purists may say about such a form as *perros jaunes,* it carries a great deal of descriptive and emotional force for the *corrido* hearer, and that after all is the poetic function of language. The ballad maker could very well have said *perros huelleros* (tracking dogs), a word also used on the Border for "bloodhounds." But *perros jaunes* is shorter and simpler. It also echoes the English language, which is the language spoken by the owners of the bloodhounds, and gives added meaning through associations that *perros huelleros* does not have. One can even find in the *au* of *jaun* an echo of the conventional Spanish way of reproducing the barking of a dog. The word *podenco,* on the other hand, would mean nothing to the Borderer, and its presence in the place of *perro jaun* would certainly be evidence of the pseudoliterary influence of the broadside hack, which is happily absent from the Border *corrido*.

"Bulldog" is usually translated as *perro buldog* (or *buldó*), with *buldog* as an adjective. *Jamón* long ago ceased to be "ham" on the Border and now means "bacon." "Ham" is *jamón piernil*, "leg ham," something like the Anglo-American way of saying "Rio Grande River."

Some other words appearing in *Gregorio Cortez* may be worth mentioning. *Calaboz'* for *calabozo*, appearing in Variants B and F, is not an exercise of poetic license. I have added the apostrophe to help the reader identify the word more easily. In Border usage, though, the word is *calaboz*, reminding one even more strongly of the English "calaboose." Upriver from Brownsville, on the American side, there is a village called El Calaboz, evidently the site of some early jail. On the Mexican side, by the way, downriver from Brownsville, there is another village, called La Bartolina.

Nublinazo is equivalent to *niebla* (mist). *Niebla* is not current on the Border, but *neblina* (light mist) is often found as *nublina*. A heavy mist is a *nublinazo*, the suffix *azo* in this case being an augmentative.

Insortar is a word that seems to belong to the Border alone. When the law declares a man wanted and sets out after him, when it puts up rewards for him and organizes posses for his pursuit, he is then considered *insortado*. The word appears in the longer variants of *Gregorio Cortez*. In a rough sense it means "to outlaw," but its origin is difficult to determine. Professor Ramón Martínez-López suggests that the word comes from *exhortar* as used in Spanish legal terminology. When a judicial officer ordered a man's apprehension, he exhorted other officers of the law to assist him in bringing the accused before justice. His official notice was an *exhortación*. There is a tendency for Latin words with the prefix *ex* to change the prefix to *ens* or *en* in Spanish, first having gone through a stage in which the *ex* was *engs*. Thus *ensalzar* was originally *exaltiare*, *enjuagar* was *exa-*

quare. Exhortar could very easily have become *engsortar,* then *ensortar.* The interchanging of *e* and *i* is common. It is very probable, as Professor Martínez-López suggests, that the Border Mexican word *insortar* may have a learned and a Latin ancestry in *exhortari.*

Proper names suffer some changes in the *corrido.* The name of the hero usually remains constant, though there are some cases when this has not held true. Jacinto Treviño and Ignacio Treviño were both ballad heroes with their own distinct *corridos,* but in recent years their two ballads have been amalgamated and the attributes of Ignacio have been given to Jacinto. If the hero's name was non-Spanish to begin with, the change is more to be expected. *El Corrido de Gregorio Dof,* from Rio Grande City, originally had as its hero a man named Gregorio Duffy [TFA P42–7]. The names of secondary personages are quickly changed. Gregorio Cortez's brother was named Romaldo, but the *corrido* invariably calls him Román. Jesús González, Cortez's betrayer, is merely Jesús in the *corrido* and in later variants becomes Juan. The names of the English-speaking adversaries of the hero do not appear at all in most *corridos.* They are rarely more than types. The Major Sheriff, and occasionally the chief of the *rinches (El Rinche Mayor),* is the main opposing character; the enemy is usually seen merely as *cherifes, rinches,* or *americanos.* The narrator himself rarely indulges in name-calling, though the characters themselves in their boasts may call their opponents cowards, *gringos,* and *güeros,* the last meaning nothing but "blond" or "fair ones."

In the Border *Gregorio Cortez* the names of Morris, Glover, and Schnabel do not appear at all. Morris, Glover, and Ranger Captain Rogers, who apprehended Cortez, are all *El Cherife Mayor.* Cortez kills the Major Sheriff, flees and is surrounded by a posse led by the Major Sheriff; he kills the Major Sheriff and flees again and finally surrenders to the Major Sheriff. In a sense they are all the same man, since each leader of a posse represents the punitive arm of the counterculture. There is more than a desire to avoid difficult foreign names in the omission of the names of American principals. The submergence of the man in his role, in his identity as the representative of the opposite culture, has a great deal to do with the matter.

Conventions which the Border *corrído* has borrowed from Greater Mexico

The *corrido,* like other folk ballads, is built on convention, not only on conventional imagery and conventional turns of language but on certain ready-made lines that travel easily from one ballad to another. Though the Border *corrido* maker had his own style, the singing of Greater Mexican ballads did have an effect upon his technique. But the fact that the conventions held in common with Greater Mexican ballads of the turn of the century are few and not of great importance is evidence of the vigor and the individuality of the Border's own balladry.

It is as Cortez is about to be captured (when the heroic action is over) that the Greater Mexican proletarian *corrido* exerts its greatest influence on *Gregorio Cortez.* As the rangers arrive, Cortez comes out to meet them and says, "Por la buena sí me llevan/ porque de otro modo no." This could almost be translated, "If you're nice about it, you can take me with you; but you won't be able to do it anyway else." It is reminiscent of the bravo of the Spanish *jácara* and of the Greater Mexican lyric *corrido,* in which the hero speaks out a whole string of boasts, telling the world what a fine fellow he is if he is treated nicely, but that he can be the very devil if he is crossed. "Don't muddy my water or you'll have to drink it!" he shouts.

After Cortez is captured, the narrator comments that the poor family is the one that is going to suffer the most. This again is in the manner of the Greater Mexican broadside, which tends to comment on the events rather than narrate them. The sufferings of the poor family, the poor mother, or the poor wife form a central theme in the ballads of prisoners, of executed criminals, and the like, and these usually are broadside *corridos* of a mediocre sort.

Gregorio Cortez, *A Study*

In the most complete oral variants of *Gregorio Cortez*, only these two conventions have survived as influences of Greater Mexican balladry; they may have been the only two. It is significant that they appear at the end, after the story is really over, and the interest stirred by the deeds of Cortez has come to an end. Later singers, in making variations on the original *corrido*, have brought into their variants other Greater Mexican *corrido* conventions, though these too are few. In the nine traditional variants that are considered in this study, only two such interpolations appear. Variant B drops the usual beginning line, "En el condado del Carmen" and substitutes "Pongan cuidado, señores" (Gentlemen, give your attention), typical of the broadside ballad, with its greater consciousness of the audience and its frequent intrusion of the narrator into his narrative. Variant E has introduced the highly traveled "shoe" stanza.

Decía Gregorio Cortez,	Then said Gregorio Cortez,
abrochándose un zapato:	As he was tying his shoe,
—Aquí traigo más cartuchos	"I have more cartridges here
pa' divertirlos un rato.	To entertain you a while."

This quatrain is found in variants of many a Border *corrido*, in *Jacinto Treviño, Ignacio Treviño,* and *Los Sediciosos,* for example. Its origin seems to be a Greater Mexican *corrido* of earlier date than *Gregorio Cortez,* one of the best Mexican ballads of the period before the Revolution, *El Corrido de Demetrio Jáuregui.* Demetrio Jáuregui kneels and prays to the Virgin before going to his death in a fight with *rurales* and soldiers. Before he rises to his feet he ties his shoe and says, either to himself or to his besiegers, "I have plenty of cartridges to entertain us for a while." Border *corrido* singers have been charmed with the quatrain, and some introduce it (unchanged except for the hero's name) into almost every *corrido* they sing, including other Greater Mexican ballads. It is misapplied, as borrowed stanzas frequently are. The kneeling to pray before battle has not been borrowed. The Border hero is made to stop in the middle of the fighting to tie his shoe, while he shouts to the enemy that he still has plenty of ammunition to entertain them for a while.

225

There is one other reminiscence of the pre-Revolutionary ballads of Greater Mexico in *Gregorio Cortez*. One of the variants of *Valentín Mancera*, which is dated in the early 1880's, begins like some later variants of *Gregorio Cortez*.

Día lunes, trece de marzo,	On Monday, March the thirteenth,
¡qué desgracia sucedió!	What a misfortune befell!

Most variants of *Gregorio Cortez*, and those that appear to be the earlier, begin with the narrator's pointing out of the scene.

En el condado del Carmen	In the county of El Carmen
miren lo que ha sucedido.	Look what has happened.

Three of the later variants included in this study have changed the second line to resemble that found in *Valentín Mancera*.

En el condado del Carmen	In the county of El Carmen
¡tal desgracia sucedió!	What a misfortune befell!

Variant C includes both forms, two opening stanzas instead of one.

It is strange that *Gregorio Cortez*, whose hero was famous for his ride to the Border, should not describe him on a horse or a mare of a certain color, as do many of the other heroic *corridos*. The honey-colored horse and the sorrel mare are the usual signs of the *corrido* hero. The legend makes much of a sorrel mare. But in none of the variants that I have ever heard is there a quatrain beginning, "Then said Gregorio Cortez/ on his honey-colored horse" or "Then said Gregorio Cortez/ on his little sorrel mare," though such quatrains are sung about other Border heroes before and after Cortez.

The honey-colored horse convention, whatever it owes to the European tradition of the white horse, appears to have come to the Border in another Mexican outlaw ballad, *El Corrido de Heraclio Bernal*, about the most famous Mexican Robin Hood before Pancho Villa. The Bernal *corrido*, which dates from the 1880's, has a series of quatrains each putting Bernal on a horse of a different color and mentioning some of the hero's qualities.

Gregorio Cortez, *A Study*

The honey-colored horse is mentioned in the next-to-last quatrain.

Qué valiente era Bernal	How brave was Bernal
en su caballo melado,	On his honey-colored horse;
peleó con tres acordadas,	He fought with three posses;
no era cualesquier pelado.	He wasn't just any tramp.
Qué valiente era Bernal	How brave was Bernal
en su caballo jovero,	On his golden horse;
Bernal no robaba a pobres,	Bernal did not rob the poor;
antes les daba dinero.	He gave them money instead.

Conventions which have been developed in *El Corrído de Gregorío Cortez*

The Greater Mexican conventions previously mentioned, though they appear in some variants of the ballad do not really belong to *El Corrido de Gregorio Cortez*. There are other conventions which one may say have been created with the creation of *Gregorio Cortez*. Made up of elements from different sources, something was added to them before they were passed on to other *corridos*. It is in the use of these conventions that the Cortez ballad shows its influence as a border-conflict prototype on other Border *corridos* and even, it would appear, on later Mexican ballads. These conventions were of course not original with the makers of the *Corrido de Gregorio Cortez*, but they were given new meaning and new force in that ballad and were passed on in changed form to later *corridos*.

Mendoza mentions a short pre-*corrido* ballad of the wars between Federalists and Centralists, about the time of the independence of Texas. It concerns a Federalist chieftain called Eustaquio Arias and has the following *corrido*-like quatrain, though most of the rest is in *redondillas*.[11]

Cuando Arias mandó llamar	When Arias sent
a don Francisco Lozano,	For Don Francisco Lozano,

[11] Mendoza, *El romance y el corrido*, p. 130.

227

llegó queriendo llorar,   He came looking as if he would
con el sombrero en la mano.   weep,
                                And with his hat in his hand.

Two conventional lines used in Border *corridos* are foreshadowed in this quatrain of the 1830's. The *con el sombrero en la mano* convention is found in *El Corrido de Kiansis* and *El Corrido de la Pensilvania,* both Border work-and-travel ballads. The conventional line *como queriendo llorar* is a favorite in Border balladry, from the old *Corrido de Kiansis* dating from the 1870's to the last *corridos* of border strife made on the threshold of the 1920's. It is in *Gregorio Cortez,* however, that the convention receives the particular form in which it is found in other twentieth-century Border *corridos,* in which it is the villain or the clown to whom the line is always attributed.

In the Federalist ballad, there is no indication that Francisco Lozano is either a villain or a clown. The picture painted of him is a rather pathetic one. Arias, one gathers, is about to have Lozano executed, though he does not relish the task; the song ends with some talk about gambling at cards in the game of life. *El Corrido de Kiansis* seems to have taken the *vino queriendo llorar* and by adding the *como* of such *romance* expressions as *dijo el rey como turbado* produced the conventional line *como queriendo llorar,* used in the Kansas *corrido* and thereafter in apposition to a *decía* line. In *El Corrido de Kiansis* the *como queriendo llorar* is given to the hero of the ballad, the *caporal.* He speaks in a voice that sounds as if he were on the verge of tears when he commands the vaqueros to head off the stampede.

Nos decía el caporal,   The caporal said to us,
como queriendo llorar: As if he was going to cry,
—Allá va la novillada,   "There goes that herd of steers;
no me la dejen pasar.   You'd better not let it by."

The tears apparent in the *caporal*'s voice are not those of cowardice, sentiment, or weakness but of frustration, the frustration of a man used to having his way. He is, needless to say, neither a villain nor a clown but the leader of the "adventurers" who are driving the herd to Kansas.

In *Mariano Reséndez*, the Border *corrido* about The Smuggler, the *como queriendo llorar* again appears, still attributed to the hero. This ballad must have been composed at the end of the nineteenth century, one or two years before the Cortez *corrido*. Reséndez is also a strong and brave man. His skirmishes with customs guards and Mexican troops make him a heroic figure. He is finally surprised, and his brother is killed in the fighting. Finding himself unable to go to his brother's aid, Reséndez allows his voice to betray the same kind of strong man's tears as the *caporal's* on the Kansas trail.

Decía Mariano Reséndez,	Then said Mariano Reséndez,
como queriendo llorar:	As if he was going to cry,
—Ay alma mía de mi hermano,	"Oh, brother of my soul,
quién te pudiera salvar.	How I wish I could save your life."

The maker of *Gregorio Cortez* gave an entirely new direction to the *como queriendo llorar* convention. He attributed the line to the Major Sheriff who comes to capture Cortez, and the context makes it evident that the Major Sheriff speaks in a weepy voice because he is afraid of Cortez.

Decía el Cherife Mayor,	Then the Major Sheriff said,
como queriendo llorar:	As if he was going to cry,
—Cortez, entrega tus armas,	"Cortez, hand over your weapons;
no te vamos a matar.	We want to take you alive."

The Major Sheriff is both villainous, because he is a *rinche,* and comic, because he is afraid. After *Gregorio Cortez* the convention becomes the sign of the villain and the clown, just as the honey-colored horse, the sorrel mare, and the pistol in hand are the signs of the hero. *Jacinto Treviño* and *Ignacio Treviño, corridos* of the 1910's, are both strongly influenced by *Gregorio Cortez*. In *Jacinto Treviño* the *como queriendo llorar* is given to the Major Sheriff, as in *Gregorio Cortez*. In *Ignacio Treviño* it appears twice in the mouths of Ignacio's less courageous companions, who call out to him in weepy voices not to fire on the rangers because he will get killed. *El Corrido de José Mosqueda* dates as an outlaw ballad to the 1880's, but it seems to have been recast as a ballad of border conflict in later times. It also has the *como queriendo llorar* convention, with the blacksmith who made the iron bars used by the outlaws to derail a train speaking in a weepy voice about his fear of being sent to prison. In the *corridos* composed about the Pizaña uprising of 1915 and subsequent years, the *como queriendo llorar* convention is standard and always attributed to Luis de la Rosa. Why the ballad makers, and tradition in general, have given the coward's role to Luis de la Rosa I have not been able to ascertain. He was one of the leaders of the seditionist movement, and with Pizaña a shaper of the plan for a Spanish-speaking republic of South Texas. Newspapers and other documents of the time show him actively engaged in recruiting men on the south bank of the Rio Grande for the enterprise. It may be that De la Rosa was a better mastermind and organizer than a fighter. Or the ballads may reflect divisions and quarrels among the seditionist leaders. It may be that De la Rosa's enemies perpetuated slanders about him in the *corridos* as did King Pedro's enemies in the *romances.* In any case, Luis de la Rosa in different ballads is shown on the verge of tears: because the raiders are going through Mercedes, because he wants a drink from the Rio Grande (taken on the south bank), or because bullets are raining too thickly on the spot where he is. In one ballad Don Luis is shown as actually in tears, during the attack by the Pizaña raiders on Norias in King Ranch.

En ese dipo de Norias	From that station known as Norias
se oía la pelotería,	Came the sound of heavy firing;
del señor Luis de la Rosa	But from Don Luis de la Rosa
nomás el llanto se oía.	Nothing but the sound of weeping.

The appearance of the *como queriendo llorar* convention in Greater Mexican balladry tells us something about the interrelationship of Mexican balladry and its Border branch. Except

230

for the *vino queriendo llorar* in *Eustaquio Arias*, presumably the ancestor of the Border convention, the latter does not appear in the Mexican *corridos* that I am familiar with (either through oral sources or through the printed works of Mexican ballad students) until the very last part of the Revolutionary period, in the late 1920's and the 1930's. When the convention does appear in Greater Mexican balladry, it follows the *Gregorio Cortez* pattern, being applied to the enemy, to a woman, or to a coward.

In *El Asalto a la Hacienda de San Juan*, a late *corrido* published by Mendoza,[12] *como queriendo llorar* appears twice, in both cases attributed to women. In one case, the similarity in language to *Ignacio Treviño*, a Border *corrido* patterned on *Gregorio Cortez*, is very close. *Ignacio Treviño* antedates *El Asalto a la Hacienda de San Juan* by at least twenty years.

Aquella mujer decía,	That woman said,
como queriendo llorar:	As if she was going to cry,
—Señor, ahi viene el Gobierno,	"Sir, the Government is coming;
no les vayan a tirar.	Take care, or they'll fire on you.
(*El Asalto*)	OR
	Please don't go fire on them."
Decía José Calderón,	Then said José Calderón,
como queriendo llorar:	As if he was going to cry,
—Ignacio, ya no les tires,	"Ignacio, don't fire on them
no te vayan a matar.	any more;
(*Ignacio Treviño*)	Take care, or they will kill you."

The other use of the convention in *El Asalto* is a variation of the first.

La esposa del comandante	The wife of the commander
decía queriendo llorar . . .	Said tearfully . . .

In *Quirino Navarro*, a ballad of the *cristero* wars of the late 1920's, the *cristeros* attack a Jalisco town and are repulsed by the agrarian forces. The *corrido* is made from the *agrarista* point of

[12] Mendoza, *El corrido mexicano*, pp. 437ff.

view. When the *cristeros* begin to lose, they call on Saint Anthony to turn the tide of battle in their favor, something that Saint Anthony fails to do.

Gritaban los de la Unión,	Those of the Union shouted,
como queriendo gritar:	As if they were going to shout,
—¡Padre, Señor San Antonio,	"Father, Lord St. Anthony,
permítenos el entrar!	Let us enter the town!"

The ballad has the *cristeros* shouting "as if they were going to shout." The maker of *Quirino Navarro* may have misapplied the *como queriendo llorar* convention, or later singers—for whom it was not traditional—may have corrupted it. The *cristeros* or Union men are the villains, though, and the convention is applied to them in the Border style. Still another *cristero* ballad, *El Corrido de Ramón Aguilar,* also written from the *agrarista* point of view, uses the convention when Aguilar, the *cristero* chieftain, is killed.

El clero y el capital	The clergy and the capitalists
andan queriendo llorar ...	Are going about on the verge of tears.

The fact that most *agraristas* were former *braceros,* many of whom had made the trip into Texas in search of work, may have something to do with the appearance of this Border convention in *agrarista* ballads.

In armament at least the *corrido* hero is in the same tradition as is the cowboy of the English-speaking culture. He is not the ranchero of the period before the Mexican War, fighting with the knife, the lance, and the lasso. He is the man on horseback armed with a revolver, the raider of the post-Cortina period. Nothing shows the relative modernity of the heroic Border *corrido* and its relationship to the cattle culture of the United States as does this typical picture of the *corrido* hero. He is seen *con su pistola en la mano,* with his pistol in his hand. Almost all Border heroes at one time or another speak or shout or boast with their pistols in their hands. If the *corrido* hero is not with his pistol in his hand, he appears *de carabina y pistola,* armed

232

with rifle and pistol. The *de* suggests such English expressions as "booted and spurred"; the hero is equipped (dressed in, one could almost say) with a rifle and a revolver. All rifles, by the way, are Winchester 30–30's, and this convention reaches far south of the Border.

The model for the *con su pistola en la mano* convention may have come to the Border in the same ballad as did *en su caballo melado*. The northern Mexican *Corrido de Heraclio Bernal*, in the series of quatrains showing Bernal on different horses, incidentally uses the line.

Qué rechulo era Bernal,	How beautiful was Bernal,
en su caballo retinto,	On his black horse,
con su pistola en la mano	With his pistol in his hand,
peleando con treinta y cinco.	Fighting against thirty-five.

This quatrain has been very well liked on the Border, and though the *corrido* about Bernal has almost disappeared, many people who have forgotten the rest of the ballad or who perhaps never knew it do remember the stanza about Bernal with his pistol in his hand, fighting against thirty-five.

Whether the convention was already current in the Border *corrido* by the time it appeared in *Bernal* there is no way of knowing, since there is so little information on the heroic *corrido* of the times during and immediately after the American Civil War. If the convention did originate with *Heraclio Bernal*, it seems to have found an immediate acceptance in the Border *corrido* but not in Greater Mexican balladry. The convention does not reappear in the Greater Mexican *corrido*, as far as one can tell, until the Revolutionary period. On the Border, meanwhile, it becomes a completely conventionalized phrase after its appearance in *Gregorio Cortez*, by being put in apposition to *decía* in the same manner as *como queriendo llorar*.

In the longer variants of *El Corrido de Gregorio Cortez*, the first lines introducing Cortez show him pistol in hand and speaking his defiance of the *rinches*. The convention in time became an essential element of the concept of the Border *corrido* hero;

Jacinto Treviño, Ignacio Treviño, Alonso Flores, Alejos Sierra, the heroes of the seditionist raids, José Mosqueda, and even the *rural* who kills Arnulfo González and is killed by him are all shown *con su pistola en la mano*. The epic hero's habit of needling his enemies into single combat by shouting insults at them was found in Border *corridos* before *Gregorio Cortez*. Mariano Reséndez was also this kind of hero.

Gritó Mariano Reséndez:	Mariano Reséndez shouted,
—Entrenle, no sean cobardes;	"Come into the fight; don't be
no le teman a las balas	cowards.
ni se acuerden de sus madres.	Don't be afraid of the bullets,
	And don't think about your mothers."

The events surrounding the *corrido* about Cortez naturally fitted this sort of idea about the hero. Cortez appears in later variants with his pistol in his hand, not justifying the killing of Morris but shouting to the *rinches* not to run away like cowards.

Decía Gregorio Cortez	Then said Gregorio Cortez
con su pistola en la mano:	With his pistol in his hand,
—No corran rinches cobardes	"Don't run, you cowardly rangers
con un solo mexicano.	From just one Mexican."

The stanza, exactly alike except for the substitution of the hero's name, is found in *Jacinto Treviño* and *Ignacio Treviño*, *corridos* about events some ten years after Cortez.

Thus the *con su pistola en la mano* convention, in the way that it was developed by the makers of *Gregorio Cortez*, became part of the standard equipment of the heroic *corrido* of the Border, typically a Lower Border *corrido* convention. The earliest *corrido*-like ballad of Greater Mexico, *El Corrido Norteño*, from Durango, shows the hero fighting rifle in hand. During the Revolutionary period the Greater Mexican *corrido* hero boasts of his rifle, usually a 30–30, rather than of his pistol. *El Corrido de Cananea*, from the border state of Sonora, has the sheriffs arrest the hero pistol in hand, "in the American style." The man pistol in hand is truly "in the American style," or the Texas style, since the revolver was originally the Ranger weapon. It is not strange that the revolver should first become an ideal weapon to the Mexican on the Lower Border, among the people who had had the most opportunity to learn about its efficacy.

The hero with his Mauser rifle or his revolver in his hand begins to appear in the Greater Mexican heroic *corrido* after Villa's defeat at Celaya in 1915 and the dispersal of his forces. *El Corrido de Benjamín Argumedo,* about the capture and execution of that general in 1916, mentions Argumedo as having "fought so long, so long/ With my Mauser in my hand." *El Corrido de Orlachía,* about a Villista chieftain in flight after Celaya, shows a man known as La Urraca defending himself from a Carrancista attack "with his pistol in his hands." *La Perra Valiente,* a companion piece, is very much like the Lower Border *corridos.* As in *El Corrido de Kiansis,* the narrator says that he wishes he did not have to remember the events (*ni me quisiera acordar*). La Perra is the hero at bay, finally dying with his Mauser in his hands. Pedro Zamora, another Villista, is the hero who escapes, getting away at the end of the ballad with the shout, "Viva Villa!" There is a series of stanzas in which Zamora and his men talk like the raiders in *Los Sediciosos,* and one of the Villistas is a timid soul, like De la Rosa of the Border *corridos.*

El Asalto a Dulces Nombres,[13] a *corrido* from the *cristero* troubles of the 1930's, has an individual hero, Julián García, who is the only *agrarista* to escape, pistol in hand, after a surprise attack by the *cristeros* on an *agrarista* village.

Valiente Julián García	Brave Julián García,
que con pistola en la mano,	Who with his pistol in his hand,
se abrió paso entre la chusma,	Made way through the mob,
dejando muerto a su hermano.	Leaving his brother dead.
Con su pistola en la mano,	With his pistol in his hand,
sin dejar de disparar,	And firing without stopping,
se abrió paso entre la gente	He made a way through the men
del cristero Sandoval.	Of the *cristero* Sandoval.

The quatrains, especially the first one, are strongly reminiscent

[13] *Ibid.,* p. 110.

of *Gregorio Cortez,* in spite of their literary flavor. The *ni me quisiera acordar* line found in *El Corrido de Kiansis* also appears in this *corrido.*

The *yo soy* tradition, the medieval hero's custom of shouting his name in battle, has also become a typical convention of the Lower Border *corrido* under the influence of *Gregorio Cortez.* In *Mariano Reséndez* we find the shouting of the name as part of the challenge to an attacking force. The Smuggler, surrounded by a detachment of soldiers, breaks out and escapes shouting:

—Este es Mariano Reséndez,	This is Mariano Reséndez,
que lo desean conocer;	Whose acquaintance you want to make;
les ha de dar calentura	You will fall ill with fever
para poderlo aprehender.	Before you can catch me.

This is not quite the *yo soy* convention, and it also includes a boast with the naming-of-the-name, not usually found in the later *corridos* of border conflict. It is in *Gregorio Cortez* that we find the *yo soy* convention in its definite form. When Cortez rides away from the scene of one of his exploits, he challenges his pursuers to follow him and adds, "Yo soy Gregorio Cortez!" Later, when he meets the Mexican who tells him how things are back home, Cortez says haughtily, "Tell me what is new. I am Gregorio Cortez." This is far from the concept of the common man. Cortez sounds not like a Border vaquero but like an old, name-proud hidalgo. It is this medieval pride in name that is the basis of the challenge as it appears in the Border *corrido,* pride in a name that has been earned through deeds and not through birth or wealth. The hero of the Border *corrido* is an uncommon rather than a common man, though it is a rude and basically democratic society that produces him.

The *yo soy* convention is continued in other *corridos* of border conflict, such as those about the two Treviños. Both Ignacio and Jacinto Treviño in their brushes with the Rangers are shown shouting out their names. The convention apparently does not play a part in the Greater Mexican *corrido,* though there are approximations to it. In *Benito Canales,* a *corrido* of 1913 or later, the hero does shout his name, but in answer to a challenge from his enemy, and not in the *yo soy* manner. The troops fighting against him shout, "Long live the government! Death to Benito Canales!"

Canales answers, "Long live Benito Canales! Death to the government!" Greater Mexican ballad heroes joke with and insult their enemies, but the *yo soy* idea is found in Greater Mexican balladry mainly in the lyric *corrido*, and then in the form of elaborate boasts in the style of the American river boatmen. Again one has to go to an early example of the Greater Mexican *corrido*, *Macario Romero*, from about 1878, to find a parallel with the Border style.

Gritó Macario Romero:	Macario Romero shouted,
—Aquí estoy, yo soy el mero.	"Here I am; I am the real one."

This is very much like the Border convention. In another variant of the Romero ballad, the hero, with five bullets in his body, has time before expiring to shout, "Long live Macario Romero!" But as is the case with the *con su pistola en la mano* and *en su caballo melado* conventions, which seem to come from *Heraclio Bernal*, the *yo soy* convention may very well have been old on the Border by the time it was used in Greater Mexican balladry. The popularity of such conventions on the Border and the little use made of them in Greater Mexico would make one suspect so. In the first two we have nothing to go by but their currency on the Border. There is better evidence in favor of the assumption that the *yo soy* convention was known on the Border before it appeared in *Macario Romero*. In the late eighteenth century, when the settlements at Nuevo Santander were still young, the New Mexican settlers were fighting Indians and writing poems about their battles. They composed a heroic play called *Los Comanches* after a severe defeat they administered to that tribe. In the play, each champion, now a Spaniard, now an Indian, tells his name and gives his boast, in the epic style as well as in the style of such *corridos* as *Los Sediciosos*. The speech of Don Toribio Ortiz, one of the Spanish captains, sounds very much like those found in Border *corridos*.

Yo soy don Toribio Ortiz,	I am Don Toribio Ortiz,
que en todo soy general . . .	General of all the forces . . .
vean si hay entre vosotros	See if there is one among you
quien me pueda contestar.[14]	Who can answer this challenge.

The source of the *yo soy* tradition on the Border is more probably *Los Comanches* or another composition like it than *Macario Romero*. One can see in *Los Comanches* another bit of evidence for the connecting link between the old Spanish heroic tradition and the heroic Border *corrido*. The Cid, charging the Moors, shouts to his knights, "Strike them, gentlemen, for the love of God! I am the Cid, Roy Díaz of Bivar!" The Spanish heroic tradition, which in the eighteenth century was undoubtedly stronger in New Mexico than it was later, probably came to the Border from that source—if the same traditions did not exist simultaneously in both frontier provinces.

The shouting of the name as a challenge was common not only in the *corrido* but in actual life. A drunken ranchero looking for a fight would stand in the middle of the saloon or the street and shout, "I am So-and-So!" Anyone who accepted his challenge would answer with his own name. An illustration of this method of challenge was reported in the Brownsville area during the hurricane of September 1933. A man whom we may call Orestes Aguirre, because though that is not his name it sounds like it, holed up with some friends in a *jacal* on his ranch to weather out the hurricane. The *jacal* was strongly built, and they were provisioned with some jugs of mezcal. As the night wore on, the supply of mezcal got lower and lower, and the wind got higher and higher. At the height of the storm, the wind threatened to blow down the *jacal*. At that critical moment Orestes picked up his shotgun, walked out the door, and poured shot after shot into the storm, shouting at it meanwhile, "Yo soy Orestes Aguirre! Yo soy Orestes Aguirre!" Soon after that the wind died down.

[14] Aurelio M. Espinosa, *Los Comanches, a Spanish Heroic Play of 1780*, comprising Vol. I, No. 1, of the *Bulletin of the University of New Mexico*, Albuquerque, 1942, p. 35.

238

Gregorio Cortez, *A Study*

Perhaps it was mezcal rather than remembered tradition that made Mr. Aguirre revert to the ancient belief that a demon rides the storm and must be fought. Frazer gives some instances of other peoples who have made war on the winds.[15] But the challenge given the hurricane came about in response to an established and conscious tradition.

There are other lines in *Gregorio Cortez* which, become conventional, show the Cortez ballad as a heroic *corrido* prototype. When the *rinches* catch up with Cortez, he exchanges shots with them and kills another sheriff. Instead of using the weaker *se balacearon* (they shot bullets at or into each other) the *corrido* says, "Se agarraron a balazos." *Agarrar* means "to seize"; so *agarrarse* is "to seize upon one another." *Balazo* can be either the sound of a bullet or a bullet wound. The suffix *azo*, however, is usually associated with a blow or a stroke, so that there is the feeling of men seizing upon each other and laying to at close range in a furious and primitive fashion in the expression *se agarraron a balazos*.

Jacinto Treviño, following *Gregorio Cortez* by nine or ten years, improves on the expression in one of the best quatrains that it contains.

En la cantina de Bekar	In Baker's saloon
se agarraron a balazos,	They went at each other with bullets;
por dondequiera saltaban	The bottles jumped into pieces
botellas hechas pedazos.	On all sides.

The Greater Mexican ballad of the Revolution, *Los Combates de Celaya*, composed some six years after *Jacinto Treviño*, puts the expression into a *romance*-like meter.

Por el lado Salvatierra	On the Salvatierra side,
se agarraron a balazos,	They went at each other with bullets;
unos tiran con metrallas,	Some are shooting with machineguns,
y otros puros cañonazos.	And others with cannon.

Other passages in the Greater Mexican *corridos* of the Revolu-

[15] James G. Frazer, *The Golden Bough*, New York, 1951, pp. 94ff.

tion remind one of *Gregorio Cortez*. When Huerta fled Mexico City in 1914, a ballad maker reported the fact in *El Corrido de don Venustiano Carranza*.

Huerta ya tiró las trancas,	Huerta has knocked down the rails;
se salió por un corral . . .	He went out through a corral . . .

It appears that *El Corrido de Gregorio Cortez,* like all folk ballads, has borrowed from other traditional sources, in this case the *romance* and the Greater Mexican ballad corpus. But unlike many ballads, *Gregorio Cortez* has created some conventions of its own, conventions related to the border conflict which was its environment. These conventions express the heroic tradition of the Border *corrido. Gregorio Cortez* passed them on to later Border *corridos,* thus fulfilling the function of a prototype of the *corrido* of border conflict, having remolded pre-existing tradition, and handed it down in a new form. Later Border *corridos* of a heroic type owe much to *Gregorio Cortez.* And as has been suggested throughout the latter part of this chapter, the Greater Mexican heroic *corrido* tradition, which does not begin until ten years after *El Corrido de Gregorio Cortez,* may owe more to the Border *corrido* than is generally suspected.

VIII: A LAST WORD

El Corrido de Gregorio Cortez has been presented as a prototype of the *corrido* of border conflict, a ballad form developed on the Lower Border of the Rio Grande. There a ballad community much like those of medieval Europe existed during the nineteenth and the early part of the twentieth centuries. Cultural homogeneity, isolation, and a patriarchal, traditional way of life made the existence of a native folk balladry possible. In discussing the Spanish border ballad, Entwistle says that the earlier *romances fronterizos* were composed under "classic conditions of balladry," being the songs "of small communities, intensely preoccupied with their own immediate dangers and successes."[1]

The Lower Rio Grande communities were just this sort of closely knit small groups, interested in their own affairs. Morley notes that most British ballads are of "limited, localized import."[2] Entwistle classifies the Montenegrin Serbs as a post-medieval folk because their social unit was a small one, the tribe or the

[1] William James Entwistle, *European Balladry*, Oxford, 1939, p. 160.
[2] Sylvanus Griswold Morley, "Spanish Ballad Problems: The Native Historical Themes," *Modern Philology*, XIII (December 1925), 208.

family state. They had no elaborate society and were isolated in the mountains.[3] The isolated, patriarchal character of the Rio Grande folk has been mentioned.

Folklorists have also noted the democratic spirit in the folk communities of medieval Europe. Vicuña Cifuentes notes that the Castilians, in the times before Spain became an empire, "saw in each peasant an hidalgo" and that plebeians and nobles were identified in the same aims.[4] In the term *pueblo* Milá y Fontanals includes not only the Spanish peasant but the "military aristocracy, which was also uneducated and extremely rude."[5] The Border ranchero also lived in a rude and egalitarian society.

The nonliterate character of the folk does not need documentary support. Balladry, like most other folk arts, depends on a society that finds its entertainment in oral form. It went into decline in Europe when the habit of reading for religious purposes, and then for entertainment, became widespread. The Lower Border people were not Bible readers, and they preferred the oral to the written word.

The Lower Rio Grande people lived under conditions in which folk cultures develop. They lived in isolation from the main currents of world events. They preferred to live in small, tightly knit communities that were interested in their own problems. Their type of social organization was the family holding or the communal village, ruled by patriarchal authority under a kind of pre-eighteenth-century democracy. And their forms of entertainment were oral. But they were not unique in this respect. Other frontier areas of New Spain, such as New Mexico, produced folk communities of the same type. The New Mexican folk communities are much older, and they preserved their isolated, individual character much longer than did the communities of the Lower Border. New Mexico, however, did not develop a balladry of a distinctively heroic type. Like most modern

---

[3] Entwistle, *European Balladry*, p. 5.

[4] Julio Vicuña Cifuentes, *Romances populares y vulgares recogidos de la tradición oral chilena*, Santiago de Chile, 1912, p. xi.

[5] Manuel Milá y Fontanals, *De la poesía heroico-popular castellana*, Barcelona, 1896, p. 395.

242

ballad areas, it maintained for the most part the traditions brought over from Europe.

It is my belief that before 1836 a balladry of the New Mexican type existed along the Lower Rio Grande, and all evidence available supports this theory. What subsequently made the balladry of the Lower Border different was the Texas Revolution and the annexation by Texas of the Nueces–Rio Grande part of the old province of Nuevo Santander, one-half of the home area of the Lower Rio Grande people. Thus a border was created, and the bitterness resulting from events that occurred between 1836 and 1848 provided the basis for a century of conflict.

In the histories of European balladries one finds the heroic ballad also arising in frontier areas where small, cohesive folk groups are in conflict with another people. The *romance*, direct ancestor of the Lower Border *corrido*, developed in Castile, where the efforts to reconquer Spain from the Moors came to a focus, and where border conflicts were daily fare for centuries. Scottish balladry also was of border origin. In Russia the *bylini* arose from the border struggles of the Russians against the nomads of the steppes. Entwistle speaks of the Akritic age in Greek balladry as "the oldest stratum of European balladry: an age when the Greek frontier was on the Euphrates and the Saracens were their enemies."[6] It would appear then that the "oldest stratum of European balladry" was also a balladry of border warfare.

The Rio Grande ballads had as their immediate models the ballad forms brought over from Spain. In its verse form, language, and objectivity of style and its restriction for the most part to men singers, the Border *corrido* resembles its ancestor, the Castilian *romance*. Occasionally one finds reminiscences not of the Spanish marches but of the Scottish border country, in tone and emphasis and in the way the hero and his background are seen by the ballad maker. The tradition and the ballad patterns are Castilian, but the social and physical conditions of the Border *corrido* were more like those of Scotland. Unlike the Spaniards, but like the Scots, the Russians, and the Greeks, the

[6] Entwistle, *European Balladry*, p. 310.

Border ballad people ended on the losing side of their conflict. Unlike the Russians and the Greeks, but again like the Scots, the Border people were not engulfed by an alien invasion. They were plagued over a long period of years by a comparatively small number of invaders, who settled down among them, often learned their language, and picked up many of their habits, and who could have been defeated but for the protection of a powerful state and a strong army. Again like the Scots, the Border people were faced by a more numerous people with a more advanced technology. The Texan's six-shooter had its counterpart in the Englishman's longbow. If the Scot was able to mount a strong attack and score some local victories, he always lost in the end to a superior army from the south. The same situation faced the Mexican Border raiders. It was the Scot, usually on the losing side, who produced the most stirring of the British border ballads. On the Rio Grande it was only the losers in the conflict, the Border Mexicans, who produced ballads.

In sum, the balladry of the Rio Grande Border was not like the Castilian, a border balladry of military victory, but like the Scottish, one of resistance against outside encroachment. The Russians and the Greeks also had balladries of the resistance rather than the victory type. But like the Spanish, they took a more national view of their struggles on the frontier. Castilian counts, Russian princes, and Greek generals led armies against the foe. The conflict on the Rio Grande, like that on the Scottish border, was most often on an individual rather than a national scale. The fighters operated in small bands, or they were individual fighting men. Morley thinks that an important difference between the *romance* and the British ballad is that the British ballad is "of limited, localized import."[7] The British ballad poetizes the exploits and the feuds of individuals rather than of nations. Its heroes were scarcely known in their own day outside a narrow region. The same may be said of the *corrido* of the Lower Border.

Here is a balladry, resembling in many respects that of medieval Europe, which developed partly in the twentieth century,

[7] Morley, "Ballad Problems," p. 208.

within the memory of living men. Though it flourished independently of newspapers and other written material, it existed side by side with them, allowing many opportunities for a comparison of written records and oral tradition, something not always possible with medieval balladry. *Gregorio Cortez* and the ballad tradition it represents offer some living evidence concerning points that have been discussed by scholars in relation to the balladries of the past. One sees the effect of social conditions in the development of the balladry of the Lower Border. A type of society similar to that of the European folk groups of the Middle Ages produced a balladry similar to that of medieval Europe. The importance of border conflict in the development of heroic balladry also is illustrated. One also sees evidence of the emergence of a dominant ballad form (given sufficient time) that replaces or assimilates other forms. Before the border-conflict period, it was the *décima* and to a lesser extent the *copla* that were the ballad forms native to the Rio Grande people, as they were to other peoples of Mexican descent. With the *corrido* also came the *danza,* another competitor. Toward the end of the ballad period on the Border, the *corrido* is dominant and has begun to replace the other ballad forms. In response to conditions similar to those which produced the *romance* in Spain, the dormant, half-forgotten *romance* tradition in America revived in the *corrido* and was well on the way to becoming a uniform corpus when the ballad period ended.

In the variants of *El Corrido de Gregorio Cortez* one has concrete evidence of the ballad tendency to develop from comparatively long originals into shorter variants. Since *Gregorio Cortez* obviously could not have been composed before 1901, its rich development of variants has taken place within a surprisingly short time, fifty years at the most. The collective imagination of the *guitarreros* and other gifted ballad singers has carved short, rounded compositions out of the longer ballad much as the action of a stream turns a rough, jagged stone into a smooth pebble. In both cases the time consumed in the transformation is less important than the ductility of the material and the amount of friction brought to bear. One often thinks that the old

European ballads took centuries to go through their changes. But a ballad sung constantly by a large group of people, learned and relearned by singers of varying talents, a ballad which is part of the life of a folk group as a whole, may change more rapidly in forty years than one preserved by a few singers may change in two hundred. Some of the ancient ballads may well have undergone their important changes in forty or fifty years.

A question that should be of interest to Mexican ballad students is the place that *El Corrido de Gregorio Cortez* and the Border heroic tradition which it represents should occupy in the whole of Mexican balladry. Unaware, it seems, of the existence of a well-established *corrido* tradition on the Lower Rio Grande, Mexican ballad scholars have viewed the *corrido*'s appearance among the Spanish-speaking people of the United States as a late manifestation. Professor Mendoza says of the Greater Mexican *corrido* in the United States: "In the border states of the South and in the industrial cities of the North, such as Detroit . . . it has given rise to the creation and the derivation of new types, which already begin to show local characteristics."[8] Mendoza's statements, made in 1954, are true enough as they refer to other parts of the Southwest and to the large cities of the North, where the *corrido* is truly a late importation, brought in with the *braceros* that have come from Mexico. On the Lower Rio Grande, however, we have a *corrido* tradition that is at least as old as the Greater Mexican, if not older.

It may even be that the Greater Mexican heroic *corrido* has been influenced by the Border heroic tradition which *El Corrido de Gregorio Cortez* epitomizes. Some data has been given in support of this assumption. It must remain nothing more than an assumption, however, because there is not yet sufficient material available to arrive at any sort of conclusions. The balladry of the Lower Border of the Rio Grande needs further investigation. A more complete collection not only of oral variants but of old manuscripts, documentary references to ballads, and like data is still needed. The balladry of Greater Mexico has received the attention of some very able literary historians and musicians,

[8] Mendoza, *El corrido mexicano*, p. viii.

246

but they have concentrated their efforts to a great extent on the collection of broadside material and ballads from other nontraditional sources. In Greater Mexico much remains to be done in the collection of oral variants in the field. The fact remains, though, that both on the Border and in Greater Mexico the *corrido* springs from the roots of the *romance*, gaining hegemony over the *décima*, as a result of special conditions, border conflict in the one case and the Mexican Revolution in the other. The necessary conditions were present on the Lower Border many years before they appeared in Greater Mexico. The heroic tradition is already in full vigor in *El Corrido de Gregorio Cortez* ten years before the Revolution.

It was a peculiar set of conditions, prevailing for a century, that produced the Lower Border *corrido*, an international phenomenon straddling the boundary between Mexico and the United States and partaking of influences from both cultures. The most important single influence on the Border *corrido* was the *romance*, though it owes a great deal to the Greater Mexican balladry as well. But the English-speaking culture also had its influence on Border balladry. The Anglo-American served first of all as a reacting agent. The most important ballads produced on the Border have to do with cattle driving and interracial struggles. The Anglo-American influenced the Border *corrido* in other ways. The concept of the *corrido* hero pistol in hand is "in the American style," as *El Corrido de Cananea* puts it. The English language affected the *corrido*, as can be seen in *Gregorio Cortez*. And the Border Mexican's attitudes about the Anglo-American and his customs became part of Border folklore. The American folklorist, particularly the folklorist of Texas, finds the balladry of the Lower Border as much his province as that of the Mexican ballad student. Transcending national boundaries, the Border heroic *corrido* belongs to Texas as much as to Mexico. A product of past conflicts, it may eventually serve as one of the factors in a better understanding.

Bibliography
and Index

Bibliography

FOLKLORE COLLECTIONS

Unpublished Sources

Collection of Lower Border Ballads, recorded on tape by the author during the summer of 1954 and comprising 363 ballads and other songs on 44 rolls of tape. This collection is now part of the Texas Folklore Archive at the University of Texas.

The author's personal collection of ballad texts, ballads without music collected from oral sources from 1941 to 1953, and including *corridos, décimas, danzas,* and other songs. In the text, specific reference is made to the source when ballads from this collection are referred to.

Phonograph Records

El Corrido de Gregorio Cortez, Vocalion record number SA 283 8351, sung by "Los Trovadores Regionales."

El Corrido de José Mosqueda, sung by José Suárez of Brownsville; collected at Brownsville in 1939 by John and Alan Lomax; found in Library of Congress collection under the title *La Batalla de Ojo de Agua,* No. 2609 A1.

La Batalla de Ojo de Agua, sung by José Suárez of Brownsville; collected at Brownsville in 1939 by John and Alan Lomax; found in Library of Congress collection under the title *El Corrido de José Mosqueda,* no record number given.

Published Works

Campa, Arthur L., *The Spanish Folksong in the Southwest,* comprising Vol. IV, No. 1 of the *Bulletin of the University of New Mexico,* Albuquerque, 1933.

Campos, Rubén M., *El folklore literario de México,* Mexico, Talleres Gráficos de la Nación, 1929.

Campos, Rubén M., *El folklore musical de las ciudades*, Mexico, Talleres Linotipográficos "El Modelo," 1930.

Campos, Rubén M., *El folklore y la música mexicana*, Mexico, Talleres Gráficos de la Nación, 1928.

Child, Francis James, *English and Scottish Popular Ballads*, edited by Helen Child Sargent and George Lyman Kittredge, Boston, Houghton Mifflin Company, 1904.

Corridos Mexicanos, No. 6, Colección ADELITA, Mexico, Editorial Albatros, S.A., 1950.

Depping, G. B., *Romancero castellano*, annotated by Antonio Alcalá-Galiano, Leipzig, F. A. Brockhaus, 1844, 2 vols.

Dobie, J. Frank, ed., *Publications of The Texas Folklore Society*, IV, Austin, Texas Folklore Society, 1925.

Dobie, J. Frank, ed., *Puro Mexicano, Publications of The Texas Folklore Society*, XII, Austin, Texas Folklore Society, 1935.

Durán, Agustín, *Romancero general*, Vol. I, Madrid, M. Rivadeneyra, 1854.

Durán, Agustín, *Romancero general*, Vol. II (*Biblioteca de Autores Españoles*, Vol. 16), Madrid, Imprenta de la Publicidad, 1851.

Durán, Gustavo, *14 Traditional Spanish Songs from Texas*, transcribed from recordings made in Texas, 1934–1939, by John A., Ruby T., and Alan Lomax, Washington, D.C., Music Division, Pan-American Union, 1942.

Espinosa, Aurelio M., *Los Comanches, a Spanish Heroic Play of 1780*, comprising Vol. I, No. 1, of the *Bulletin of the University of New Mexico*, Albuquerque, 1907.

Espinosa, Aurelio M., "Los romances tradicionales en California," *Homenaje Ofrecido a Menéndez Pidal*, I, 299–313, Madrid, Librería y Casa Editorial Hernando, S.A., 1925.

Espinosa, Aurelio M., "Romancero Nuevomejicano," *Revue Hispanique*, XXXIII-84 (April 1915), 446–560; XL-97 (June 1917), 215–227; XLI-100 (December 1917), 678–680.

Espinosa, José Manuel, *Spanish Folk-tales from New Mexico*, Memoirs of the American Folk-lore Society, Vol. XXX, New York, G. E. Stechert and Company, 1937.

Fawcett, F. Burlington, *Broadside Ballads*, London, John Lane the Bodley Head Limited, 1930.

Frimont, C. Herrera, *Los corridos de la Revolución*, Mexico, Biblioteca Enciclopédica Popular, Secretaría de Educación Pública, 1946.

Kennedy, Charles O'Brien, *American Ballads*, New York, Fawcett Publications Inc., 1952.

Lang, Andrew, *Border Ballads*, London, Lawrence and Bullen, 1895.

Lomax, John A. and Alan, *Cowboy Songs and Other Frontier Ballads*, New York, The Macmillan Company, 1938.

Bibliography

Lomax, John A. and Alan, *Folk Song, USA*, New York, Duell, Sloan, and Pearce, 1947.

Lomax, John A. and Alan, *Our Singing Country*, New York, The Macmillan Company, 1941.

Lucero-White, Aurora, *The Folklore of New Mexico*, Vol. I, Santa Fe, Seton Village Press, 1941.

Mendoza, Vicente T., *Cincuenta corridos mexicanos*, Mexico, Ediciones de la Secretaría de Educación Pública, 1944.

Mendoza, Vicente T., *El corrido mexicano*, Mexico, Gráfica Pan-americana, 1954.

Mendoza, Vicente T., *El romance español y el corrido mexicano*, Mexico, Imprenta Universitaria, 1939.

Mendoza, Vicente T., *La décima en México*, Buenos Aires, Establecimientos Gráficos, 1947.

Menéndez Pidal, Ramón, ed., *Cancionero de romances impreso en Amberes sin año*, Madrid, 1914.

Menéndez Pidal, Ramón, *Flor nueva de romances viejos*, Buenos Aires, Compañía Editora Espasa-Calpe, 1938.

Morley, Sylvanus Griswold, *Spanish Ballads*, Holt, 1911.

Olrik, Axel, *A Book of Danish Ballads*, translated by E. M. Smith-Dampier, Princeton, Princeton University Press, 1939.

Owens, William A., *Swing and Turn: Texas Play-party Games*, Publications of the Texas Folklore Society, 1936.

Percy, Thomas, *Reliques of Ancient English Poetry*, edited by Charles Cowden Clarke, Edinburgh, William P. Nimmo, 1869, 3 vols.

Robb, John Donald, *Hispanic Folk Songs of New Mexico*, Albuquerque, The University of New Mexico Press, 1954.

Santullano, Luis, ed., *Romancero español*, Madrid, M. Aguilar, 1943.

Schindler, Kurt, *Folk Music and Poetry of Spain and Portugal*, New York, Hispanic Institute, Lancaster Press, 1941.

Vázquez Santa Ana, Higinio, *Canciones, cantares y corridos mexicanos*, Mexico, Imprenta M. León Sánchez, 1925.

Vázquez Santa Ana, Higinio, *Historia de la canción mexicana*, Vol. III, Mexico, Talleres Gráficos de la Nación, 1931.

Vicuña Cifuentes, Julio, *Romances populares y vulgares recogidos de la tradición oral chilena*, Santiago de Chile, Imprenta Barcelona, 1912.

Wells, Evelyn Kendrick, *The Ballad Tree*, New York, Ronald Press Company, 1950.

Zárate, Manuel F. and Dora Pérez de, *La décima y la copla en Panamá*, Panama, Talleres de "La Estrella de Panamá," 1953.

COMMENT AND CRITICISM

Campa, Arthur L., *A Bibliography of Spanish Folk-lore in New Mexico*, comprising Vol. II, No. 3, of the *Bulletin of the University of New Mexico*, Albuquerque, 1930.

Dobie, J. Frank, *Guide to Life and Literature of the Southwest*, Dallas, Southern Methodist University Press, 1952.

Entwistle, William James, *European Balladry*, Oxford, Clarendon Press, 1939.

Espinosa, Aurelio M., *El romancero español*, Madrid, 1931.

Espinosa, Aurelio M., *La ciencia del folklore*, Habana, Cultural, S.A., 1929.

Fife, Austin E., and Redden, Francesca, "The Pseudo-Indian Folksongs of the Anglo-American and French-Canadian," in the *Journal of American Folklore*, Vol. 67, No. 265 and 266, pp. 239–251 and 379–394 (July–December 1954).

Frazer, James G., *The Golden Bough*, abridged edition, New York, The Macmillan Company, 1951.

Howard, James H., "The Tree Dweller Cults of the Dakota," in the *Journal of American Folklore*, Vol. 68, No. 268, pp. 169–174, April–June 1955.

Menéndez Pidal, Ramón, *El romancero*, Madrid, Editorial Páez, no year.

Menéndez Pidal, Ramón, *Poesía juglaresca y juglares*, Madrid, Tipografía de la "Revista de Archivos," 1924.

Menéndez Pidal, Ramón, *Poesía popular y poesía tradicional en la literatura española*, Oxford, Imprenta Clarendoniana, 1922.

Michaca, Pedro, *El nacionalismo musical mexicano*, Mexico, Tesis premiada por la Universidad Nacional de México, 1931.

Milá y Fontanals, Manuel, *De la poesía heróico-popular castellana*, Barcelona, Librería de Alvaro Verdaguer, 1896.

Morley, Sylvanus Griswold, "Spanish Ballad Problems: The Native Historical Themes," in *Modern Philology*, Vol. XIII, No. 2, pp. 207–228 (December 1925).

Pérez Martínez, Héctor, *Trayectoria del corrido*, Mexico, 1925.

Pound, Louise, *Poetic Origins and the Ballad*, New York, The Macmillan Company, 1921.

Slonimsky, Nicolas, *Music of Latin America*, New York, Thomas Y. Crowell Company, 1945.

Sokolov, Y. M., *Russian Folklore*, New York, The Macmillan Company, 1950.

Thompson, Stith, *The Folktale*, New York, The Dryden Press, 1946.

Thompson, Stith, *Motif-Index of Folk Literature*, Indiana University Studies, No. 96, 97, 100, and 101 (June 1932, September 1932, June 1933, and September 1933), Indiana University, Bloomington.

Thompson, Stith, *Antti Aarne's The Types of the Folk-tale, Translated and Enlarged*, Ann Arbor, Edwards Brothers, Inc., 1940.

Torner, Eduardo M., "Del folklore español, Persistencia de antiguos temas poéticas musicales," *Bulletin of Spanish Studies*, Vol. I, No. 2, pp. 62–70 (March 1924).

Bibliography

HISTORICAL REFERENCES

Primary Sources

Interviews

Aréchiga, (Mrs.) Desideria, at 807 East 8th street, Austin, Texas, on April 14, 1955.

Aréchiga, (Mrs.) Nora, at 1009 East 9th street, Austin, Texas, on April 14, 1955.

Briseño, (Mrs.) Martina, at Brownsville, Texas, on August 16, 1954.

Canales, J. T., at 335 East 10th street, Brownsville, Texas, in December 1953.

Cortez, Valeriano, at 2514 East 3rd street and 390-B Deep Eddy Apartments, Austin, Texas, on June 4 and June 6, 1955.

Flores de Garza, (Mrs.) Josefina, at 32 East Levee street, Brownsville, Texas, on August 3, 1954.

Johnson, J. W., at Webb County Courthouse, Laredo, Texas, on August 26, 1954.

Manzano, Eduardo, at Brownsville, Texas, in December 1951.

Sánchez, Serapio, at 4707 Reyes street, Austin, Texas, on April 16, 1955.

Villarreal Cortez, Pantaleón, at Matamoros, Tamaulipas, Mexico, on July 24, 1954.

Letters

Canales, J. T., to author, dated Brownsville, Texas, March 6, 1953.

Canales, J. T., to author, dated Brownsville, Texas, March 17, 1953.

Cortez, Louis, to author, dated Houston, Texas, August 7, 1955.

Garza, Marcelo, to author, dated Brownsville, Texas, July 7, 1955.

Paredes, Lorenzo, Sr., to author, dated Brownsville, Texas, March 6, 1954.

Paredes, Lorenzo, Sr., to author, dated Brownsville, Texas, March 18, 1954.

Official Documents

Appeal by Gregorio Cortez of Del Rio from conviction of rape; District Court of Val Verde; affirmed. Case No. 4688, April 1917, Records of the Texas Court of Criminal Appeals, Texas State Library, Archives Division, Austin, Texas.

Application for Pardon No. 28220 and related papers, entitled The State of Texas v. Gregorio Cortez, filed July 8, 1913, by F. C. Weinert, Secretary of State, Texas State Library, Archives Division, Austin, Texas.

The official correspondence of Governor O. B. Colquitt, Texas State Library, Archives Division, Austin, Texas.

The Southwestern Reporter, containing all the current decisions of the Supreme and Appellate Courts of Arkansas, Kentucky, Missouri, Tennessee, Texas, and Indian Territory, permanent edition, June 3–July 1, 1903, Vol. 74, St. Paul, West Publishing Company, 1903.

The Texas Criminal Reports, Cases Argued and Adjudged in the Court of
Criminal Appeals of the State of Texas.
   Vol. 43, reported by John P. White, Austin, Gammel-Statesman
   Publishing Company, 1903.
   Vol. 44, reported by John P. White, Austin, Gammel-Statesman
   Publishing Company, 1904.
   Vol. 47, reported by Rudolph Kleberg, Chicago, T. H. Flood and
   Company, 1908.
   Vol. 82, reported by Rudolph Kleberg, Austin, Von Boeckmann-
   Jones Company, 1919.

Theses and Dissertations

Buckner, Dellos Urban, *Study of the Lower Rio Grande Valley As a Culture Area*, Master's Thesis, University of Texas, 1929.

Cowling, Annie, *The Civil War Trade of the Lower Rio Grande Valley*, Master's Thesis, University of Texas, 1926.

Crawford, Polly Pearl, *The Beginnings of Spanish Settlement in the Lower Rio Grande Valley*, Master's Thesis, University of Texas, 1925.

González, Jovita, *Social Life in Cameron, Starr, and Zapata Counties*, Master's Thesis, University of Texas, 1930.

Guerra, Fermina, *Mexican and Spanish Folklore and Incidents in Southwest Texas*, Master's Thesis, University of Texas, 1941.

Holden, William Curry, *Fray Vicente Santa María: Historical Account of the Colony of Nuevo Santander and the Coast of the Seno Mexicano with Introduction and Annotations*, Master's Thesis, University of Texas, 1924.

Huckaby, George Portal, *Oscar Branch Colquitt: A Political Biography*, Doctoral Dissertation, University of Texas, 1946.

McArthur, Daniel Evander, *The Cattle Industry of Texas, 1685–1918*, Master's Thesis, University of Texas, 1918.

Smith, Cecil Bernard, *Diplomatic Relations between the United States and Mexico Concerning Border Disturbances During the Diaz Regime, 1876–1910*, Master's Thesis, University of Texas, 1928.

Vigness, David Martell, *The Lower Rio Grande Valley, 1836–1846*, Master's Thesis, University of Texas, 1948.

Vigness, David Martell, *The Republic of the Rio Grande: An Example of Separatism in Northern Mexico*, Doctoral Dissertation, University of Texas, 1951.

Webb, Walter Prescott, *The Texas Rangers in the Mexican War*, Master's Thesis, University of Texas, 1920.

Books

Bartlett, John Russell, *Personal Narrative of Explorations and Incidents in Texas, New Mexico, California, Sonora and Chihuahua*, New York, D. Appleton and Company, 1854.

Bibliography

Canales, José T., *Juan N. Cortina, Bandit or Patriot?*, San Antonio, Artes Gráficas, 1951.

Dobie, J. Frank, *The Flavor of Texas*, Dallas, Dealey and Lowe, 1936.

Dobie, J. Frank, *The Mustangs*, New York, Bantam Books, 1954.

Ganoe, William Addleman, *The History of the United States Army*, New York, D. Appleton and Company, 1924.

García y Cubas, Antonio, *Atlas geográfico, estadístico e histórico de la República Mexicana*, Mexico, Imprenta de José Mariano Fernández de Lara, 1858.

[Giddings, Luther], *Sketches of the Campaign in Northern Mexico*, New York, George Putnam and Company, 1853.

Goldfinch, Charles W., *Juan N. Cortina 1824–1892, a Re-Appraisal*, Brownsville, Texas, Bishop's Print Shop, 1950.

Gutiérrez de Lara, L., and Pinchon, Edgcumb, *The Mexican People: Their Struggle for Freedom*, New York, Doubleday, Page, and Company, 1914.

Herrera E., Celia, *Francisco Villa ante la historia*, Mexico, 1939.

Informe de la Comisión Pesquisidora de la Frontera del Norte al Ejecutivo de la Unión, Monterrey, Mayo 15 de 1873, Mexico, Imprenta del Gobierno, en Palacio, 1877.

Martínez Caro, Ramón, *Verdadera idea de la primera campaña de Tejas y sucesos ocurridos después de la acción de San Jacinto*, Mexico, Imprenta de Santiago Pérez, 1837.

Mena Brito, Bernardino, *Felipe Angeles federal*, Mexico, Publicaciones Herrerías, 1936.

Mena Brito, Bernardino, *El lugarteniente gris de Pancho Villa*, Mexico, Casa Mariano Coli, 1938.

Núñez Mata, Efrén, *México en la historia*, Mexico, Talleres Gráficos de la Nación, 1951.

Parkes, Henry Bamford, *A History of Mexico*, Cambridge, The Riverside Press, 1950.

Pierce, Frank C., *A Brief History of the Lower Rio Grande Valley*, Menasha, Wisconsin, George Banta Publishing Company, 1917.

Salinas Carranza, Alberto, *La expedición punitiva*, Mexico, Ediciones Botas, 1937.

Webb, Walter Prescott, *The Great Plains*, Boston, Ginn and Company, 1931.

Webb, Walter Prescott, *The Texas Rangers*, Cambridge, Houghton Mifflin Company, 1935.

Pamphlets

The Chapa Pamphlet, 48 unnumbered pages in Spanish, an account of Gregorio Cortez's life up to 1913. Lent to the author by Sotero R. Pedraza, 1201 Jackson street, Brownsville, who bought it from a San Antonio book store in 1914. No publisher's data but last page advertises the Chapa Mercantile Company, owned by Col. F. A. Chapa, the publisher of *El Imparcial*.

257

Newspapers

Austin American-Statesman, Austin, April 6, 1952.

Austin Statesman, Austin, July 1913.

Beeville Bee, Beeville, Texas, 1913.

Beeville Picayune, Beeville, Texas, 1913.

Brownsville Herald, Brownsville, Texas, 1901.

Corpus Christi Caller, Corpus Christi, 1901, 1902, 1903, 1904, and September 4, 1953.

El Imparcial de México, Mexico City, 1901.

El Paso Herald, El Paso, 1913.

El Popular de México, Mexico City, 1901.

Houston Chronicle, Houston, 1913.

San Antonio Express, San Antonio, 1901, 1902, 1903, 1904, 1905, and 1913.

San Antonio Light, San Antonio, 1913.

Seguin Enterprise, Seguin, Texas, 1901 and 1902.

Index

259